ALL TIME LOW

DON'T PANIC, LET'S PARTY:
THE BIOGRAPHY

JOE SHOOMAN

MUSIC
PRESS

Published by Music Press Books
an imprint of John Blake Publishing Ltd
3 Bramber Court, 2 Bramber Road,
London W14 9PB, England

www.johnblakebooks.co.uk

www.facebook.com/johnblakebooks 🄵
twitter.com/jblakebooks 🄴

First published in paperback in 2016

ISBN: 978 1 784 1 8985 3

British Library Cataloguing-in-Publication Data:

A catalogue record for this book is available from the British Library.

Design by www.envydesign.co.uk

Printed in Great Britain by CPI Group (UK) Ltd

1 3 5 7 9 10 8 6 4 2

Papers used by John Blake Publishing are natural, recyclable products made
from wood grown in sustainable forests. The manufacturing processes
conform to the environmental regulations of the country of origin.

Every attempt has been made to contact the relevant copyright-holders,
but some were unobtainable. We would be grateful if the appropriate
people could contact us.

For Hustlers everywhere

CONTENTS

INTRODUKTION

*I*magine you are an alien.

You might have green or blue skin, eighteen eyes and ten tentacles. It's up to you. Your spaceship can be a ten-thousand-metre-long cigar, or an undulating multidimensional packet of crisps, or in the shape of a Flying V rock guitar, with strings that resonate with the music of the spheres to propel you on your adventures.

It's up to you.

Imagine that your adventures have brought you to an unassuming solar system situated in the backwaters of the Western Spiral Arm of the Milky Way Galaxy. There are eight-and-a-half planets, one mid-sized sun and plenty of asteroids to hide behind.

Something, however, is different about this system.

The third planet from that reasonably normal sun is a lovely green-blue colour. It also seems to be radiating energy waves in a way no other celestial body in these parts does. You turn on the spaceship's internal universal translation system. Handy things, those. Yes, it's certainly tuning in to something unique. Something that could only be created by reasonably intelligent life forms. You turn up the Megafractic Speakerator units on your elvisty-twelve earpods and you hear: 'Merry Christmas, kiss my ...'

What was that?

You zoom in to the planet, turning on your invisibility shields as you go. You rush towards the surface, through the upper atmosphere, taking advantage of a nice big hole in the ozone layer that beckons you in. That was thoughtful of this species, you think, as you see a continent ahead of you that the Universal Mapalator tells you is called North America. Closer still, you see that this place is called the United States. Your ship starts to brake as you centre in, circling ever closer: Maryland, Baltimore, Towson.

And you find the source of this sound, this melodious construction of effervescence, humour, visceral beats and awesome sneakers. Four life forms, being roared at by thousands more life forms.

This species is already unique. They are chanting: 'All Time Low'.

You turn on the Backtime Widgetspickler and rewind to the beginning of this phenomenon. The numbers roll back on the Earth Calendator, and it stops in Earth Year 2003.

CHAPTER ONE

BEGINNINGS
AND ENDINGS

Alexander William Gaskarth was born in Harlow, Essex. His father, Peter Gaskarth, had been previously married, as Alex told an interviewer from *Rock Sound*. 'He had kids when he was very young and ended up separating from his first wife; initially he married her when he realised they were having kids but it didn't work out. I was born quite a bit later so I have two half-sisters and a half-brother. My sisters are a lot older than me as my dad didn't remarry until sometime later.' Nonetheless, he said that his life was normal even though his siblings were all rather older; in the same interview he explained that when the time came for the family to move to the United States in 1995 his sisters were old enough to do their own thing in the UK, but his half-brother, Tom, was closer in age and came along too. 'He definitely acted like a big brother to me but we were just a few years too far apart to really be close,' said Alex. 'We just missed out on that serious brotherhood/sidekick thing but he was always great to be around and it was awesome to have someone to learn from.' That move to Townson, a small part of Baltimore, Maryland, was to have a tragic element, as Tom – just twenty-one years of age – passed away when Alex was twelve. One can only imagine the depth of the devastation.

Jack Bassam Barakat was born in Lebanon in 1988 and has three siblings. His family had moved to the United States. 'My mom escaped the [civil] war with my brother and sisters,' he explained to Talking with Soup. 'It was literally like out of a movie. She picked up my brother and sisters, who are ten years older than me, got in the Mediterranean, got in a hovercraft [to Cyprus], mid-bombings ... my dad was in the US practicing medicine ... [We] somehow got to Canada and the US. It was wild, man, crazy.' His folks, he explained, were normal citizens of the country but like thousands of others were suffering from the bombings. 'We barely made it out,' he added. The civil war ended in 1990. His parents moved back to Lebanon much later once they were retired and the kids were all grown up and settled. Jack added that he goes back to visit and the country was more stable two and a half decades later.

Once in the United States, Jack's school career was relatively uneventful, although he did explain to Buzznet that he had got into a scuffle or two along the way. 'I got suspended once for punching a kid in the face cause he took one of my gf's [sic]. It was after school. I was an idiot. 8th grade,' he recalled, also explaining that he used to 'hang in the library in the morning'. He also revealed a rather inventive way of getting the academic side of school taken care of. 'I would ask the nerdier kids to do my homework from the night before. I gave them tickets to local shows a lot,' he said. That energy would soon find a new outlet: Jack became an active guitarist in various knockabout bands while in high school, inspired by Tom DeLonge of Blink-182. 'I just loved the way that he had the careless attitude onstage, and he had this punk swagger that I guess you can only get from growing up in southern California. I idolized his moves,' Jack told Mousertime. 'Billie Joe Armstrong is another great frontman, who can captivate an entire audience while singing and playing the guitar at the same time. He is also another idol of mine.'

It was at Dulaney High School that Jack realised he had compadres into the same kind of music, one by the name of Marc Shilling, a bassist and vocalist. So far, so Blink … the pair teamed up briefly with a drummer Jack knew by the name of Ionnaris 'Yanni' Giannaros before realising that another guitarist was needed. Alex Gaskarth, handily, was also a big fan of Blink-182, as he told WeLoveDC: 'Blink-182 is definitely the band that inspired us to be a band and probably was the most responsible for us being the band we are today. They really taught us that it was okay to have fun being in a band and playing music.' And so the first line-up was complete.

Alex was in no doubt about what he wanted to do with his life. 'Doing music was kind of the do all end all for me,' he told an interviewer for *Rock NYC Live and Recorded.com*: 'I really didn't have any other aspiration at the time and I just knew that I wanted to make it work. To be honest [if I hadn't made it], I'd probably [have dropped] out of college, working a shitty job. I didn't always know I wanted to do music, I got more into music in high school. I always sort of liked the idea of psychology so I thought of being a therapist or someone who helps other people.' Which, as we shall see, isn't all that far from the truth ...

Luckily for the rising pop-punkers, the support from high school was unrelentingly positive; there was even a scheme that assisted directly in the group's ability to rehearse. 'The guidance counsellors were very supportive and actually allowed the three of us to do a "work study" program where we would leave school early to go to band practice,' Alex told WeLoveDC in 2011. 'We've all said it before but this band wouldn't be where we are if it wasn't for the amazing support of our parents. Heck, our mothers used to drive with us on tour [...] I think they're really proud of everything that we've accomplished so far and hopefully they know how much we appreciate all of their help.' The band's influences are pop-punk in general, but as Alex mused later during a Reddit Ask Me Anything (AMA), there were many other groups that he admired: 'I was inspired by so many different artists and genres. Blink and Green Day got me into the kind of music that we play, but beyond that, I'd say I was molded by The Beatles, Queen, Pink Floyd, Nirvana and Genesis,' he wrote. Later, both Jack and Alex were interviewed for *Beat the Scene* about the group's origins. In a typically lively mood, Jack took up the baton. 'Me and Alex met in the 8th grade. We started separate Blink-182 cover bands and in 9th grade we all came together to form the ultimate Blink-182 cover band.' Not to be outdone, Alex countered with his own take on it: 'Jack harassed the other 50 percent of the band and convinced them to join, against their will, I think. Eventually, after we learned pretty much every Blink song, New Found Glory song and Green Day song there [was] to know, we started writing our own music, and it kinda caught on.'

The new band's membership evolved further as Robert Rian Dawson joined as permanent drummer after meeting Jack, reportedly, in French class. Like Jack, he sports a tattoo of heroes Blink-182, so is a perfect fit. Marc Shilling also bowed out of the picture at an early stage with Zachary (Zack) Steven Merrick slotting in on backing vocals and bass, thus completing the line-up that still stands strong today. Alex later explained to *deaconlight.com* how it panned out: 'We met in high school. Jack and I knew each other from eighth grade, and once we got into our freshmen year we met Rian, who went to our high school, and Zack, who went to a different high school but was in the same grade, through a mutual friend. We found him and added him as a member of the band last just because we didn't have a bass player. [Before All Time Low] we kind of messed around with different combinations of people but it was never really a real band.'

Some names to conjure with in the early days included Fire in the Hole, NeverReck, the Coincidentals – all of which were short-lived high-school pickup bands featuring some of the current members. Marc and Jack remain good friends and can sometimes be found cheering on the Baltimore Ravens American football team. Jack explained in 2012 that the band were big fans of their local side. 'When we're home, we try to go to every game. When we're on the road, we try to watch every game,' he told *espn.com*. 'Sometimes that can be difficult. In Japan, it was 2 a.m. and all of us were curled up in our hotel room trying to watch a game on one of the laptops.'

The group's first recordings – in Rian's basement on some crappy gear – according to a later interview included a cover of the theme song from *Friends*, which, said Alex when asked by the Daily Chorus, was the first song the band ever did. Early shows included Battle of the Bands and people's parties, he explained. The first cover the band ever played, Rian said later, was Anti-Flag's 'Angry, Young and Poor'. That song is a pretty harsh-punk slab of youthful frustration and a lot more politically charged than those with which All Time Low were to become associated.

First things first, however, and, as everyone knows, the most important part of being in a band is selecting a cool name, isn't it? Fortunately, New Found Glory had a cool, if rather downbeat, song called 'Head On Collision' about a breakup. One of the memorable lines featured those three little words that mean so much: all time low. Add some capitals and you've got one of the best-loved bands of the past decade and a half. As Jack put it when speaking to jenaeistoday: 'It's a band that we admired so we kind of took that line and it stuck.' Simple!

CHAPTER 2

EARLY DAYS, SKOOL DAZE

*T*echnology and specifically, the ability to be in contact with other like-minded souls worldwide has featured in the band's career from a very early stage, with the group very *au fait* with the possibilities of the Internet even back in 2003. The first sign of the group's presence in the electronic ether was in June 2003 when an online mailing list was available on long-dead Internet portal, Geocities. Ryan Wapner, a merchandise specialist and promoter of concerts in nearby Pennsylvania in those early days, explained to me how bands of that era including All Time Low took advantage of the proliferation of cheaper and faster Internet access in order to hook up with fans.

[It] was a unique time. You had MySpace and PureVolume really in their prime, so (personally) I think finding new acts was a lot easier, especially within your immediate surrounding region. Outside of that though, I think new artists were extremely hungry then, at least going into that time, and would really go out of their way to make their local followings something worth talking about. Then MySpace really brought on the ability to have fans before you've even played a show, and I think that kind of motivation I spoke of really fell off for a while. Things are coming back around though, and new artists in my area are really building up regions again before they set off for the opposite coast.

Wapner's opinion on the band's subsequent success is that the band, which he first promoted in 2005, were savvy on all counts even in their nascent years. 'Their shows were engaging and they were writing great songs by themselves, both right from the start,' he told me. 'They built upon that, grew organically, but also supplemented with the social media boom, and took a changing tide in music trends by the reins.' From the band's point of view, that engagement with its fans took many forms, as Alex explained to Pup Fresh. 'I think you just have to get out there and let people know about your band. We would always be out at shows handing out CDs and fliers, meeting fans and as many touring bands as we could. We were lucky to develop a good local fan base and became the local band that promoters added when a tour would come through to help with ticket sales. That allowed us to meet a lot of touring bands, and that really helped us out.'

On 9 November 2003, visitors to the former All Time Low website were treated with tantalising news from the group that a four-song EP had been recorded and would be available in mid-November, with merchandise also to follow. The group signed off the update explaining that a full album was in the planning stages.

That year, in many ways Year Zero for the band, came to a close with gigs at St. John's (alongside Absolute Stereo System, Capitol 9 and Underscore), The Recher Theatre and a 30 December outing alongside 451 and Fire in the Hole, the venue of which is lost to posterity. Underscore – and in particular their singer, Matt Flyzik – were to prove something of a pivotal player in the game. Also recorded for posterity is an early biography on the now-defunct website, Talentmatch, which summed up the approach of the boys succinctly: 'All Time Low is an energetic, 4-piece band from Baltimore, MD. Their music varies from catchy, pop-punk anthems, to slightly more aggressive rock ballads. Using their youth to their advantage, All Time Low may just be the next big thing.' The site also listed four early demo tracks: 'We All Fall Down', 'Light the Way', 'The Next Best Thing' and 'My Paradise'. There's also a very early photo of the band posing on a bridge.

The New Year dawned with the band still promising that merchandise was imminent, while the aforementioned PureVolume biography from January 2004 explained what the group had been up to, listing gigs during late February and early March at various venues including the Oracle Clothing Show on 12 March 2004. Indeed, an April update expanded on the growing attention that the band was drawing: 'Having made a name for themselves locally, All Time Low is now expanding, fan bases forming nation-wide, until finally, the world is taken by storm. With tours being planned, and cd's [sic] on the way, it's well worth keeping your eyes on this one.'

The quartet expressed their delight online with an update thanking fellow groups Bangarang and Next Day Flight for a great gig from 21 March at the Recher Theatre in Towson. There was also an onstage guest with ATL: Joe from Supergiant MD, soon to be renamed Bury Me Standing. The camaraderie between the two bands was so strong that there were even plans to release a split CD. Other live appearances in March, April and May included an acoustic special at St. John's Church with Underscore also popping up again; Sidebar Tavern, alongside Hopeless Records artist Digger; the Thunderdome and The Nation in Washington, DC, alongside Never the Machine Forever. The second of June was also to bring the band's biggest gig to date, at the Ottobar, where All Time Low backed Stars Hide Fire, Armor for Sleep and Midtown, all bands making waves in the industry at the time. Having cut their teeth at a local level, All Time Low were rightly attracting the attention of record labels themselves.

CHAPTER 3

A RECORD DEAL?
DON'T MIND IF I DO, SIR

Matt Boylan, a Baltimore music fan and musician, noticed a gap in the market as far as independent and rising bands were concerned. That gap was a record label dedicated to the growing scene of Maryland and further afield. So he stepped in and created Emerald Moon Records in order to publicise the bands he loved. Matt was in it for the love of the music and had played in several groups, including The Suburbanites, The Jigawatts and Athens is Burning. With his strong understanding of what was needed and a stellar work ethic, there was nobody better to launch a label. Emerald Moon's first release was a compilation called *From the Land of Pleasant Living*. The name of the compilation is a nod to Baltimore's National Bohemian Beer, for which those exact words were used as a slogan.

The nineteen tracks included contributions from familiar

and not-so-familiar scenesters like Silent Film, Thin Dark Line, Driving in Silence, Downside Risk and, with a track named 'Last Flight Home', none other than All Time Low. It was released on 27 August 2004 and, as such, marks All Time Low's first official release on a record label. Of the release, a reviewer known only as K. From Galveston, TX, wrote on Interpunk that it was 'actually a pretty good comp that features punk, hardcore, indie as well as several other varied forms of rock'. K. namechecked Silent Film, Athens is Building [sic] and Bled Across Miles as having the best songs. However, the other bands were 'quite good as well', he felt.

Matt was keeping things independent, using the web wisely with promotion and distribution through PureVolume, *Punkhardcore.com*, Punknews, Interpunk, SmartPunk and *Pheer.com* – all useful places where bands, fans and labels could congregate to swap news, source tracks and of course sell records. Stephen Dufresne of Hometown Anthem, an early Emerald Moon band, recalls the impact that the record label was to have on the scene. 'Matt Boylan took care of things that we either didn't know anything about, or didn't have the capital to make happen,' he said in an interview for this book. 'Our agreement with Matt was that he would fund the pressing of the album in exchange for a percentage of each sale. He also took care of getting our album on websites like SmartPunk, Interpunk and iTunes. Right now [a decade and a bit later] it probably doesn't seem like much, but this was before digital distribution was the norm.' Switched on from the start, Boylan's label was breaking new ground in the online markets.

There was more good news for fans of All Time Low very

soon, with the announcement by Emerald Moon on 9 October 2004 that the band's new EP was available. Matt's animated joy at the sound and sight of the record was genuine. The EP was called *The Three Words to Remember When Dealing with the End.* An irresistible guitar lick heralds the first song 'Hit the Lights (Tribute to a Night, I'll Never Forget)', which then quickly kicks in with energetic punk-pop guitars, multiple layers of vocals, accomplished stops and starts, double-time drumming alternating with guitar chugs, sweeps and an early demonstration of the band's leanings towards music of epic scale, with a breakdown before a final chorus-based coda. It's an impressive start and shows that this is a group that has honed its ideas on the masters of the genre, including Blink-182 and Green Day. Second track, 'The Next Best Thing', marries a classic sense of melodic chords with a frantic, but smooth, guitar lick, opening up into a tale of breaking up from a bad relationship. Again there are excellently delivered vocal melodies, rhythmic play and sonic beefiness at work that belies the youth of the band that created it. The pre-final chorus solo starts as if it's from a beginner player of the guitar, but with a great sense of humour and timing kicks in to some brilliant axework. 'Last Flight Home' starts off with an excellent bass and vocal interplay, then more vocal interplay between the lads that is much more than just straight harmonics on the same rhythm – the maturity of the songwriting and arrangement at this early stage certainly shows why label boss Matt Boylan was so excited about the second record to come out on his label. Rian Dawson puts in quite the shift at the end with some banging double-kick playing. The fourth and final track, 'Memories that Fade Like Photographs', starts off in harder mode with a series of stops and starts that mark the song out as the most experimental so far in the All Time Low canon, while retaining the aural temptation to jump up and down. Indeed, there's a hint of Angels and Airwaves' expansive sensibility on show that pointed to many possibilities ahead. All in all, the EP was streets ahead of most bands at such an early stage of their career.

It made quite a splash both at the time and later on, including a gushing retrospective review by justsurrendrfan on AbsolutePunk. The reviewer was much enamoured with the writing and musicality on show, especially considering the group was still in high school. Also worthy of praise was the group sounding like they were playing the songs and enjoying themselves rather than indulging in a swish production job. The EP, said the reviewer, started on an upbeat with 'Hit the Lights': 'The first three songs all have such momentum of a speeding train. "Last Flight Home", and my personal favorite, "Next Best Thing", stick in ones [sic] head more with each additional play. The final track, "Memories that Fade Like Photographs", is the closing song that knocks one out of its socks,' ran the review. The reviewer concluded by praising it as being as good as anything else on the pop-punk scene of 2004 and urged fans to take repeated listens to a record that even staunch All Time Low followers may not always put up there with their favourites. One piece of trivia: the band had a temporary fifth member, singing backing vocals on 'Memories that Fade Like Photographs'. That would be one Matt Flyzik. Him again! As for the EP title, those three words to remember are rumoured to be 'All Time Low' and/or 'I Love You'.

Alex Gaskarth later told Dan Campbell's Talking with Soup

video interview series about how the Emerald Moon hook-up happened. '[Matt] was fronting bands money to go into the studio to record ... we had never done anything before [...] we were fifteen, sixteen [and went into the studio with] Paul Leavitt.' He went on to say that there was no formal record contract signed between the band and the label but that the cost of the studio, which he estimated at around a thousand dollars, had been paid by Emerald Moon and had got the ball rolling. Other bands on the label that Alex namechecked included Hometown Anthem from Jersey, with whom All Time Low would go on their first proper tour. '[Matt] signed bands that he was friends with [...] and the music that he was in to [...] it was cool and opened up a lot of doors on a basic level.' That meant increased contact with lots of other bands active on the scene, enabling them to book shows in different geographical areas, which undoubtedly helped the group expand its activities. Jack has said in the past that he considered ATL to be one of the first bands to take significant advantage of the Internet, telling Mousertime in a 2011 interview that they 'basically started our entire band via the Internet. Before MySpace Music even existed, we had a band MySpace page. We were one of the first fifty bands on PureVolume, and we really built everything from the Internet. That's how we started talking to record labels, that's how we booked our first tours. Without the Internet social networking, like Twitter, we definitely wouldn't be where we are today. It is a huge part of the band.' He also noted that thinking positively and being prepared to work extremely hard were key elements of the group's subsequent success. That, and preparing to record a full-length album follow-up to their debut EP as 2004 moved towards 2005. Hometown Anthem's Stephen Dufresne, who went on to work for Snapchat, sees the time as a transitional one in terms of the net. 'The Internet was becoming a more powerful tool to reach people, but you didn't have smartphones. At the time you had things like a Sidekick, which were limited in their internet capabilities. We put together physical press kits and were mailing them to promoters and venues that were along our proposed route. We'd use MySpace and PureVolume to find bands in certain areas and try to do show swaps with them. Our personal contacts outside of our own areas were limited, but we were able to make the best of the situation.'

In nearby Pennsylvania, Ryan Wapner was just beginning to book bands for gigs in the area. 'I started setting up local concerts in 2005,' he says. 'I was fifteen. All the shows were in alternative spaces, due to the area really lacking a proper all-ages venue. Baltimore had something similar around the same time happening at a church called St. John Hamilton's.' Looking back, Ryan remembers how the first promotion together came about: 'We were all in high school at the time, and I was setting up local DIY concerts in Central Pennsylvania. A band I had booked numerous times called Underscore [Matt Flyzik who would tour manage ATL for many years fronted this band] was coming back, and they had asked if their friends, All Time Low, could play the show as well. I of course said yes. I think this was right before [debut album] The Party Scene came out ... I would book them in my hometown by just emailing Jack. That first EP and full length really got the attention of everyone, I think. I remember thinking that these guys who were the same age as myself had a record that could hang with some of my favourites at the time. Right from the start the songs were there, the production was there, the catchiness was there, and the releases to follow just expanded on that.'

On that note, it's time to take a look at the debut album of this already-accomplished, still-schoolkids, making-a-splash band of buddies.

CHAPTER 4

AN ALBUM?
TOO RIGHT, GUV

The first full-length record by Jack Barakat, Alex Gaskarth, Rian Dawson and Zack Merrick has to go down as one of the most accomplished pop-punk debuts in history. With tight playing, subtle arrangement, great vocals and above all a bunch of instantly catchy songs, it's streets ahead of what you'd expect from a band still unable to get a legal drink or even drive themselves to gigs.

The whole caboodle begins with the epic, growing 'Prelude', guitar chords ringing out while underneath the bass and drums push at their limits, ready to soar, before the track scrunches itself up as if a tape has been suddenly stopped. Alex then introduces the title track, 'The Party Scene', a call to arms if ever there was one. While guitars chugs underneath, the vocalist tells the tale of moving forward, fulfilling potential, staying out late, seeing the sunrise, girl trouble, being seventeen and letting the bad parts of life go. It's both a comment on teenage life and something of a manifesto for the career to come.

'Lullabies', as the title suggests, begins with a close-microphone, soft delivery – intimate as anything else thus far in the band's career – before hurtling into a spiky, jumpy, first verse that itself then melds into a typical All Time Low punch and counterpunch of holding back, mid-paced energy, a break, then sweet release. The lyrics are delicate, heartfelt, talking of life and missing someone who is no longer there. Alex sings that he feels that a part of him is now missing, but that he cannot learn from this missing someone who is no longer there. He misses this person and vows to see the person in dreams. The usual reading of this song is that it's a tribute to Alex's sadly passed half-brother, Tom. It is an extremely affecting song and performance that is full of emotion and a rawness that is very beautiful, very sad and extraordinarily powerful in its own right as a piece of music, but even more so with the knowledge of that terrible family tragedy.

'Hometown Heroes, National Nobodies' is the fourth track on *The Party Scene*, and we're back to the sound of a band on the brink of a major step forward in their career. It's a pure and straightforward song for and to the fans from the perspective of a rising group. The song talks about the vibe and energy created between a band and its fans, particularly in a live arena, dancing all night, rock 'n' roll and getting into a real groove of rocking out.

'Circles' brings us back to the thorny issue of relationships, specifically the fact that often things come to a natural end; images of autumn and being inspired run alongside a wanting to start again – hence the circle of the title.

Next up is the two-minute 'Interlude', featuring more AVA-like soundscapes, some *Star Wars*-style laser noises and a sort of musical ellipsis as the album catches its breath ready for 'We Say Summer'. The song features a set of lyrics predominately about getting up and out and at 'em – which is certainly true of the start of a new relationship, and equally true of a band ready to conquer the world. It's a big statement about not caring for consequences and having eyes on the prize – success. Equally true once again of a relationship or a band.

'Break Out! Break Out!' takes up that theme with energy and relish: this is the time to get in that car and get to the big city, following dreams. It's a chance for All Time Low to reflect on how far they'd come so far as a band, as well as a vow not to let that hard work slide, because it is time to break out and not to look back. The time has come for this band and you either get on board or get left behind.

The acoustic guitars come out in 'Running from Lions', proof that a good song can be played stripped down to handclaps, a few sets of vocals and a couple of guitars and still be as effective as a full-on, wall-of-sound production. It also shows the band's natural skill with vocal arrangements: this track demonstrates a real sense of voice as instrument. That means long, sustained notes underneath the vocal, contrapuntal passages, even different lyrics as call and response in order to serve the song as best they can.

When the full electric band set-up returns for 'Noel' it seems to come in with double the force as a result. It's a classic All Time Low blend of multiple riffs, multiple drum rhythms, stops, breakdowns and then building up to the ultimate release of a cracking, crackling chorus. This is a song for the live arena: a song to get crowds jumping in the air with the sheer visceral joy of being alive. Even on record it is almost visible coming out of the speakers and setting the dust of the day dancing in the light of the rays of the sun.

'I Can't Do the One-Two Step' is another song dedicated to making the most of what you have when you have it and identifying chances to go and seek something better in life. Another statement of intent from the band, all about belief, looking for more than the same old, same old and committing to getting out there and having no regrets about it. 'The Girl's a Straight-Up Hustler' is the last 'proper' track on the album and is a stone-cold classic take on a bad breakup. Its self-referential lyrics talk about a certain girl for whom the protagonist has written songs, even if he's sick of doing so, and the fact that it all is ending. Again, the image of staying seventeen reappears, this time as a negative phenomenon, while the protagonist moves on to bigger and better things rather than remaining caught in amber and never developing, never moving forward.

There's just time for a hidden track, 'Sticks, Stones and Techno'. As you'd probably expect from the title, the song's based on an electronic dance beat and vocoder-vocals. The synth strings and dancefloor feel are playful and unexpected at the end of a record that is one of those rare beasts: a brilliant debut. 'Sticks, Stones and Techno' isn't exactly the best bit of electronic dance music ever made, but as the work of a young bunch of musicians looking to expand their horizons it's a sign that they'd not even started yet.

Released on 19 July 2005, *The Party Scene* drew some reviews from contemporary outlets. Again, AbsolutePunk was on the case, with one Drew Beringer praising the band of seventeen-year-olds as having produced an album 'Filled with great melodies, catchy sing-alongs, and energizing guitar hooks.' The reviewer praises Alex's vocals as having 'no trace of a whine'(!) and compared 'Hometown Heroes, National Nobodies' with 'old school NFG, minus the annoying vocals'. Also worthy of praise was 'Break Out! Break Out!' – a song that Beringer rated as his favourite. 'Running from Lions', meanwhile, showed range and great vocals and 'The Girl's a Straight-Up Hustler' reminded the reviewer of Northstar for its slow build-up. As for 'Sticks, Stones and Techno', that was a fun end to 'a stellar pop-punk album'. Tellingly, and with some insight, the reviewer rated All Time Low as having the potential not just to emulate but to overtake the likes of Cartel and The Academy Is... A later review from an unnamed fan on Ultimate Guitar called it 'brilliant from guys in their senior year of high school'. Because of the small initial run of CDs – around a thousand – it's become quite the badge of honour to be in possession of an actual physical copy of the album, and a decade or so later it's not uncommon to see auction websites listing copies of the LP for hundreds of pounds or dollars.

Two videos were subsequently produced to boost the release. *Circles* was directed by Matt Grube at the Sheffield Institute for the Recording Arts and begins with a bored-looking band in black and white sitting on the sofa before the action cuts to the familiarly energetic quartet giving it loads in a live set-up. We cut between that sofa and various shots in wide angle of the band themselves, individual musicians all getting their place in the sun in the serious business of rocking like anybody's business, interspersed with the boys messing about with cushions, sofa-diving on top of each other and generally having as good a time as any bunch of clearly good friends of their age would do under the circumstances. There's nothing subtle about the video – and there isn't meant to be. It's a band doing what a band does best: delivering a song to the best of its abilities and looking pretty cool doing it.

The video for 'The Girl's a Straight-Up Hustler' is more of an extravaganza, with the group playing in front of what appears to be a kind of posh graduation party with great-looking people holding cocktails and watching the group get its freak on. It has echoes of the famous Nirvana video for 'Smells Like Teen Spirit', albeit without the sheer madness of the Seattle band's film's descent into complete chaos. Good-looking girls circulate around the band, and manfully the boys manage to somehow keep relatively cool and keep the song going. As the track develops, the party truly does begin, with the stage area being completely invaded by the now-dancing hordes, balloons all over the place and even some crowd surfing. It all ends with a disconsolate girl looking regretfully at the consequences of her actions, something that is entirely in keeping with the tone of the lyrics. Those who have an eagle eye may spot Matt Flyzik in a small cameo. For a group on a relatively tiny label, the whole idea of making a video shows how far technology had come as well as the willingness to present the band as a fully formed entertainments unit rather than 'just' a live band.

Talking of playing live, the group's first proper tour was with Hometown Anthem, which was booked largely by personal contact; Jack even posted to AbsolutePunk with a list of confirmed dates and a whole bunch of possible free dates in various towns over July and August 2005. Ryan Wapner, looking back a decade, says he can identify one of the main reasons the boys have been such a successful unit. 'Both back then and now are similar in the sense of being very fun and they have always been very engaging. There was no production back then, so they were intimate, playing five feet from you. Even now they do a great job of making their shows very special, and even though there is a massive amount of production involved, and huge numbers of fans, their shows are still very engaging.' That is a sentiment genuinely shared by the Anthem boys, as guitarist Stephen Dufresne recalled for this book. At the time, he remembers, there was something of a transition from Drive-Thru Records bands to the Fueled by Ramen label. He namechecks bands including Punchline, The Academy Is... and Paramore as influential. Over in New Jersey, names like Hidden in Plain View and Madison ruled the roost, with Hometown Anthem also upcoming:

Bands like Hidden in Plain View and Madison are the ones that come to mind. During this time we were still playing a lot of VFW halls and smaller clubs, but we would occasionally open shows for larger acts that would come through the area. There was a promotion group called Tri-State Punk that really helped us transition from pay to play shows to setting a guarantee. We played two shows at the same local venue in the same week and were able to draw a few hundred kids in total. After those shows we were their first choice to be the local support for acts like Silverstein, Spitalfield, Park, and whoever else they had coming into town. It was a time when the scene was really starting to take off, so you started to see a lot more people take notice. The venues started to get bigger, from the Wayne Firehouse to places like Birch Hill and Starland Ballroom. The crowds were great around this time. Most weekends you would find us on a show with bands that we were friends with, so if you had 200 people there, most everyone was friendly with each other. I can't really recall any fights or problems that happened at these shows. The Baltimore music scene was unknown to me before All Time Low. Even though it's only a three-hour drive, it's not an area that we played until we started touring on a regular basis. When we met All Time Low, we would play places like St. John's Phoenix and Hamilton with them.

Indeed, the first time Hometown Anthem met the All Time Low boys, he says, was when they first shared a stage. Both bands at that point were on the Emerald Moon books and Hometown Anthem were looking to get on to the Flipside Festival in Virginia. All Time Low's suggestion was that they come down and meet the promoters, which didn't work out all that well, says Stephen. 'We weren't able to formally jump on the show, so in the middle of All Time Low's set we jumped in and started playing. The promoter wasn't too happy about that and we got booted from the venue and subsequently didn't get added to Flipside.' Wonder why? Still, continues the axeman, Matt Boylan had high hopes for the two bands and suggested they tour together, which felt like the right thing to do.

Both of our albums were being released on the same day and we had similar followings in our respective regions. We had done some show swapping leading up to the tour, so our relationship had grown over those months. They were a very friendly, outgoing group. I feel like there was a quick friendship between our bands because at that time, we were in similar situations. We were both new signings to Emerald Moon Records and prepping to write our first album. We ended up going to the same guy, Paul Leavitt, to record our first releases.

The bands certainly travelled in comfort, says Stephen, with All Time Low getting themselves around in a fifteen-seater van that the Hometown Anthem man describes as

the most insane tour van I've ever seen. Anyone who has seen it can attest to it. This was a band that was certainly touring in style. There were a few TVs and a killer sound system for blasting music or playing video games. When we toured they brought their friend James with them. He was over 18 and I think they made a compromise to bring him along. There were some dates that someone's parents would also be there. It was really cool to see how supportive their families were right from the start.

During the summer dates, Alex later recalled, the two bands managed to sneak into one of the dates on the influential Warped Tour. He told Rocksound.tv that while the Anthem and All Time Low were on a day off they joined lots of the other bands playing the touring punk festival and drove their van in, unhindered by the fact that they didn't have any passes, contacts or other ways in. This sense of mischief is altogether in keeping with the Can Do/Why Not? attitude of the groups at the time. As a result of their successful sneaking in to the fest, they managed to watch From Under the Cork Tree – a group that was really on the way up at the time – and Fall Out Boy on the main stage. Alex was much enamoured by the treelike ones, calling their set, finding their set inspiring and off-the-wall in equal measure.

That sense of inspiration was allied to Alex's self-confessed growing frustration with what he legally still had to spend his term-time days doing – being of an age where school was compulsory. Speaking to Mammoth Press in 2007, the singer reflected on how it had been in those pre-graduation days: 'I personally felt like a caged animal all through high school – the daily repetition just wasn't for me, so there was often conflict between my priority, which was the band, and my effort in classes,' he mused, adding that he 'did manage to get through, obviously, so it wasn't all bad. I paid my dues and now I'm on to better things.' The tour had begun with dates in the New Jersey area, which was good in terms of crowds as it was more or less a hometown gig for Hometown Anthem, but not all the gigs were to prove quite so user-friendly, showing the value of merchandise for any bands looking to pay their way around. 'Once we got outside of our comfort zone, you saw how touring life really was,' Stephen Dufresne explains.

We played a few shows with a handful of people there and we'd do our best to sell a few CDs to make money to get to the next place. Fortunately, the first night of our tour was our record release party in NJ. We sold a ton of merch, which really helped us. All Time Low had their album and a single T-shirt. Pretty much the same that we had. However, even at this early stage it was clear that All Time Low were moving up to another level. Outside of our areas, we were initially drawing a comparable number of people. Over the course of the tour, you could see more and more people coming out for All Time Low, their MySpace friend count was climbing at a rapid pace, various websites were talking about them, and the album was selling well on *Smartpunk.com*. You could sense that their momentum was going to pick up as soon as the summer was over.

There was just time to fit in a few remaining 2005 dates with a clutch of other names including the Anthem, Sound the Alarm, The Hint, Second Start, Fox Troutsy and various other cool-named groups over the Thanksgiving period, before 2006 dawned with a revamp of the band's website, where the All Time Low crew had now picked up a gig booker – Ron Opaleski of William Morris – plus a street team run by someone known only as Charlene and, possibly most importantly, management through Keith Lazorchak of Absolute Management. *The Party Scene* had been re-pressed and restocked on SmartPunk in time for the Sonar club gig on 21 January 2006, where other bands included Gatsby Gets the Green Light and Eleven:54.

Touring always did bring both rewards and some difficult clashes, as was the case for a couple of gigs in February 2006 in Pennsylvania and New Jersey, which Jack had to miss due to a commitment in Canada that required his attention. So, for the gigs at Altoona and Vineland that Friday and Saturday, bassist Zack moved up to guitar and bass was handled by a certain person credited only as Nano from MySpace – almost certainly the nickname of Mariano Tissera, who would become co-manager of the band in due course. March dawned with some awesome news – that the band had gone back into the studio to work on some old and new songs, and that a tour was planned alongside Transition during April. The group would also be on at the Flipside Festival but the biggest shout of the lot was the confirmation that they would be joining the hugely influential VANS Warped Tour that summer. All Time Low were now attracting interest from a clutch of other labels so it's time to introduce a group who had a great hook-up with what would turn out to be their perfect record company.

CHAPTER 5

HOPELESS IS THE BEST WORD IN THE WORLD

Amber Pacific were a band formed in 2002 near Seattle, Washington state. By 2005, the group had signed to a label called Hopeless Records. Hopeless was formed in 1993, down in Los Angeles, with a view to releasing everything punk, alternative, rock and just downright fun stuff. A contract with someone like that was and remains one of the golden goals of any young band, due to the label's understanding of the scene, contacts, energy and support for its signings. Amber Pacific's debut emo/pop-punk album *The Possibility and the Promise* was released on Hopeless in May 2005 and, as is the way of things, the group was out touring in order to support the record. Jack told AbsolutePunk that the bands had met at a show in Virginia Beach: 'We all took a liking to one another and kept in touch from that day on, so as we began to attract the attention of certain labels, Amber Pacific took it upon themselves to pass our music on to Louis at Hopeless. We heard from him very shortly after that, and the rest is history.' As quick as you like, then, Hopeless jumped to the front of the queue and secured the signature of the group in March 2006. The official news – described as 'stellar' by the band – was broken on 28 March 2006 in an announcement on All Time Low's own website. The band had been somewhat ducking questions about it for a while. The update noted that the group had travelled extensively, meeting a host of record labels over the last few months, and had finally plumped for Hopeless/Subcity Records, home of Avenged Sevenfold, Melee, Thrice and of course Amber Pacific. The joy was palpable in the band's words, which referred to the label's family feeling and the sense of belief shared by all sides. Hopeless suggested that initially it would be preferable to put out an EP, rather than an album, which would give listeners a chance to get on board with the All Time Low aesthetic while at the same time allowing the group to continue to develop musically, get more experience touring and also accommodate the small matter of graduating from high school and breaking free of those bonds at last. The first fruits of the collaboration would be an EP called *Put Up or Shut Up*, a seven-track effort comprising five existing songs, re-recorded, plus two new ones, which was slated for release in the summer of 2006.

More good news came in May with a battle of the bands called WHFS Big Break at the Recher Theatre on 18 May. This was the group's opportunity to share the main stage at the HFStival with the likes of The Misfits; Coheed and Cambria; Panic! At the Disco; and, er, Kanye West. By now, All Time Low had already passed Fall Out Boy in terms of the

PureVolume charts, which reflected the number of times the band had been played on that website, so they were certainly picking up fans. The Big Break contest took place on 18 May 2006 ... and guess who won? Yup, our quartet of heroes – could there be any other result? This meant they opened both days of the festival, an annual bash backed by the East Coast radio station that was once the largest event in the area. All Time Low played on 27 and 28 May at the huge Merriweather Post Pavilion in Columbia, Maryland, and over the weekend over forty thousand people attended. To say the band was on the up is probably an understatement at this point.

Another milestone was to follow very quickly: the 25 July 2006 release of the band's Hopeless Records debut, *Put Up or Shut Up*. The title was taken from a lyric in the track 'Break Out! Break Out!' and itself is a statement of intent in that the line in question talked about not wasting time and getting out there to live the dream. So far, so good. As had become the norm, the EP was recorded with Paul Leavitt, but then taken for mixing in Atlanta with Zach Odom and Kenneth Mount at Tree Sounds. The result is an even more radio-friendly, bigger- 'phatter'-sounding band with a definite energy refined by an understanding of studio work and by that all-important time spent on the road living with the songs inside and out, night after night.

The EP begins with a new song, 'Coffee Shop Soundtrack', a tuneful ditty about a liaison that in typical All Time Low style has a bittersweet reflection on love, secrets and youth. Next up is the re-recorded 'Break Out! Break Out!', which takes the rougher-edged viscerality of the version on *The Party Scene* and adds a sheen of confidence that speaks to the continued success of the band and its growing master plan. 'The Girl's a Straight-Up Hustler' shows Alex's voice with a richness that had only been hinted at before, a boy who has become a man. The band as a whole here is notable for its tightness, particularly in the more stripped-down moments, as All Time Low begin to move through the gears towards that all-important chorus. There's an opportunity for Zack to really show off some of his chops here, with some ace turnarounds and bass fills that enhance the song without it becoming intrusive. And is that a hint of The Beatles in the coda's arpeggio?

'Jasey Rae' is the next track and it is a song that has lasted the years. In a Reddit Ask Me Anything (AMA), Alex noted that, yes, it was about a lass: 'Jasey Rae is a girl from Altoona, PA. We used to play these tiny VFW and Church halls, and she was a girl I had a crush on for a short period of time. Back then, every crush feels like a big deal, and her name happened to sing really well!' So in a sense, though this awesome pop-punk love song was named after one particular girl, it represents a universal human condition. Playing-wise, the control within the band as they slow down together towards the end is spot on.

The reworked 'Running from Lions' is next, keeping up the vibe and the dance-along nature of an EP that is both a summation of what the musicians have done before and a definite nod to the future, Zack's bassing here moving into another gear altogether. The last track proper on the release is an equally powerful version of the resonant 'Lullabies', here presented with a warmer, lusher sound than its first airing and if anything more jumpy-angular guitar stabs in the pre-chorus.

When Alex sings about feeling as though a piece of him is missing it is impossible not to feel for him. What is evident here, too, as with 'Jasey Rae', is the ability of the band to create songs, lyrics and vibes that may originally have come from personal experience and transpose those into moments, experiences, songs that other people can relate to from their own lives.

Reviews of *Put Up or Shut Up* were varied. A review on the usually supportive site AbsolutePunk was written by one Gabe Gross and began unpromisingly with the comment that the writer was more or less certain that 'fans will write you off as another band faking it for recognition'. The review went on to slate the perceived derivative nature of All Time Low, held up here as something of an avatar of a scene that the somewhat jaded-sounding reviewer seemed to be sick of. However, despite ripping into the band's so-called copyism, the reviewer had to admit that 'their music is so incredibly addictive, so much so that listening to it over and over again is rather enjoyable. And as a pop music enthusiast, this is so disheartening.' The review pointed out that five of the EP tracks had previously appeared on *The Party Scene* and concurrently praised 'Coffee Shop Soundtrack' and 'Jasey Rae' as good steps in a songwriting direction. A reviewer on Punknews.org was equally dismissive, hammering the band's efforts with the thought that 'it's hard to be a pop-punk band that's even somewhat memorable, I understand that, but these songs leave so little an impact it's often hard to remember they're playing at all.' Again, however, 'Jasey Rae' and 'Coffee Shop Soundtrack' were praised. Alex's vocals reminded the reviewer of another vocalist, Kenny Vasoli of The Starting

Line, albeit that Vasoli seemed to have 'something extra' to offer. The writer lambasted All Time Low for being off-key and lacklustre, concluding damningly that 'they're able to hide a lot of the inconsistency with simplicity, but only so much can be held back before becoming painfully evident that the substance is lacking.' Ouch!

On the positive side – and there is a rather large positive side – Sputnikmusic were bang into it. The reviewer here said that it was an album that was user-friendly while being memorable at the same time. As well as the 'catchy, relaxing and fun' sound, the harmonies in the vocals were great, the bass was sturdy and the drums solid as you like. More than that, there were some 'respectable guitar melodies' in evidence. 'Riffs are not only catchy, but also very precisely executed and wonderfully written. There is never an abundance of riffs, yet at the same time rarely a drought; as the band always uses them when the situation calls for it. All of these are factors that help make *Put Up or Shut Up* a joyful listen.' Which is a lot more like it, no? The review went into great detail about the tracks one by one, taking the songs on their own merits before concluding that the band seemed to have a good idea of where they were going in general. There was also a good combination of riffs, basslines, sections and arrangement, and while the sound was not groundbreaking, wrote the reviewer, the tone was very consistent in terms of vocals in particular: 'Things sound polished, catchy, and most importantly enjoyable; which is a lot to say since all four members graduated high school in 06! *Put Up or Shut Up* gives listeners a hint at what success the future might hold for the Maryland quartet.'

There were more encouraging words on Allmusic,

the reviewer also referencing one of the band's near-contemporaries, this time to the advantage of the Low: 'All Time Low plays unabashedly earnest and summery pop-punk like the Starting Line used to play before they took a stab at "maturity" and experienced severe growing pains.' The writer said that the record was 'practically pleading to be repeatedly blared from the car stereo over that last high-school summer before senior year starts. Their music reeks of youthful exuberance and fleeting innocence (though all of this should come as no surprise since the guys signed on with Hopeless during the final months of their senior year).' The band, thought the reviewer, was certainly influenced by the likes of Green Day and Blink-182, unabashedly so, which was to their credit. The review ended on a positive note saying that All Time Low had the room and time to refine their craft and grow. On Ultimate Guitar, meanwhile, users of the site were able to upload their own reviews, and a website writer known as Velorium Camper felt that the time was right for the group to kick on to a new level. 'Coming from a scene in Maryland that is not highlighted as often as other scenes (New Jersey, SoCal, etc.), All Time Low have been working hard from day one to make it big. It shows, and is paying off,' the reviewer wrote, not unreasonably, while getting in an early hipsterish note by saying that they actually preferred the older versions of the re-recorded tracks. Another reviewer, xdeline!, said that it was a definite step forward for the band. 'If you listen to the [*Three Words to Remember...*] EP first, then to this, you will never go back again. There is so much more harmony used in singing, which adds so much depth to the sound.' Contemporaries such as Boys Like Girls, Cartel, Taking

Back Sunday and Valencia were namechecked as stylistic counterparts to the lyric writing and the reviewer gushed in conclusion that 'all tracks on this CD are just amazing, and I would recommend this CD to anybody.'

The reviews continued through the years, with a much later summary appearing on Altpress, this time looking at Fall Out Boy and New Found Glory as touchpoints for the group, to the extent that Alex's vocals on Coffee Shop Soundtrack were reminiscent of FOB's Patrick Stump. 'Jasey Rae' was more like 'New Found Glory', felt the reviewer, particularly because of the 'spinning choruses and layered pop-punk guitar riffs'. In retrospect, or should that be 20/20 hindsight, this reviewer, writing in 2010, called *Put Up or Shut Up* 'the middle ground between a cover band obsessed with Blink-182 and a career of originality'. In other words, a band really and truly finding its own way in the music industry.

Neufutur agreed with that shout: 'While it still is up in the air whether the band is able to maintain this momentum for future recordings, this disc shows nothing in the way of flaws that may stand in front of the band. Pick up this album, give them a year, and then pick up the LP; chances are that you will not be disappointed.' Rockstar Underground caught up with Alex and Jack at a concert at The Stone Pony in Ashbury Park, New Jersey, and the guys were in full-on buddy mode, messing around and leaning in for *faux*-kisses, displaying the closeness and confidence of a group totally at peace with each other; it'd be impossible to tour so extensively were they not so comfortable in close proximity. Rian and Zack hung around in the background trying to put their bandmates off. 'We're brothers,' announces Jack at one stage, receiving a kiss on the cheek from his mate – and though it's all in fun there's obvious love there. Nano is also pictured eating an apple and joining in the general joshing. The interviewer was much enamoured of 'Coffee Shop Soundtrack'. 'Without giving too much away,' Alex explains, 'it's naughty ... a situation where a person already has another individual in their life ... it's kinda about those secret meetings you have with this person at coffee shops, very out of the way.' Jack, meanwhile, compares it to the relationship between the Montagues and Capulets in *Romeo and Juliet* – a nice reference to throw in and definitely not what one would expect from the dunderheaded one-dimensional pop-punks that some would seek to portray them as. Typically of the band, however, when the interviewer says that she's 'fickle', Jack asks if that means 'poop'. Alex corrects his buddy that 'faecal' is the word he's thinking of. Cheeky!

With the EP now out and roaring, All Time Low kicked on with a few dates alongside The Killing Moon, then hopped on to the VANS Warped Tour for a series of East Coast-based gigs. Alex told an interviewer for Punktastic that it'd been an extremely busy but amazing time: 'It's an all-day event, so playing is just part of what comes along with being on the tour. A baby band like ourselves generally have to bust ass promoting the time and stage on which they play, to get as many kids out as possible.'

And as with any band on the up, there was work to be done: Jack and Alex put on their shortest shorts to hand out flyers about the band, which led to a lot of interest from people who hadn't previously heard of the group. Crowds duly improved, Alex explained, and then the process was repeated with the band members heading out into the crowd to sell CDs to their new buddies: '[It is] the same concept as flyering but with a persuasive, manipulative, disgusting salesman twist,' he said, somewhat tongue-in-cheek. 'Sinister, I know, but you'd be amazed at what an iPod and some jazz-dancing can do.'

After Warped, All Time Low were one of the support bands to Amber Pacific, who'd been instrumental in hooking the Baltimore boys up with Hopeless in the first place. Dates ranged from Tacoma to Seattle from August to October, and other bands included Sherwood, Over It and Just Surrender. Set-lists to several of the gigs have been uploaded and if SetlistFM is to be believed, the concert at Club Impact, Tacoma, on 15 August 2006 was pretty similar to the EP's contents: 'Coffee Shop Soundtrack'/'Running from Lions'/'The Party Scene'/'Lullabies'/'Break Out! Break Out!'/'The Girl's a Straight-Up Hustler'/'Jasey Rae'/'Damnit (Growing Up)'. And yes, that last track was a cover of the Blink-182 song, from the 1997 album *Dude Ranch*. That latter track's lyrics deal with the passing of years, moving on, and a breakup with a girlfriend all at once – making it well within the All Time Low canon, not to mention being one hell of a crowd-pleaser at the same time.

Not that the tour was without its troubles: a concert at Cape Coral, Florida, at The Hinge venue on 11 September, was beset by technical problems as All Time Low hit the stage first, only to find out that there was no electrical power onstage. Undaunted, the boys duly performed acoustically. Once the power came back on, the band returned at the behest of second-on-stage Just Surrender in order that fans should experience the electric version of All Time Low. The band always liked to do things a bit differently live, with balloons, silly string, daftness and fun prominent in their live gigs. 'We don't like to replicate the CD exactly,' Alex was quoted as saying on Jambase. 'We make a thing out of being almost theatrical on stage. We try to turn the whole place into a party every time. We want to be everybody's friend. I think we try to keep everything really positive and have a good time. We've come to party!' And so they did.

The dates continued through to November, at which point our young heroes were due to start thinking about entering the studio again. This time the desk-meisters would include one Matt Squire, as the band began writing some brand-new songs for that most precious of things: a new album.

CHAPTER 6

DON'T CALL IT A SOPHOMORE ALBUM, THAT TERM SUCKS

Matt Squire's musical chops are impressive in themselves, with stints in several nearly successful independent, alternative and metal bands. Perhaps the most recognisable of those was the near-miss post-hardcore act Boston, which made waves in the mid- to late nineties before encountering a sadly familiar tale of label shenanigans and a subsequent band split prior to what would have been the release of their debut album. It was, however, a good learning experience for Squire, a guitarist by trade, who had always had an interest in the recording process. That blend of knowledge of the ins and outs of musicianship, a technical prowess and an innate understanding of what makes musicians tick made for a successful move into engineering and production and by 2004 he had established his own studios, SOMD, in College Park, Maryland. It all made him an ideal producer for All Time

Low's second full-length album, alongside the ever-inventive Paul Leavitt.

History notes that recording began on 18 April 2007, but it began in a manner that was anything but smooth, as Alex noted later in LiveDaily: 'We went into the studio hoping to record about fifteen songs and it got stripped down to about three. So we had to do a lot of writing there in the studio. I think it came together really well, and we're all really happy with the way it came out. You just need to turn it up loud and just enjoy it!' Never a bad piece of advice in punk rock, sir. Thematically, the singer was in something of a tongue-in-cheek mode when he told a LiveJournal interviewer that the new album had been inspired by '2006/2007. Some romance, some action, some murder mystery ... that's about it.' In the same article he explained how the songs generally came together. 'Writing wise, we all contribute to the music. I usually come up with the core lyrics. I can't write drums, so Rian takes care of drumming.' The live experience was as strong as ever; the boys spent most of March and early April on the road alongside Valencia, Secret Handshake and Just Surrender. Ryan Wapner remembers how it all went down. It's an experience he clearly recalls fondly. 'That entire first tour is exceptionally memorable. I think that was right between *Put Up or Shut Up*, and [second album] *So Wrong, It's Right*. I think Valencia and ATL were switching on and off for the direct support slot. I made some lifelong friends on that tour, and really learned a lot.' The merchandise expert and promoter said that he remembered it being quite a big deal that year.

$$6 \times 9 = ?$$

[It was an] incredible line-up, and most of the artists had new records coming out or albums in the works, so there was a lot of buzz about it. Industry folk coming out, sold out shows, and it being a ton of fun. I was young back then, and it was my first full coast-to-coast tour, so I'm sure I overlooked a lot of stuff like that. Tour schedules can vary a lot depending on whether you are a headliner or a support band, in a van or a bus, or have multi buses and trucks, and if there are things like in-store performances and press too.

He added that a typical day touring in a van was usually something along the lines of

- wake up at hotel or friend's house
- drive two to six hours
- gas station or fast casual brunch/coffee
- load in/set up [of the band's gear, PA, guitar stacks, etc. and maybe a soundcheck]
- find dinner/wander around the venue vicinity/coffee
- doors
- show
- load out
- drive two to twelve hours
- sleep.

Which does show the relentless nature of the beast. Not everybody is suited to life on the road, but All Time Low's constant willingness to subject themselves to the privations of the pavement marks them out as being worthy contenders indeed.

Meanwhile, sales of *Put Up or Shut Up* continued at an unprecedented pace. The world was beginning to wake up to this hard-working, fun-loving, pop-punkin' bunch of mates. The album begins with the breakneck speed of 'This is How We Do', Rian's irresistible drumwork driving a joyous, romping introduction to the band and the album complete with gang vocals from a host of mates including Matt Flyzik, The Dangerous Summer, Dan Dori, Jason Park and Alex Grieco. The lyrics talk about loving life, raising glasses and partying with the people. Rarely has there been a stronger statement of intent for an album ready to make the breakthrough.

'Let it Roll' could be read as a tour diary of sorts, sleepless nights and friendship, the lure of home and the brotherhood of friendship. Zack's on grand form here with a solid and yet eager bassline that features all the right turns in all the right places. It's a song about restlessness, about the passage of time and underneath it all the realisation that nothing lasts for ever – so enjoy it while it does. Timeless sentiments and again a lyrical maturity that often wasn't necessarily associated with All Time Low at this point.

'Six Feet Under the Stars' threatens briefly to turn into Motörhead's 'Overkill' before settling down into a more plaintive, mid-tempo tale of late nights, one-night stands, youth and getting into perhaps unwise situations. 'Holly (Would You Turn Me On?)' features co-writing credits from Dave Katz and Sam Hollander for both the music and additional lyrics. This concept of opening up the doors to musical collaborations was to return time and again in the group's activities and in this case the result is the kind of irrepressible pop-punk track that could be the soundtrack to a thousand surf video shows.

The Beach's simple guitar intro nods to The Ramones and launches into another love-relationship-based song which has the optimism of the summer burnt through it; you may leave the beach and the sun behind physically, but the memories remain. A fine sentiment indeed.

'Dear Maria, Count Me In' marks another milestone for All Time Low in that it has become one of their absolute classic tracks over the years. It's easy to see why: the spacious arrangement allows the lyrics and the sentiment to flow as the band frames a tale of breaking out, taking the world on together and claiming a version of the American Dream. It's pretty much a perfect slice of mid-late 2000s pop-punk with its variations in tempo, chord progressions and intimate but identifiable words checking all the right boxes. 'Shameless', meanwhile, deals with the underside of life; walking on a tightrope between doing what's right and getting led astray – by a woman, of course. 'Remembering Sunday' features a duet between Alex and Juliet Simms of the band Automatic Loveletter and begins with an acoustic tale of a character who hasn't been sober for some days; the girl whom the character is with leads him 'upstairs'. Strings, bass and drums enter as the tale moves on. The narrator is looking for a girl who was with the main character; he remembers the day was a rainy one and in retrospect the clouds were significant. Simms takes the main vocal for the last verse, a soaring, scathing admission that she is never coming back as she's thousands of metres above the ground and over him in a physical as well as emotional sense. The narrator, meanwhile, accepts that it's time to go home. In a later interview, Alex admitted that the song was about an actual experience with a girl, and revealed that, despite its themes of mortality and never returning, the girl in question was literally on an aeroplane and that no inference to her having passed away was intended. There is also a reading that points to a possible subtext of the tragic loss of Tom here, although as ever it's up to the listener to decide – which, of course, is the central point of all art.

'Vegas', which immediately follows, is also about the same girl and a missed opportunity to get married. Letting go also feels good and friendship is deemed the most important thing, after all. What the song also does is up the pace again following the relatively plaintive 'Remembering Sunday'.

'Stay Awake (Dreams Only Last for a Night)' is in some ways the flip-side of the album opener, dealing as it does with feeling the pressure while still trying to remain confident. The singer admits he isn't yet the captain he wants to be, but he's determined and dedicated enough to stay on course. Musically, there's a great breakdown in the middle where the band sings in close harmony before the gang comes back in to reassert its intent to live it up. A final chorus keeps that bunch o' shipmates on board to reinforce the point.

'Come One, Come All' is another road-fever ditty that redirects a washed-out feeling and frustrated protagonist's paranoid ire towards a particular DJ whose choice of tracks is hardly helping matters. A quick holiday, however, would do the trick just as well as burning down the radio station in question. Lest anyone should mistake All Time Low for sociopaths, of course, there's just time for another bona fide classic, 'Poppin' Champagne', to reassert the band's avowed intent to rise, to kick against the pricks and to ignore the naysayers, the bad TV and the moments of self-doubt because there certainly is a place for dreams and beliefs to come true. Like the track opener, it's shot through with the optimism and determination of a group still relatively at the start of their careers. In case anyone was in danger of taking the whole thing too seriously, the band warned on the cover art that anyone making illegal duplicates of the album would have their houses set on fire by the boys – a brilliant detail in an album that is full of excellent moments.

This time around, the media response was largely very positive. AbsolutePunk said that while the pop-punk sound was hardly new and had been done before (although what hasn't?) the album was absolutely loveable. Indeed, the reviewer called it, 'Somewhat of a throwback to the glory days of pop punk, an album full of youthful, summer-y, hook-laden songs that just begs to be listened to in a car, volume at 11, windows down and all.' Noting that sales of *Put Up or Shut Up* had now reached an impressive 60,000, the review went on to praise many tracks, including 'This is How We Do' ('There is a certain swagger about the group that is undeniable') and the anthemic 'Stay Awake'. The record got better on repeated listens and although the writer acknowledged that there would be naysayers as to the perceived generic nature of the album, it was refreshing that the band stuck to their roots to deliver what they wanted to do. The reviewer was convinced enough by the record to state with some certainty that All Time Low were definitively poised to become a major act.

Allmusic picked up on other influences, saying that, 'The quartet, fronted by affable singer/guitarist Alex Gaskarth, also nods to vintage hardcore on occasion, as evinced on the blazing opener "This Is How We Do".' The set of songs was sharp, sincere and sensitive, felt the website.

Alternative Press (*AP*) said that the band wasn't out to rip up the rulebook, but that they 'write pitch-perfect pop-punk anthems designed for sunny days at the beach/mall and evenings under the stars/influence [...] really freaking well.' The respected mag gave the album three and a half stars out of five before the reviewer began to riff on the deliciousness of the band's confections, concluding that '*So Wrong, It's Right* manages to stay sweet without drowning in genre clichés. And you know what that means: No cavities!' Which is good news for the listeners if not for the bank balances of the dentists, anyway.

Sputnikmusic was also on board with the momentum starting to build around the group, noting that 'they play their style of pop punk better then [sic] many acts ever will.' The lengthy review discussed the tracks in some depth, noting that the band had its own unique sound, Alex had an instantly recognisable voice and that even 'Remembering Sunday' as a slower track was 'truly touching'. The writing, felt the reviewer, was superb throughout the album and the lyrics were also excellent. All in all, All Time Low had kicked things up to another level. Again, the conclusion was that this was definitely a group looking to the stars: '*So Wrong, It's Right* succeeds because it constantly has so much going for it. There is no weakness to be pinpointed here and it is for that reason that All Time Low will be the front runners in the pop-punk world sooner as opposed to later.'

Hybrid Magazine contexted the rise of the band alongside the appearance in the mainstream of Plain White Ts. Here the reviewer noted that 'the band has made strides in their Sugarcult-dipped punk and their Cartel-coated emo-rock. Their music has reflections of a number of power punk bands before them and shows a huge amount of youthful energy that a contemporary generation of rock fans can latch onto and relate to immediately.' Other contemporaries included Taking Back Sunday and Red Jumpsuit Apparatus and the riffs were fat while the rhythm secured things with a surge of power. The music, said the writer, would become relevant to the newer generation of lovers of rock and pop-punk, and she praised the 'kinetic energy' generated therein.

All that being said, there were always a few misery-guts reviewers, such as Punknews, whose writer called it 'another uninspired disc devoid of any authenticity'. The writer said that the band was 'made for teenage girls', and went on to slam the group as having 'successfully removed all the remaining endearing qualities of the genre'. Perhaps realising the ranty nature of the review, the Maryland writer acknowledged that he did not like the band and signed off with a simple acknowledgement of his venting: 'I feel so much better now.'

As did the many listeners who'd loved the album on first – or subsequent – listens. That includes the naughty people who took advantage of the all-too-common phenomenon of an album leak – that is, an unofficial and definitely illegal placing of the record online by persons unknown. It was out two weeks earlier than planned. As Rian later told the Daily Chorus: 'If people are going to download it, they are going to download it. Either before it comes out or after it comes out ... they are probably going to buy it when it comes out anyway.' Such is the nature of the modern music game. Alex responded in the same interview that he wasn't going to pay for a copy, either.

During 2007 and even more widely circulated around the official release (25 September) came a slightly (but really, seriously, not very) risqué press shot of our gallant heroes wearing nothing but Y-Fronts, and in the case of Alex, for some reason a pair of white sneakers. While it's undeniable that the band is comprised of some good-looking and talented young chaps, it was hardly hardcore pornography. That didn't deter Magnolia Middle School of Harford County, Maryland, however, who spotted that picture adorning the locker of a fan named only as Rea. The humourless authorities suspended the pupil for three days as a punishment. Rea told reporters, 'I'm annoyed and bothered by the fact my principal called the picture "porn". I've seen way worse Chris Brown pictures.' Alex responded that he was equally upset that anybody could take offence at the shot. 'We tried our very hardest to look as sexy as possible and I think that maybe the administrative figures responsible for suspending the student were just jealous of our dashing, young physiques. I don't see any harm in carrying that particular picture around in a school environment. In fact, I've been speculating that studies may prove that the picture actually stimulates brain activity, and promotes greater levels of success in the classroom. But that's just one theory ...' And may the Lord have mercy on us all. Alex also said that the band had got bored of seeing other groups in posed shots, looking angry, with the same vibe: 'What if we took that serious picture and were naked? ... Why not do something just a little bit scandalous? Why not?'

With the album now out and roaring into the consciousness

of an even wider set of minds, it was time for the band to get back out there and tour, tour, tour to support it. Given the excellent EP sales, they were now attracting some real attention as they moved through the gears to accelerate their careers to the fast lane. The world seemed at their feet, so it was time to get out on the road – and get in the air, too – over a year that would prove to be another massive breakthrough for an act that, let's not forget, had only finished high school a matter of months previously.

CHAPTER 7

MEDIA MADNESS

Never ones to shy away from the hard yards, All Time Low's schedule for 2007 was a packed one. The boys weren't shy to talk to the media either, with increasing interest on both sides of the pond. During the summer on the VANS Warped Tour Alex was interviewed by MusicplusTV and explained that everyone was starting to feel the pace of the Warped dates a little, but that it was also a sad time to be parting from new friends. He added that the band would love to do the whole tour next time, proving that there was a medium-term plan in place already and that the ambition remained. The singer talked about how cool it was to be hanging out with New Found Glory, who were also on the tour and of course from whom All Time Low had gained their band name. Rian had played poker with some of the guys in the Glory, and the groups became lasting friends. The

Warped dates were a prelude to going out on the road proper with a debut tour of the UK alongside the Plain White Ts for ten days, then tours with The Starting Line and Boys Like Girls. The next significant time off, Alex explained, was over Thanksgiving – which in 2007 was 22 November. Given that this interview took place during August, that was quite a busy schedule but such are the demands a band on the up must adhere to. When asked how they kept up with their schedule Alex said that the band was full of youthful energy (he was the oldest at nineteen) and stoked about the possibilities of the future.

The Daily Chorus had a relatively rare full set of the four boys on board for another Warped-era interview in which Zack gave an insight into the touring process: 'It's all different for everyone … I like to work out. The worst thing is possibly a long drive where you don't get to shower for two days.' Rian's favourite thing about touring was seeing the fans so happy. Sagely, Jack spoke of the importance of engaging with everyone, from other bands to promoters to employees of fast-food establishments. Rian chipped in with the observation that while some people might say that the band was in some way lucky, having been signed straight out of high school, in fact they'd put in a lot of work up to that point. 'You're gonna play some of the crappiest shows in the world and some of the crappiest tours but everything helps,' he said. Another thing to do was to learn from more experienced groups, as Alex told *Vancouver 24 Hours*. The Warped Tour in particular featured bands that had been touring for a number of years, which created an ideal chance to share experiences, ask advice and get things about the industry straightened out. In the same interview, the singer was asked what it was like for a young band to be surrounded by girls. 'It's definitely cool,' said Alex, somewhat unsurprisingly. 'We're not super-indulgent of those kinds of things; the rock star life is definitely not what it used to be ... shit happens, but I won't talk about it.'

Buzznet were also on board, asking the boys to introduce themselves and tell the fans what their favourite cheeses were. For the record, Alex likes Mozzarella, Jack's a Parmesan dude, Zack is a Cheddar-head and Rian's flava is the Swiss cheese with the holes in it. That's classy journalism, right there, folks! Alex also told a story that speaks volumes as to the sense of daftness in the group – on a recent visit to Disney, encountering long queues, the band decided to rent a wheelchair to enable them to cut into lines. He said he felt terrible about pretending his legs didn't work. Inevitably, Jack was spotted while taking his turn in the wheelchair: by a fan wearing an All Time Low T-shirt. A picture of this incident exists somewhere ... Zack, sensibly, went surfing instead of participating in the Disney shenanigans and Rian claimed he had no part in the incident. 'We are bad people,' Alex said. 'Don't listen to our music.' As if.

The group had also won the Energiser competition on the tour, which meant a precious extra ten minutes of stage time. Being voted for by the fans it was doubly satisfying. On the Phoenix date, Jack had gorged on toast and jelly without having enough water to drink, and in the humidity and heat the inevitable happened and, whoops, up came the snack again! The guitarist, now a couple of pounds lighter, got back onstage and continued playing. 'It was really confusing from my perspective,' said Alex of the incident. '... I kept glancing to my right and he wasn't onstage … he comes back after the song and [says] "I just threw up."'

Another tour story concerns merchandise guy Vinny Vegas, who chased down three girls who had stolen some All Time Low gear from the van. Rian, not to be outdone, told the world about Jack having chipped his tooth on a Tootsie Roll, a particularly soft American candy. This necessitated a call to the guitarist's mum, according to the drummer. Chaoszine spoke to Alex and Jack on 11 October, the pair looking a little tour-weary as they were asked a series of questions including one about bad reviews. '[Some] reviews say it's a solid pop-punk record but it's not original,' Alex began. 'But we're not trying to be Led Zeppelin or Radiohead or whatever. We play pop-punk.'

A more serious and responsible side of the band was on show in a quick interview undertaken by PETA (People for the Ethical Treatment of Animals). Alex began by making the point that bringing a creature of intelligence into your home came with responsibility; he derided the small proportion of terrible dog owners who were breeding or keeping their animals in order to perform in illegal fights. He also put his weight behind campaigns to try and force change within those sections of the fast-food industry that had a bad reputation in terms of how they treated their source animals: 'The less people that stand for that kind of action, the more will change,' he noted. Fur was also in the firing line, the singer making the point that in these technologically sophisticated times there was no reason to kill animals just for their pelts when alternatives such as synthetic furs could quite easily be manufactured. Times had also changed in the schoolroom, where the established practice of taking dead frogs, for example, and dissecting them to find out how their innards were put together, was outdated. Jack added that he'd had to do that in school and the process was next to useless as a learning experience. 'You learn just as much by just looking at a picture,' he said. The short interview ended with the pair encouraging people to educate themselves by signing up to receive more information about these tricky moral quandaries.

A different kind of moral quandary was addressed directly by Alex following the band's video for 'Six Feet Under the Stars' being voted by fans on to TRL for airplay as part of a *Jukebox* video. The idea was that in some way the group was 'selling out' by doing so; on 10 December, Alex revealed his new plan to upload regular video blogs and introduced his first one by noting that dialogue and even disagreement was good. He explained what it meant to him to 'sell out' as a band. He said that the group were all very happy that the fans had voted the video on to TRL, albeit he had not seen it himself. However, there had been conversations on social media between factions of their fan base, who were either stoked that All Time Low were getting mainstream success or derisive for the exact same reasons. 'I'm not getting paid for it,' Alex said. 'Should I be?'

He asked for a definition of what 'selling out' meant in 2007, because his own definition was that an artist sold out if they changed their creative process or mindset purely for financial rewards. He still lived with his parents, he pointed out, meaning that he couldn't possibly have sold out – unless someone somewhere had not given him his wad of cash for the TV appearance. This mixture of tongue-in-cheek fun, down-to-earth trying to understand, and most of all willingness to engage the world in dialogue is something that permeates the career and work of All Time Low. They-am what they-am, as Popeye might say. Unless he'd sold out and started eating cabbage instead after a huge sponsorship deal, of course.

As the year came to a close, the group were named in *Alternative Press* as One of the Bands You Need to Know in 2007. Other notable names from that list included the brilliant Cold War Kids, Hot Chip, Silversun Pickups and The Horrors. The annual list of a hundred bands was seen as one of the touchstones for the current crop of upcoming acts, and on the back of the group's successful year it was inevitable that the Baltimore boys would be included. With sales still rocking on and gigs coming thick and fast, the New Year looked set to provide more challenges, more opportunities and a whole lot of fun along the way.

CHAPTER 8

THIS TIME IT'S (NOTHING) PERSONAL

*T*he year 2008 got under way with our favourite foursome out on the road – of course – and enjoying the experience immensely. Billboard carried tour diaries from the group, as All Time Low, for the first time, were touring as headliners. The other acts on the tour included Just Surrender, with whom Alex got up on stage nightly to sing 'I Can Barely Breathe', 'Every Avenue' and 'Mayday Parade'. The band also made a huge effort to continue meeting their fans with a run of in-store appearances at record shops and other venues where they'd converse with people of a similar mind. This personal contact between the band and its fans is one of the endearing parts of a career based on mutual respect and is the polar opposite to the old version of untouchable rock stars who'd never get close enough to do something so demeaning as actually talk with the people buying their records and tickets. It's also one of the reasons why All Time Low are so loved by their many supporters. An in-store event is by nature less high-octane than a gig and quiet enough to have those conversations, of course.

There were some typical tour pranks on show, too: Just Surrender's Jason Maffucci was to be the recipient of a sandwich punch while the bands were having a quick bite at Denny's. This daft game involves one main rule: if a sandwich is unprotected, it must be punched unless its owner has covered it or is holding it in their hands. The game begins when the first bite is taken. You pay for your slackness in leaving uncovered bread snacks, and rightly so.

An incident did occurr when the tour bus stopped so that the travelling party could collectively take a wee, and then drove off without the drum technician, Alex Grieco. Oh the scamps! Later, Every Avenue's van got covered in cake and Just Surrender's bus was decorated with shaving cream. All Time Low didn't get away with it, though: their own bus was covered in a variety of silly substances like string and bananas, plus some extremely unsavoury ones that had originated in the bodies of their tour mates.

Slightly more worrying was an incident on the way to a show at The Intersection, Grand Rapids, Michigan on 19 January 2008. Up there, the average temperature at that time of year is something like -6°C so inevitably the band found itself caught in a snowstorm. The multi-talented Matt Flyzik was on driving duty that night and somehow managed to keep everybody alive even as the van spun round completely, skidding through a total of 720 degrees. The trailer holding the band's gear skidded and hit the tour bus, which added to the danger, but as luck would have it, due to the conditions, the highway traffic was moving at a slow enough pace to ensure no other vehicles were involved in what could have been a terrible accident. Not that Alex Gaskarth was perturbed – he didn't even wake up from his slumber as the excitement was going on.

Nicer news was always on hand, however, with the band finding out that their gig at Crock Rock Cafe in Allentown, Pennsylvania, had sold out, making for an audience of 1,300, nearly double the crowd the last time they'd played there. Another boost for gig-goers was the appearance of Ryan Kinley, ex-Matchbook Romance, at The Polish Club in Poughkeepsie, who joined the boys onstage for their rendition of 'Damnit', the Blink-182 cover.

The boys' video for 'Dear Maria, Count Me In' was also starting to make a few waves. It has a rather risqué setting of the group playing the song at a strip club as a band. But there are also other versions of the quartet on show wearing dodgy wigs and deep in a strange, 1970s vibe, watching the performer strut her stuff, while giant bunnies and bees lark about and the barman – a clown – fixes drinks. The band are collectively enthralled by the Spanish-looking model playing the part of the exotic dancer. A chimp also has a go at pole dancing but, in the absence of any underwear in which to tuck notes, sadly goes untipped. A mock-brawl breaks out which culminates in the band being first handcuffed to a pole then finally leaving the club – along with the chimp. Obviously. The video began to be shown on TRL and then broke through to a host of MTV shows including *Discover and Download* and *Music Choice Fresh Crops* and playlisting on *Big Ten* and *MTV Hits*, which signalled another major breakthrough for the group. The song was also featured as part of the *Take Action! Volume Seven* CD/DVD release on Hopeless/Sub City on 4 March 2008, with proceeds from the twenty-track and twenty-video compilation going to the non-profit charity Do Something, one of the biggest campaigners for opportunities for young people and social change worldwide.

Amid this whirl of television work was the excellent step of debuting on *Jimmy Kimmel Live* on 7 March. The influential TV show host plugged the band's album before introducing a live performance of 'Dear Maria, Count Me In', and then Kimmel held up the album to the camera once more and the band launched into 'Six Feet Under the Stars'. A great way to introduce themselves to a very wide television audience and doubly beneficial as another tour was about to start.

This time it was the *Alternative Press* tour, which they were co-headlining alongside The Rocket Summer. Other bands on the bill included The Matches, Sonny Moore and Forever the Sickest Kids. In an interview with a Buzznet blogger, Alisa Reed, Alex said that it was great to be headlining a gig in front of 1,700 fans: 'Obviously though the other bands are a huge part of it, but it's cool to be at the top of the bill and, y'know, feel like it's your tour. It's awesome,' he said. He went on to say that the sold-out House of Blues gig was testament to The Rocket Summer's and Forever the Sickest Kids' local fan base, alongside All Time Low's growing legion of supporters. The singer mentioned that he felt like the band were on their way towards their goals but not quite there yet. When asked about whether he was able to enjoy his own music as a fan, Alex explained the difficulty of objectively listening without critiquing his own stuff: 'It's weird to sit down to listen to it to enjoy it. Sometimes I do try to sit back and listen to it from like the perspective of "y'know, if it wasn't my band would I enjoy this CD and would I listen to it?" I think I would.' No doubt about it.

The growing fame of the group was also under consideration, with Alex admitting that he had Googled himself only to find that some non-press photos taken by mates had somehow become part of the ever-sharing Net. In fact, sometimes these shots were the only proof that certain nights actually did happen, he reckoned. His dream supergroup, he added, would be Bryan Donahue from Boys Like Girls on bass, Shawn Harris from the Matches on guitar, Travis Barker of Blink-182 on drums … and Elvis Presley up front. Now that would be something to see. Mind you, the live experience of the *Alternative Press* tour was pretty great in itself, gathering some decent reviews for the package of emerging bands, although, as ever, there were still some holdouts, including a reviewer for Mishmash Magazine who somewhat harshly felt All Time Low were '[a] disappointment and actually wound up leaving a bitter taste after the show ended. Most of their songs were trite and juvenile although they did close their set with a near ballad that, while I'm sure intended as heartfelt, came off as insincere when preceded by their early work.' Gah, some people just won't be told, will they?

High Voltage had a much better idea of what it was all about: 'ATL are no strangers to rave reviews and I can definitely see why. The pop-rock-based band couldn't go onto the stage without a more than memorable introduction including Eazy E's 'My 6-4' and a backdrop with a few not so G-Rated words adorning it. Their set was definitely one of the major highlights of the night.' Which was much more like it. The reviewer particularly enjoyed 'Coffee Shop Soundtrack' and 'Dear Maria, Count Me In', concluding that they would definitely advise anyone to watch All Time Low live, as it was worth the money plus the 'neck cramps from all the dancing'. Which does beg the question somewhat where the writer learnt his dance moves, but to each their own.

One little factoid from the 2008 tour is that Sonny Moore played his first tour under his own name after having left previous band From First to Last. Nothing particularly earth-shattering about that little morsel apart from the fact that Moore was later to find another level of fame (and music) entirely under the name of Skrillex.

All Time Low also appeared as cover stars of the April 2008 edition of *Alternative Press* magazine with the blurb saying, 'Maryland's entry in the pop-punk sweepstakes have come to testify, like Blink-182 before them, [that] life is one glorious poop joke. No worries, because there's a legion of fans who think ATL are indeed, the shit.' It was the magazine's eighth annual 100 Bands You Need to Know issue, the previous year's version of which had of course been a big help to the quartet's ever-growing reputation.

The band were interviewed by *Rock Scene* on 24 April with the tour in its final couple of weeks, and the interviewer got a little more than she bargained for when enquiring as to what the group would ask their fans if given the choice. After some messing about, Alex came up with, 'Why do you write so much homosexual fan fiction between Jack and I?' – at the same time grabbing his best mate round the shoulders in a mildly flirtatious way. Indeed, this phenomenon was something that was beginning to crop up around most culturally current groups of performers in the fields of music, movies and entertainment. There's a large community of writers who play with the idea that there is more to the relationships of their favourite bands/film/TV stars than meets the eye and these imagined trysts can be extremely explicit. Such is the nature of fandom and the Internet, and really as long as nobody's getting hurt it's a pretty harmless activity.

Another poser for the band concerned which question they would like to be asked, but have never been asked. 'Are you good at Jenga?' was Jack's quick-as-a-flash response, bringing giggles from all concerned. So there's a vital thing for any journalist worth their salt to consider next time an opportunity to chat with a band crops up.

The power of video and social media was strong, Alex said, after a fan named Cody Carson uploaded a video to Alex's YouTube channel. Basically Cody asked if he could get onstage and sing with the band. The song would be 'Coffee Shop Soundtrack', and Alex said, well, yes you could, sir. The dream came true on 2 May 2008 at Cleveland House of Blues, Cody providing a super-high energy vocal as the crowd sang along with his every word. The young man clearly had a bright future ahead, making the very most of his moment in the spotlight by getting the crowd to clap and sing along as he spent his time clambering on monitors, doing star jumps along with the rest of the band and throwing some goddamned cool shapes while he did so. 'That was fucking rad,' Alex said, advising the dude to go get a drink of water and compose himself. What a moment for any fan. The *Alternative Press* tour came to an end in early May 2008, but for All Time Low there was no such concept as 'resting' – it was back to Europe for a summer of gigs and festivals.

Another pivotal moment in 2008 was when Rian got himself a tattoo of the Blink-182 dancing bunny. The tattooing process was filmed and put online by All Time Low and, as it happened, Blink's bassist and vocalist Mark Hoppus, a hero for the band, actually saw that video, which he reblogged on his own personal website. After that, Rian and Hoppus started to email each other, which escalated into the respective managements talking to each other and finally into what was something of a holy grail for Alex *et al* – the chance to work with Hoppus on some music. Needless to say, it was a huge thrill for all concerned, as a song was co-written with the intent that the material would appear on All Time Low's next album, which was starting to be discussed among the band. 'It was a really cool experience,' Alex told *Artisan News*, '[...] getting to know him, seeing [...] a dude that I idolised for so long, seeing his process of writing songs. It was very cool.' He added that he hoped Hoppus, at the time fronting Blink-182 offshoot +44, might also appear on said new record.

Back to the live arena first, however, and a quick couple of weeks in the UK, headlining a number of established venues in conjunction with Cobra Starship. Broadway Calls were the other band on the bill and the package duly delighted all who attended. A measure of All Time Low's success is the band's constant urge to be out there working and they duly filled in a rare off date with a last-minute opening slot being added to a gig headlined by The Movielife. Also at the gig on 19 May 2008 was a reviewer from Punktastic, who said of the Low's five-song set that it was 'fun, sugary pop-punk' and while not being totally the writer's thing, he still found himself singing along to 'Dear Maria, Count Me In' along with the rest of the crowd. All in all, wrote the reviewer, it was a great start to the gig.

Following the UK dates, a brief ten-day tour was set up alongside Hit the Lights, Valencia and There for Tomorrow, known as *The Shortest Tour Ever*, with the usual tongue-in-cheek titling. The band was getting ready for the Warped Tour 2008, of which they were becoming something akin to old hands, although still of a very young age. TheyWillRockYou grabbed Alex and Jack to talk about the phenomenon of young bands playing alongside their older predecessors. Alex said that initially it had been a bit tricky but conversely the industry had changed and younger groups were now getting signed straight from high school and going out on tour, following directly in the footsteps of the Baltimore boys. 'I think it's going to become more of a regular thing, cause I think the sooner you start the better you are going to be at that prime time, when it's time to actually go to that next level,' he said. Jack added that the group had been going for five years and had been signed to a label for two years, so the experience was there.

Also in the interview was a reference to the guys' caring side; All Time Low had autographed a guitar, which was sold for the More Than A Zodiac Sign campaign to benefit the American Cancer Society. Other charities with which the band were associated were Keep a Breast, To Write Love on Her Arms, and Invisible Children. The Warped Tour, said the singer, was a really great way to hook up with people doing such good work for their fellow human beings and subsequently not just to understand what the charities were all about but also to be able to help.

Typically for the band, though, a moment later Alex and Jack were discussing the fact that one of their favourite pranks of late had been killing We the Kings, who had apparently resurrected themselves after having had their heads lopped off live on stage. The boys were joking, of course – unless We the Kings are, in fact, zombies, which could very well be true. Aim for the heads! Again, typically of the boys, the conversation then veered off into a very revealing moment in which they told the interviewer that because of their tour schedule, the concept of rehearsing in their folks' basement was old news: they simply got out on stage and gave it everything.

Addicted2Shows lived up to their name with a gushing review of All Time Low's appearance at Los Angeles, where they were live on the Hurley stage. And the moshpit was in full effect, with a packed crowd losing their sandals, crowd surfing and falling over. 'All Time Low's set was fun, energetic, and definitely dance-worthy,' wrote the reviewer. 'There was a dancy, sweaty mix out there on that black top with even a little bit of circle-pit action which is great to see at Warped Tour.' Standout songs included the full, uncensored version of 'Poppin' Champagne', which had been bleeped for TV, 'Six Feet Under the Stars', and many other anthemic tunes. 'Fun, sweaty times,' concluded the write-up.

Following the heady days of the Warped bandwagon, All Time Low played a couple of dates on the mtvU Video Music Awards Tour – Katy Perry was also on the bill – then the boys jetted back over to the UK for gigs at London Scala and Nottingham's Rescue Rooms on 25 and 26 August, returning for two more mtvU dates in Texas. The next set of dates would be alongside Mayday Parade, The Maine and Every Avenue in October, giving the band a rare breather of around a month in between. The name of the tour this time was highly ironic: The Compromising of Integrity, Morality & Principles in Exchange for Money, harking back perhaps to Alex's blog of around a year previously. The group also put out a new video, *Poppin*, a remix of 'Poppin' Champagne'. Their linguistic skills were also improving, with 'Feeding the Pony' a new addition to the band's lexicon, taught to the boys by the naughty people at *Flecking Records Magazine*. As this is a family publication, you're gonna have to look up the definition yourselves, but please don't tell us you haven't been warned, OK?

For October read Rocktober, at least according to Music Choice, which put a series of rockin' videos and shows on air during that month: the edition of *Fresh Crops* was dedicated to All Time Low. The director of the station, Justin Prager, said that the month-long celebration was 'Music Choice's proudest moment yet for original Rock music content'. Fair play! A bizarre but truly collectible item was also shortly to go on sale, with a limited-edition set of two-inch models of each member of the band being made available. Yes, you too could have a tiny, white-panted vinyl avatar of our quartet sitting on your desk – if you were one of the lucky 1,500 who managed to grab the set.

Regardless, the reaction to the Principles... tour was pretty good. A Buzznet reviewer caught the show at Ventura Theater, Ventura, California, on 30 October, and despite being a relatively new convert to the group she 'effing loved it'. The writer said that the experience of watching the band was a bit like hanging out as friends. The difference was that 'they happen to interrupt your conversation with a few songs. I've never seen it done like that before, with such a fun, easygoing atmosphere. I like it, and it works well for them.' As much as the songs were great, she said that the bits in between were equally fun. For example, Alex and Jack had a competition as to who could spin their guitar round the most. Alex said that if he won, the crowd would have to get naked. He did win; they didn't.

Some typical humour was also on show when one of the cannons set up to fire confetti was triggered by accident midway through a song. Alex said that this kind of premature firing was something that Jack was very familiar with. Jack's response? Unprintable (but it was actually 'Fuck you'). Indeed, that same phrase was put into action again when he confiscated a phone from a fan who was speaking to her friend during the gig. The night ended with Jack picking Alex up and threatening to chuck him into the audience.

The fun continued through November, too, as seen in another write-up from the gig at Sayreville's Starland Ballroom right on the other side of the country, in New Jersey. Once more, there was standing room only. The band was in making-mates mode with the audience, giving the gig an intimate feel as group members spent time, 'tossing to them water bottles, guitar picks, and lyrics that spoke directly to each and every teen enthralled in a vicariously thrilling night [...] Their performance was fearless, fervent, and of course exceptional', reckoned the writer. Alex left the stage exhorting everyone to live life as if it were a party. Excellent advice, sir!

On a more sombre note, Mark Hoppus posted a blog

concerning two recent tragedies associated with Blink-182: the death of their long-time producer Jerry Finn and a plane crash that took the lives of two of the band's friends, Che and Little Chris. Travis Barker, drummer of Blink, and DJ AM, another close associate, had survived. As a result, the previously strained relationships between the band members had been somewhat healed, leading to rumours of a reunion for the three-piece who had been so influential in the career of All Time Low.

Hoppus also found time to introduce the Baltimore group onstage for the 2008 mtvU Woodie Awards on 12 November. The band was up for a Breaking Woodie gong, but was beaten to it by There for Tomorrow, who ironically now are pretty much There Yesterday, having split up in 2014. Other names to conjure with in that category were Lykke Li, Tyga, and We the Kings. In any case Alex and the boys put on a splendid rendition of 'Poppin' Champagne', rocking the stage as only they could.

Bassist Zack Merrick had been a busy chap, too, creating a clothing brand called Amerrickan in order to provide cool clothes for himself and of course his like-minded mates and fans. In a later interview with the ever-excellent *Alternative Press*, he explained that the idea had come from pictures he'd made from photos he taken on tour. He was friends with one Jonny Smith, who owned Kill Brand. Smith used one of those images on a T-shirt, which drew the attention of Zumiez, an online retailer. Initially, explained the bassist, the clothing line was dubbed the Zack Merrick collection by Kill Brand, until Ryan Ogren from the group Runner joked that a shirt could be created with the legend 'I AM-

Merrick-AN' on it. 'Inspiration comes from whatever just pops in my mind. Ironically, some of the things I have said in interviews we put on T-shirts, and people seem to really like them. I mostly wear plain T-shirts, so it's fun to try and design something on a blank canvas,' said Zack, who added that the designers at Kill Brand could knock up pretty much any design within hours. One example was a rather lame visual pun in which a cat was wearing one of those helmets that deliver beer through tubes to one's waiting mouth, but in lieu of the booze it was ketchup, or as the logo had it, cat-sup. Ouch! Zack also explained that he had been inspired by Ray Lewis of the Baltimore Ravens, someone he rated as being extremely motivated, certainly not a quitter and having leadership qualities. As far as those who wore his clothing line's output goes, Zack added that wearing an Amerrickan T-shirt usually meant that the person was a fan of All Time Low and also that they felt part of something unique given that the line is not a faceless corporate creation.

And so an extremely busy 2008 began to draw to a close, but not before Alex appeared alongside members of the Chiodos, The Rocket Summer, Relient K and good old Mark Hoppus on a special cover version of The Verve's iconic 'Bittersweet Symphony' by Ace Enders and producer Chris Badami. The track was released on 2 December in order to benefit the VH1 Save the Music Foundation, which buys new musical instruments to help kids in school learn to play. 'I have known most of the musicians who are a part of this for years or have played shows with and have become friends with them,' Ace explained. 'Most importantly we wanted to put together a group of people who respect and don't take advantage of their importance in the music business and the effect they have on the fans who look up to them.'

There was also the news that All Time Low were to play MTV's New Year party show, hosted by the equally prone-to-nudity Miley Cyrus. Other acts included The Academy Is… and Metro Station. More great news was that the group had been named *Alternative Press*'s Band of the Year 2008 – an accolade that came with a cover appearance scheduled in that influential mag for January 2009. Oh, and there was also the small matter of the announcement that a new album was being scheduled. Producers this time, according to rumour, would be Matt Squire, Butch Walker and David Bendeth.

CHAPTER 9

COLLABORATION AIN'T A DIRTY WORD ... UNLESS YOU'RE DOIN' IT RIGHT

The band went into the studio sessions with a number of finished tracks but also a number of ideas ready to be fleshed out. The sessions began on 20 January, which was the first time the boys had picked up their instruments for three or four weeks. Given how tight they had become as a band in the previous non-stop year, it wouldn't take long for it all to come back together as they began to learn the new stuff. Also on the list of things to do was multiple signing of posters such as the 300 Jack did on 20 January while Alex and Matt Squire worked on some guitar parts.

Jack had been a busy boy, also heading into the realms of style with his own clothing line. He'd teamed up with Glamour Kills to design and offer cool clobber that he'd like to wear, much in the same mindset that launched his bandmate's Amerrickan work. The title of the collection was a blend of

Jack Barakat and Glamour Kills, under the acronym JAGK. The logo could be printed in any number of different fonts – there were hoodies, slim Ts and a lot of colourful expressions of joy and music. As with Zack's stylings, this would prove to be a new way for the artist to express himself through a different form.

Zack was happy that the sessions were in Huntington Beach, California, where it was 20°C (80°F), rather than in their snowy home state of Maryland, where the temperature was less than half that. The studio process sometimes involves a lot of waiting around for other band members to work on their individual instrumental or vocal parts with the engineers, who twiddle with the magic buttons, and the producer, who has a more creative overview of the process. In the case of the new All Time Low sessions, the order of the day was to record rough demos for the band and then listen to them with a critical ear. On 22 January Squire and the band sat down and listened to what had been recorded over the previous couple of days, and then the boys set up their gear and jammed out the songs as a whole in order to get to grips with the material. This helped the demos to evolve into a more solid arrangement, because as soon as Rian started to record his drum parts, the structural side of the songs would be difficult to significantly alter.

The tracking process – in which each member records his part separately to build up the final sound – is generally how most bands prefer to record, because it means multiple takes can be recorded, even to the extent of 'dropping in' for a few bars to correct any snarl-ups. For drums, though, having a solid and ultra-tight arrangement to play is absolutely crucial, as it is the bedrock of the rest of the recording when done this way. Even when bands record live in the studio, the amplifiers and drums and vocals will usually be isolated from each other in separate sound booths in order to leave the possibility for additional takes of an instrument that may have a flubbed note or two.

To start with, then, the boys were in this pre-production process before heading to the main studio, called The Lair. Anyone reading the boys' blogs at this juncture, which were live on the Glamour Kills website, would have been bemused by Jack's entirely jocular announcement that the new album was going to sound like an old-school metal LP. Hmm ... Anyway, by early February, Zack was cracking on getting his bass sound sorted with Butch Walker. Being such a solid player of his instrument meant that he managed to get his main basslines hammered out in just a few hours, meaning bass and drums were down relatively early. Rhythm guitars were ready just a couple of days later and things started to sound like songs.

Another feature of studio work is that the concepts of night and day become meaningless. There is usually a touch of clockwatching going on – time is definitely money – but there are also long stretches that need filling with entertainment and waiting for your own turn to get creative. This the boys did by variously watching movies including *The Passion of The Christ* and ironic/guilty pleasures like *Oprah* and *The Fresh Prince of Bel-Air*, or at least accusing each other of doing so. A short break in the video updates was caused by Matt Flyzik having to briefly head back to Baltimore, before the news restarted in late February once the group were back on relative home turf in the New York area. The recording was punctuated with some letting off steam; or, if you're All Time Low, letting off actual fireworks in a car park.

There was also a rumour going around at the time that the new album would be coming out on giant label Interscope. This may have been unwittingly given credence by Alex, who felt it necessary to go on to AP.net to set matters straight. Basically he'd given an interview at the Grammy Awards in which he appeared to say that Interscope would put out the LP, but in fact at the time he'd had trouble hearing the question due to the surrounding hubbub on the red carpet. 'To put an end to it – The next record is coming out on Hopeless – Its [sic] gonna be awesome,' he wrote on the site. True at the time but, as we shall see, that record label is still a major part of the story.

Recording was completed by 17 March and a week later fans heard the first fruits of their heroes' labours with the lead single from the album, 'Weightless', being put online through AbsolutePunk with a video simply showing the lyrics. It came out on iTunes on 7 April. This three-and-a-bit minutes' track has become one of the band's most loved songs, and deals with wanting to get out there and take the world by the scruff of its neck, banishing negativity and maybe wanting to never grow up. It's another signature track that has a great loud/quiet contrast, massive-sounding guitars courtesy of Matt Squire's sessions, and a real sense of forward movement in a career still gathering momentum day by day. By 10 April it was at Number 10 in the iTunes Alternative Chart, which wasn't a bad start at all.

After all that time in the studio the band must have been

raring to get back out there and experience the instant hit of the electric vibe that is a live tour. This time, the band wouldn't be headliners but actually one of the support acts to the (at the time) more well-known Fall Out Boy. The gigs on the Believers Never Die, Part Deux US tour would also feature Cobra Starship, Metro Station and Hey Monday for most dates. Bizarrely, perhaps, rapper 50 Cent (that's about 32p sterling at current exchange rates) would join the tour for five dates in April. Billboard.com picked up the story and frontman Patrick Stump explained that the rapper had 'been talking for a while about doing something together. We definitely like hip-hop a lot, and I think a lot of people know that at this point. We've toured with Paul Wall. We've had Lil Wayne on our record. I worked with Gym Class Heroes extensively. So I think it works.'

Not unreasonably, the band advised that should anybody really object to Fiddy's set they could go to the concession stand, the bathroom or presumably the bar instead. As for the rapper, he was up for the challenge and with typical gusto explained what was going to happen. 'This will be a major moment in music history,' Contactmusic quoted him as having said. 'Joining forces with Fall Out Boy, one of the most dynamic rock bands in the industry, will be an exciting and historic event for rock and hip-hop. This is a chance for me to bring my music not only to hip-hop fans, but to a broader music audience.'

Dates duly began in Phoenix, Arizona's Mesa Amphitheatre on 3 April 2009. The headliners first took to the stage dressed in suits, with singer Patrick Stump wearing a wig, apparently in a statement against corporate America. Mock-riot police were also in evidence as bass player Pete Wentz said the crowd was welcome to the 'corporate retreat' and that the plan was to get everybody rich so they could buy a yacht. 'But most importantly, you gotta learn how to thrill them first,' he added. The band went offstage after three songs to change back into more familiar Fall Out Boy clothing, with Wentz coming back to explain it was all about showing how the rich treated the poor and that people's attention should also be on starving folk in other countries like the Republic of Congo and Sri Lanka. Deep. A guest star on the song 'Sugar, We're Goin' Down' was Hey Monday's vocalist Cassadee Pope – remember that name. As for All Time Low, the Sacramento City College's online reviewer summed them up thus: 'All Time Low was pretty good, I've never really listened to them before, but they had good energy, but still opening act status.' Hmm, just you wait, old chum ... just you wait!

Still, Outloud were a lot more into the band, noting that the crowd at the 21 April gig in Pompano Beach, Florida, was very quickly jumping about and joining in with the vocals, particularly during 'Weightless'. 'Being a bit of a "glory hog" as Alex Gaskarth put it best, Jack Barakat decided to take a stroll while playing and ran around the venue with teeny boppers chasing him down,' wrote the reviewer. 'All Time Low stole the spotlight of the show with their antics and fun-loving attitude on stage.' The website had to add, however, that as South Florida's outdoor gigs had a no-cursing policy that presented a few problems for the Baltimore lads, for whom the odd salty word or two was pretty much part of their usual lexicon.

Fiddy, meanwhile, had appeared at the Dallas gig on 14

April before missing the Orlando show because of studio obligations, and then the Houston gig on 18 April had to be pulled altogether due to bad weather. The gigs, however, were coming at their usual speed and All Time Low, as was becoming the norm, only got better as time went on. A review of the set in Chicago's Allstate Arena on 9 May got the boys' music and approach spot on, praising them and saying that they 'continue a tradition of teen angst bands that somehow come off as adorable instead of pathetic. Their quirky awkward songs really speak to a disenfranchised youth but still enable them to dance.' The well-researched writer noted that songs included 'Stay Awake', 'Circles', 'Weightless', 'Jasey Rae', 'Poppin' Champagne' and, of course, 'Dear Maria, Count Me In'. The review went on to say that rather than being possibly a one-hit wonder, the group really did have a bright future ahead of them.

More rain blighted the gig at the Lifestyles Communities Pavilion in Columbus, Ohio, but the packed crowd didn't care. A critic glorying in the name Cassie the Venomous was also in attendance. Not that Cassie was being particularly venomous in her observation that the lads provided the most sincerity and genuineness of the whole night. There was, Cassie wrote, 'no ostentation (save for a hot pink bass guitar that was just sweet), no awkward theatrics – shirts stayed on and everything! The band members treated the crowd to an intimacy that the previous bands had not provided when the guitarist jumped into the audience and also when he somehow managed to get to the lawn and stand in front of it.' Which is fairly typical of Jack's onstage demeanour, is it not?

A fan called Bryan Peters had the experience of fronting the band once more at the gig in Milwaukee on 16 May, leading them in their cover of Fall Out Boy's 'Sugar, We're Going Down' when Alex went offstage briefly for personal reasons. Bryan – a 'normal guy' from Appleton, Wisconsin – posted a short video online following the experience, wearing the same T-shirt that he'd had on that night (presumably having washed it first) and showing the drumsticks that Rian had given him as a memento, calling it a 'dream come true' to have been pulled out of the crowd to step into the limelight. Rian and Zack were cool, he noted, adding that he hoped Alex was feeling better now. 'I hope you suffer no more anxiety attacks. You're an awesome singer.' Bryan also said that he hoped the many people who had come up to him after the gig to congratulate him would see his video response. He also put in a plug for his own band, called Page Two, which interested folk could find out more about on MySpace. The site, however, was quickly superseded by other forms of social media, including Twitter.

Contemporaries of All Time Low, Metro Station, made a point of being visible online. And while vocalist Trace Cyrus and Alex were to lock horns in 2015, Cyrus summed up the general feeling among upcoming acts in 2009.

'We used to spend loads of time on the Internet finding new music, it's one of the most fun things to do, but it's hard to do when you're on the road so most of the bands we see are the ones we play with on the road,' explained the brother of Miley.

Twitter accounts [–] that's the next main thing. You can do it from your cellphone and it's really simple. We used to be on MySpace all the time but now it's so hard to get a connection on the net on tour. But we love finding new bands – it's very different to how it used to be for us. Twitter is a very instant thing, you can put things out and everyone gets to read it. It's a great way to speak to the fans and we do competitions on there too for tickets and stuff. Day-to-day stuff, we can tell people what they're doing, send out pictures and make people think they're involved with the band. It's a cool connection with the fans.

All four members of All Time Low are very active users of social media and could be described as digital natives, particularly in comparison to previous generations of less tech-savvy musicians. Indeed, as Billy Ray's boy says, the potential to connect with fans in a much more direct manner is one of the things that means so much to the Baltimore chaps; they'd never been the kind to shy away from the very people who were buying their records and concert tickets and merchandise. And if nothing else, it was a great way to find out where the best parties were going to be, potentially, wasn't it? Metro Station later went on to tour for the rest of the year alongside Miley and shared the work ethic of All Time Low.

'We're trying to be one of the biggest bands in the world,' Trace continued. 'We've been on the road for two years and we're not going home any time soon. We're going to make the second record and keep touring. We don't have holidays. We'll be in one place for a month when we're recording and that's as close as we get. Live shows are instant gratification, you feed off the audience while recording in the studio. You do the same thing over and over again and it just clicks cause we all want the same thing.' These words could easily have come from the mouth of Alex, Jack, Rian or Zack: modern pop-punk bands were definitely of the opinion that success was something that came through hard work as well as catchy, jumparound songs to get crowds off their feet and into the stratosphere. The Believers Never Die, Part Deux tour came to a close on 17 May at the Roy Wilkins Auditorium in Minneapolis.

By now fans were absolutely buzzing about the prospect of the new album and in true Internet style a tracklisting was 'revealed by the band' on 16 May. According to a report on Alter the Press!, *Nothing Personal* would be released on 7 July and would feature twelve songs in the following order: 'Weightless'; 'Keep the Change, You Filthy Animal'; 'Damned If I Do Ya (Damned If I Don't)'; 'Lost in Stereo'; 'Stella'; 'Therapy'; 'Walls'; 'Hello Brooklyn'; 'Sick Little Games'; 'A Party Song (The Walk of Shame)'; 'Break Your Little Heart' and 'Too Much'. (The site reported two weeks later that the actual running order was going to be: 'Weightless'; 'Break Your Little Heart'; 'Damned If I Do Ya (Damned If I Don't)'; 'Lost in Stereo'; 'Sick Little Games'; 'Hello Brooklyn'; 'Walls'; 'Too Much'; 'Keep the Change, You Filthy Animal'; 'A Party Song (The Walk of Shame'; 'Therapy'.)

Excitingly, the band then jetted off to Japan for gigs at Club Quattro venues in Tokyo on 25 and 26 May, Nagoya on 28 May, and Osaka Shi on 29 May, along with Set Your Goals. The next stop was Australia in June – which is the winter over in the Antipodes. The Aussie tour was part of the Take Action! Initiative and the Hopeless Records CD/DVD came out in Australia too. For those shows, the set was 'Six Feet Under the Stars'; 'The Beach'; 'Jasey Rae'; 'Shameless';

'Poppin' Champagne'; 'Coffee Shop Soundtrack'; 'The Party Scene'; 'Remembering Sunday'; 'Holly (Would You Turn Me On?)'; 'Umbrella' – a cover of the Rhianna track and 'The Girl's a Straight-Up Hustler'. Encores were 'Weightless' and 'Dear Maria, Count Me In'. The local music was provided by Stealing O'Neal, a quintet whose pop-punk was firmly in the same vein as the Blink/Green Day/All Time Low triumvirate.

FasterLouder was on hand at a couple of gigs to report on proceedings. First, the concert at The HiFi, Brisbane, on 4 June. 'All Time Low have two pretty guitarists with slick haircuts, a fan's D-cup bra slung over their mic stand and some fairly standard emo pop punk tunes,' wrote the reviewer, who went on to compare them unfavourably with Set Your Goals. She also noted that at one point Zack's bass was making the walls rattle, such was its power. As usual, the bands were having fun onstage; Joe Saucedo, bassist with Set Your Goals, jumped onstage in his pants with a poster strapped to him saying he was 'Hotter than Alex', before that cover of 'Umbrella' went down really well with the crowd. Later, Michael Ambrose, drummer with the Goals, helped the boys out with 'Weightless', prompting the writer to sum up the band's appeal to its fan base. '[They have] great vocal harmonies, kickin' rhythm section and guitar-around-neck-swinging abilities. The annoyingly poptastic 'Dear Maria' gets the obligatory encore thrashing, right before half the audience turns into pumpkins,' she noted. Cool! Wait, what?

No vegetable-based metamorphosis was in evidence at the Corner Hotel, Melbourne on 6 June, with another reviewer from *FasterLouder* praising the band's presence and tightness as a unit. 'We decided to take the time to get drunk in Melbourne,' an unnamed band member was quoted as saying, which was no doubt true after the gig, which featured 'Alex Gaskarth providing crisp, near perfect vocals, and Jack, Zack and Rian showing great musical talent'. During the gig, Alex stepped in to challenge a fight that had broken out in the middle of the moshpit, telling the perpetrators that, 'You come to these concerts to get laid, not to fight. I don't care what he did. Just leave it ... I don't want to have to deal with this shit.' At which point things calmed down a little. Jordan Brown, vocalist with Set Your Goals, got onstage to assist with some backing vocals before guitarists Dan Coddaire and Audelio Flores took over guitar duties for 'Dear Maria'. Jack took the opportunity to do one of his now nearly obligatory dives into the crowd. They clearly loved him already for one of his more, uh, playful introductions to songs, when he'd said prior to 'Holly (Would You Turn Me On?)' that it was 'about a blowjob ... in the back of a Subaru ... Alex's mum's Subaru ... Except it wasn't Alex's mum in the car ... it was his dad.' What a scamp!

Following the Australian leg of the 2009 live extravaganza, the boys travelled for a gig in Hawaii at the Pipeline Cafe in Honolulu on 12 June, then a pair of dates in Madrid and Barcelona a couple of weeks later. New material was still popping up online, too, with 'Damned If I Do Ya (Damned If I Don't)' hitting MySpace, followed by a demo version of 'Hello Brooklyn'. Talking of New York, the boys also busied themselves recording a special set for MTV Unplugged. The tracks were 'Remembering Sunday', 'Weightless', 'Damned If I Do Ya', 'Coffee Shop Soundtrack', 'Dear Maria, Count Me In', 'Lost in Stereo' and 'Jasey Rae'. That little lot proved that the group had several bona fide classics already to draw on, with plenty more to come. Things had been pretty hectic so far for the band, but they were about to ramp up even further with the release of what was, in many ways, their breakthrough album.

CHAPTER 10

THE ALBUM DROPS

The first time the new album was available in its entirety was on 30 June 2009 as a stream on MTV's *The Leak* (if you happened to be in the United States) although a five-minute trailer was more widely available in which the boys talked about several songs including lead single 'Weightless'. Rian said he was happy that it was the first single and Zack added that it got a great reaction. 'It really fucking rocks, and that's about all that matters,' he said. The band explained that rather than writing together as previously it was more the case that the album had come from individual bits written while travelling and touring. Alex said he felt like that process had definitely had an effect on the record and Jack explained that there had been several producers involved. Different producers kept the process sharp, and being able to record in different places also helped the band keep it together rather than feel as though they were glued to one location for a long period of time. The new album was a step forward, the band agreed, because there had been the opportunity to draw on the experience and creativity of different producers, plus to explore different ideas and approaches. It was, they believed, the best record the band had made to date. The trailer ended with a montage of people saying how the band sucked, were ugly, had no future in the industry – but that was nothing personal.

The album came out on 7 July in the United States but the UK had to wait until 14 September to grab a copy. It begins with the aforementioned 'Weightless', with its initial Adam and the Ants-esque intro and massive guitars truly launching another All Time Low classic-to-be. The band then launches into 'Break Your Little Heart' with some of the most vitriolic lyrics written to date. The song talks about a girl who, though good-looking, is not worth the trouble; the protagonist is going to break her heart and it won't be pretty. The album title is taken from this track. As with the album opener, it's a Matt Squire production and features some multi-tracked guitarwork that adds a nice textural layer. And was that a synth in there too?

Butch Walker was at the helm for 'Damned If I Do Ya (Damned If I Don't)', which has a hint of Blondie about it and a nice, mid-paced beat that allows the track to really expand into its sonic space. This one's all about the build, whether ascending in volume, adding or taking away instruments, or the hand-damped guitars that are a signature sound of the band and the genre.

'Lost in Stereo' is one of two tracks under the production

overview of S*A*M & Sluggo (the other is 'Hello, Brooklyn'). That pairing of Sam Hollander and Dave 'Sluggo' Katz had previously collaborated with Cobra Starship on the track 'Snakes on a Plane (Bring It)' from the cult movie starring Samuel L. Jackson and, well, a bunch of snakes. Over the years they'd worked with Metro Station, Katy Perry, Gym Class Heroes, Boys Like Girls, Good Charlotte and more, and were named by *Rolling Stone* magazine as Hot List Producers of the Year, 2008 – some accolade indeed. The track has something of a 1980s feel at times, in a good way of course, with lyrics about a girl dancing to the radio who is definitely something of a handful – but a worthy handful.

'Stella' follows, another Squire production with words that veer between exhaustion, getting wasted, wanting to be taken home and staying out late, getting fucked up. Those gang vocals near the end and stadium rock drumbeat are pure Queen, too: 'We Will Rock You', indeed.

'Sick Little Games' is Butch Walker's second production and a very catchy track with some stark lyrics about life in the spotlight. It's the realities of fame and playing the game of celebrity while at the same time trying to keep grounded and experiencing moments of doubt. There's a telling line near the end in which Alex wonders how he ended up on stage, trembling and anxious. Given the demands of the road, it's inevitable that a sense of unreality develops and once more it's a song that hides some really insightful and personal sentiments beneath an emo-tinged pop-punk ditty.

'Hello, Brooklyn' is a paean to the coast-to-coast party vibe, featuring of course someone to kiss and the fact that when the world ends, that'll be a party too. The phased guitars are space age and intriguing additions to the All Time Low sound here; the song romps along with a gleeful energy that is unmistakably ATL.

'Walls' is a collaboration with David Bendeth and introduced by an arpeggio-like synth figure before heading into a song about hooking up with an old flame for something more than lust. It's love of a deeper nature that the protagonist needs now, and he's not the youngster who was naive at the start.

'Too Much' (Squire) picks up the sentiment and again utilises that epic 1980s synth sweep, a neo-disco beat and Georgio Moroder-style tinkling synth figure and hand claps. The texture builds towards the chorus, where it falls, and the processed vocals have a hint of vocoder about them, used to excellent effect creatively. It's not until the second pre-chorus that the guitars really kick in and even then they're there more as a way to increase the depth of the song rather than to lead it. 'Too Much' is a track that really does show how far the lads had come creatively and on its own merits fully justifies their new modus operandi in the studio. It's experimental in relation to the group's previous work without being so completely different as to be out of place.

'Keep the Change, You Filthy Animal' (Squire) pulls it all back into familiar guitars and vocals territory straight away. It's a song about fakers, people telling tales, little secrets and bitchiness. The boys here are rapier-sharp in their playing, the legacy of so much time on the road refining their skills as musicians. They rip through a classic pop-punk ditty voraciously, but star of the show is Rian, whose rhythms and drum figures are complex and fantastically played.

'A Party Song (The Walk of Shame)' is another one from

the Matt Squire sessions and kicks in almost unexpectedly straight after its predecessor with some more gang vocals in an instant singalong moment. All about one-night stands – having human contact for the night to feel better – it's certainly got some poignancy about it amid the bravado.

The album ends with the Bendeth-produced 'Therapy', a quiet and introspective number sung beautifully by Alex and with some lovely acoustic work, including gorgeous harmonics. Zack's on marvellous form with a sensitive bassline as the song gradually builds into what would be a full-blown rock ballad in another group's hands but here is a lush tale about keeping a brave face but feeling completely different inside. It's easy to read this as a song about doubt at the success of the band's career and feeling like a fraud in front of so many fans, but equally it could be about a relationship gone sour.

The reviews started to come in faster than ever before. Good old AbsolutePunk's reviewer found it made him hark back to 2002, when at the age of sixteen he was cruising around listening to New Found Glory, The Starting Line and Blink-182. That, he said, was a good thing because *Nothing Personal* was set to be All Time Low's breakthrough record. He wrote that the producers and the band had delivered twelve songs that 'sound crisp, smooth and dynamic'. 'Weightless', he wrote, packed a 'Tyson-sized punch', and while most other pop-punk bands wished they were able to write as good a hook, there were even better ones to come including the instantly catchy 'Damned If I Do Ya (Damned If I Don't)'. Bands namechecked in the review included Jimmy Eat World, New Found Glory and Plain White Ts in the final track, 'Therapy'. The album, according to the review, did have its low points, including

'Hello, Brooklyn' and 'Too Much', which the reviewer felt was a missed opportunity. All in all, the conclusion was that it was a step forward and that All Time Low would reach the heights of Fall Out Boy and Paramore.

Alternative Press, the magazine that had given the band two album covers in 2008, commented on the fact that Walker, Squire, Bendeth and S*A*M & Sluggo had not only production but also co-writing credits on the album. 'In effect, nothing on this album was written strictly by All Time Low. So how did this affect the band's youthful exuberance?' they asked. Well, to start with, the Blink-182 influence wasn't so strong on this record. Jimmy Eat World, New Found Glory and Motion City Soundtrack were more obvious touchpoints. 'Damned...' and 'Sick Little Games' were both stormers, reckoned the writer, massive pop-rock tracks that highlighted the excellent vocals. 'This is new territory for the brash, young band, and they pull it off better than haters would want to believe' was the verdict there. However, the S*A*M & Sluggo tracks didn't do it for the writer, who felt that betwixt those very high and very low points the stuff in the middle was pretty darned good. 'Too Much' was given props for being a great step forward as '[a] slow, electronic-tinged number showcasing Gaskarth's Justin Pierre-esque timbre – unfortunately, as with the entire album, his vocals are Auto-Tuned and Vocodered far beyond what they should. (Note to all future producers: This kid can actually sing – let him, already!)' The album, concluded the writer, wasn't the band's ultimate effort but it was definitely better than what had preceded it. There was creativity on show that would serve them well, he felt.

Billboard gave the album a score of 65 out of 100 and said

that it 'plays like a veritable pop-punk frat party': '"Stella" is a bouncy, booze-fueled anthem and "Lost in Stereo" tells a tale of unrequited love.'

The UK later got on board when the record came out in Blighty, with the mighty *Kerrang!* magazine giving it a KKKK review (that's four out of five, noise fans) and saying it could make the band as big as My Chemical Romance and Fall Out Boy. '"Weightless" is a three-minute rush of punk smothered in pop fairy-dust,' the magazine printed, 'as are "Damned If I Do Ya (Damned If I Don't)", "Lost in Stereo" and "Stella".' The album was more of a party than a riot, the review continued, and while 'Therapy' wasn't as dramatic as maybe it could have been, the overall experience was that of a group having one hell of a time, and inviting you to have one too. It was for fans of the likes of Fall Out Boy and Simple Plan, the reviewer concluded.

Rock Sound, another venerable institution, bewailed the lack of the collaboration with Mark Hoppus but said 'Stella' and 'Break Your Little Heart' were fine tracks. 'It was always going to be tricky, topping an album as catchy as *So Wrong, It's Right*, but All Time Low have nailed it with their third offering, *Nothing Personal*,' was the verdict.

The Washington Post said that the record company ought to cancel any vacations by its publicity department because the album was destined to bring the media spotlight to the boys. The reviewer felt that the songs were 'so jaunty and their lyrics about first love, betrayal and parties so angst-filled you can easily imagine them playing in the background of the TV shows *The Hills* or *90210*. Expect to hear the high-school/college crowd blasting the tunes at top volume as they cruise around town this summer.' 'Lost in Stereo's earworm of a chorus was praised and while the songs were relatively straightforward it was all good clean summery fun. The reviewer chucked in a couple of different bands to reference here: the Go-Gos and the Romantics.

Alter the Press! said that the record's 'slick production and singalong choruses are spread throughout', praising the hooks of 'Weightless', a 'pure and perfect slice of pop-punk pie'. Somebody's clearly hungry again, but never mind. The writer also loved 'Break Your Little Heart' and 'Damned...' but 'Too Much' featured a lifeless vocal from Alex and while 'Therapy' was a heart-string tugger, it followed some filler songs. Nonetheless it was an album full of happiness and good pure pop-punk.

Someone at Punknews enjoyed the album, describing it as nearly really good. 'Some of the compositions, harmonies and compiled melodies are excellent and often highly infectious,' wrote the journalist. 'Most of the tracks have a good upbeat vibe and are well-executed. This is not "bad" pop-punk by any means, and there are a number of moments where you can't help but say "damn, that's catchy". But, there is a massive problem. This album is horribly over-produced. As a result, it doesn't just sound like bubblegum pop; it almost tastes of it.' 'Too Much' and 'Lost in Stereo' were big ballads that ruined the whole album and the lyrics weren't hot either. Despite this it was a good pop-punk band making the music, even if they were at risk of sounding generic.

Another circumspect review was delivered by Punktastic, whose short review would state that *Nothing Personal* was a 'great pop-punk record which will be lapped up by all those fans who loved the first album, but not the step up you'd kind of hope for'. Expanding on the point, the reviewer felt that the group had delivered, in effect, *So Wrong, It's Right, Part Deux*. It wasn't destined to be a classic, felt the writer, but that probably wouldn't stop the fans making them one of the more prominent bands of the year.

On About Entertainment, the writer also made reference to the perceived familiarity of the sound that ranged between Weezer, Fall Out Boy and basically any group associated with the VANS Warped Tour. The producers were some of the biggest hitters of the day, wrote the reviewer, which resulted in 'a highly commercial sound'. But sadly, not so much of a distinctive one.

A quick word here for Under the Gun, whose writer called it a sophomore release – which was (a) incorrect and (b) a horrible turn of phrase that ought to be banished. That aside he referenced the good-looking boys and stagecraft as two reasons why the new album could help the popularity of the group no end. Indeed, the reviewer said that the band had grown both sonically and as writers. 'Alex Gaskarth's voice radiates as if made to be the voice of a new generation,' gushed the writer. 'Where Blink-182 defined the lives of those of us born from 1984–89, ATL's quick wit, rhyme scheme, and honesty rattles in the bones of everyone from 15–24 yr. old, and probably farther than we can even begin to express.' The album's diversity was praised, as were 'Too Much' and 'Therapy', which reminded the writer of Third Eye Blind, but 'Stella' and 'Sick Little Games' were a little over-simplified in comparison to these. The final thoughts were that while long-term fans would say this is the third album (because there were two albums released before it, presumably?) it had overcome 'the feared "Sophomore slump"', which sounds like something that could be cured by (a) realising that it was indeed album number three, or (b) a course of Viagra. The reviewer gave it nine out of ten anyway, so we'll let him off.

So much for the reviews. We want to know how the record fared in the charts, don't we? Oops, here comes a new chapter!

CHAPTER 11

2009 IS YOURS, IN CAPITALS

Number 4, that's where.

Not in the Alternative Charts, the Pop-Punk Charts or the Sophomore Albums that are actually Third Albums Charts. That's Number 4 in the Billboard Top 200. First-week sales? A cool 62,992. In other words, a pure and simple crossover into true mainstream success. What a moment for a band that, let's remember, were only three years out of high school. Alex and Rian spoke about the achievement in an interview with *Artisan News* a little later that summer.

'Insane,' said Alex. 'My mom finally believes me that I actually did something with my life.' Rian responded that it was incredible and that the band had 'always had super-low expectations so for something like that to happen it's kinda like the world's about to end.' Alex added that the hard work had paid off and that at the start of it all they never dreamt that things would be such a success. He explained that the album was always going to be an important one but that musicians needed to balance high expectations with being prepared to roll with the punches and take things as they came. Rian agreed and noted that if it hadn't worked out, the band would have needed to be philosophical about it. But of course, it had been great. As for that ever-present accusation of selling out, the drummer's view was that perhaps it was down to certain people wanting in some way to keep their early discovery of a band to themselves, which while awesome of course was only one side of it. Ultimately, the *raison d'être* of any band was to reach as many people as possible, wasn't it?

Alex joked that he and Rian would go to a Less Than Jake gig and yell out that that band had sold out. 'A lot of people throw that word out, but the fact of the matter to me is that we would be selling out if we were compromising and no longer playing the music that we actually enjoyed playing,' he reasoned. On the contrary, Rian said, they were totally enjoying playing their new tracks – if they'd sold out, and were doing it just for the money, then that would be obvious from the live experience. And it wasn't, so they hadn't. The question, of course, was a perennial one for groups that had come from humble beginnings but in all honesty it would be better directed at those who found their fame through the empty seduction of the countless conveyor-belt identikit TV talent shows, where fame at all costs is the key and kids as young as twelve claim it's been their lifelong dream to be sacrificed to sarcastic English money-men in their fifties who wear trousers up to their nipples.

Another great little vignette was when Good Charlotte's

Joel Madden tweeted that his ideal world tour would feature his band, Boys Like Girls and All Time Low. He said he'd love to start in February and take five bands out altogether. Intriguing stuff, sir.

Nothing Personal's lead single, 'Weightless', received a remix by The Secret Handshake in early July and the video for the song proper came out on 6 July. It begins with Alex getting talked at by four girls who are given various captions like Stalker, Get a Restraining Order, etc. The captions are tongue-in-cheek throughout, showing the inner monologues of the band members, crew and fans. People are shown saying they'd rather be watching other bands, the merchandise guy says he would rather *be* in a band, plunging necklines are critiqued, stage invaders punched, Twitter updates indicated (most of which are saying that the band sucks in one way or another) and Jack is accosted by groupies. The whole thing is hilarious, even more so towards the end when Pete Wentz of Fall Out Boy tweets to none other than Mark Hoppus that All Time Low are merely a Fall Out Boy rip-off. A world-weary Hoppus, meanwhile, is thinking that both Fall Out Boy and All Time Low are ripping off Blink-182. At the end, everyone is labelled 'loser', before the legend *Nothing Personal* takes over the screen. The whole thing is a clever take on what people might be thinking but don't feel comfortable voicing out loud. In this, it's comparable to the hit TV comedy series, *Peep Show*, which explores similar territory. Plus, of course, it features the band rocking out with their fans, which gives a real indication of what an actual gig is like.

A Behind the Scenes video was released at virtually the same time, showing from behind the camera how the album was pulled together: the lads off-duty, grabbing a bite to eat, getting their instructions from director Matt Stawski, who had previously worked with Anti-Flag and Train. Jack explained that the band had viewed the work of a lot of different directors and had selected Stawski because the company Refused TV had previously done great videos for America's Sweethearts and Fall Out Boy. Stawski would go on to direct videos for the likes of CeeLo Green, De La Soul, AFI and The Wanted as his career took off even further.

In the video, Zack is seen sitting around, waiting to be called into action, and he reckons the makeup artists will not be happy with him sweating as he jumps around wielding his lovely pink bass guitar. The video gives a really good insight into the non-linear process of making a video, with scenes being set up and shot out of their narrative order. Quote of the video probably goes to Jack, who comments that every time he sees beautiful girls, he wants to eat sandwiches. The fourteen-hour shoot, Rian observes, was a long day but possibly the best they'd ever done, after which he hands out sticks to some of the fans – who, being good-looking and female, probably made Jack want to order a 12". That's a twelve-inch sandwich, of course.

Even though the lead single was out, the band still continued to put new music online, including 'Toxic Valentine', through their MySpace account. The boys also made their MTV *Unplugged Secret Shows* session available, plus a session from their *Live from MySpace Secret Shows*, the EP of which could be purchased through *Shockhound.com* only, as a package with a new T-shirt. Merch, ahoy!

The road beckoned once more with the 2009 VANS

Warped Tour, which for the boys began on 19 July. This time, however, the quartet would be playing the Main Stage (with one appearance on the Hurley.com stage for the hell of it). As ever, the chaps were happy to be interviewed by the media. One such chat happened at Salt Lake City, a couple of weeks into the bash, where Alex and Jack chewed the fat with 921theedge. The interviewers noted that in comparison to 2008, the band was now all over MTV, playing on the big stage and basically kicking it up to the next level. Alex and Jack looked at each other in happy bemusement. 'You tell me, man,' said the singer when asked what was going on. 'I don't know, it's been a blur and a real crazy ride.' He added that the band had their own expectations to try to live up to as regards the album and that the process had assisted them in exploring their ideas while also looking to appeal to a wider audience. He went on to say that the *MTV Unplugged* set had been superb, although the band had only got the opportunity to do it because somebody major, possibly Amy Winehouse, had pulled out. Given that his band was a genuine top ten act in the making, that's probably something of an understatement, but the humility still shone through.

The *Unplugged* sessions now had a two-decade history, with names like Dashboard Confessional, Nirvana and Paul McCartney having previously performed. Jack and Alex mused that, in terms of status, All Time Low must be one of the least famous bands at the time to have featured on the prestigious show.

Stripping the songs down in preparation took all of one day, and since acoustic shows weren't the group's usual preference, they generally did them only with Alex and Zack involved. In rehearsals, Rian got there straight away so it was a matter of Zack and Jack working together to sort out the guitar parts. The energy on the main stage was amazing, said the interviewer, who then asked what was next. Alex said that hopefully there wouldn't be too many new songs for a while because that had been the focus of much of the recent past and his brain was essentially full at this point.

Rian and Alex talked to Rock Show Addiction at the gig in Fresno on Wednesday, 19 August in pretty cuddly form as the three sat together on a very small couch. The boys had been enjoying the after-party and Alex observed that 'Too Much' is first about a heroin overdose, then about his and Rian's relationship, for which he received first a slap and then a kiss on the cheek. The interview became sillier as Rian picked up the mic and took the questions sheet from the young interviewer. Rian said it had been an honour when Aaron Gillespie of Underoath guested with the band onstage at the Seattle gig during 'Dear Maria, Count Me In' – Gillespie being a seriously awesome drummer. 'If I'm a three out of ten as a drummer,' he said, 'he is like a nine.' So modest! Mind, the tour was a cracking one, featuring Bad Religion and NOFX, by this stage veterans of a scene that enabled the likes of Blink and Green Day to really break through; as such, they could be seen as grandparents, great grandparents, ancient ancestors of All Time Low.

An All Time Low track appeared in an interesting release during August, too, with 'Toxic Valentine' being part of the soundtrack to a movie called *Jennifer's Body*. The writing of the track is credited to Alex, along with No Doubt bassist Tony Kanal and Golden Globe winner Jimmy Harry, who was famed for his work with the likes of Madonna, Pink, Weezer, Kylie Minogue and Santana – another indication, for sure, that the band were moving in ever more rarefied atmospheres. As for the movie itself, it's all about a high-school cheerleader who gets possessed by demons, while her best buddy is trying to stop her killing all the dudes in her class. You know, the usual stuff. It also features a kiss between co-stars Megan Fox and Amanda Seyfried that goes on for a full minute. For plot reasons, of course. There were in fact rumours that Joel Madden or Pete Wentz were going to be cast in one of the lead roles, but in the end the musicians lost out to Adam Brody. The venerable broadsheet the *Guardian* thought it was a decent high-school horror that also featured some satire. 'A struggling indie band want to sacrifice a virgin to Satan in return for mega-selling fame,' advised the writer. 'But Jennifer, as played by Fox, is no virgin, and the evil ceremony turns her into a parasitic vampire who destroys lives – as opposed to simply doing so metaphorically in her pre-vampiric state as a total beey-otch.' Convinced yet?

Another achievement in the Game of Rock and Fame was unlocked with a nifty manoeuvre on 13 August as the band appeared on Conan O'Brien's mega-famous show with 'Damned If I Do Ya (Damned If I Don't)' – the interviewer and comedian called the performance 'absolutely fantastic'. By contrast, the band found time to judge the New England stop of the MTV VMA Tour at which newcomers Gentlemen Hall were voted by the panel as Breakout Boston Artist of 2009 and the Hall were subsequently covered on MTV and MTV2.

The Warped Tour – skateboarding, moshing, making out and drinking – was also over and so it was time to look to

European dates once again. There was some intrigue on 5 September as Ryan Ogren of good mates Runner announced on his Twitter feed that for a couple of shows on the European tour, he would be playing bass for All Time Low, filling in for Zack. Ogren was the dude who'd named Zack's clothing label, and a good mate, so the world took it with plenty of salt.

The Euro dates of what was called the Glamour Kills tour began on 16 September over in Sweden, two days after *Nothing Personal* finally came out officially in the United Kingdom. The gig on 17 September at the Kulturbolaget in Malmö was reviewed by Rockfreaks, who began the review in wonderment at the sheer number of girls aged sixteen or under queuing at the gig hours prior to doors opening. For the first time in several years, even the twenty-four-year old writer was asked for ID when buying an alcoholic drink. The bartender explained that 'there were probably only three people at the entire 750 capacity venue who were eligible to buy alcoholic beverages.' The Audition were the support band but while they went down well, the writer felt that the Baltimore boys were in 'an entirely different league'. The set began with 'Lost in Stereo' and the venue was filled with a happy energy, the boys jumping about, running around, providing songs with which to sing along and dance and generally being completely likeable. 'It helps, of course, to have a few albums' worth of great material to pick from,' continued the writer, namechecking 'Six Feet Under the Stars', 'Break Your Little Heart', recent single 'Weightless' and 'Remembering Sunday', which Alex played solo and acoustic in the early part of the song before the lads joined him. Of course, the encore of 'Dear Maria, Count Me In' was the biggest hit of the night, with the crowd singing along so loudly that earplugs were needed to survive, in the opinion of the writer. Indeed, the only thing that the Rockfreaks reviewer could find to complain about was that the gig didn't go on for longer.

The dreaded question of jetlag was on the group's minds when interviewed by *Venice Magazine* prior to the Backstage Club, Munich, on 20 September. 'We're all on weird time schedules,' said Alex. 'None of us wakes up before three in the afternoon, and we don't go to bed before six in the morning. The jetlag is definitely crushing us right now.'

Alltimelowexposed.com caught up with Jack and Rian at the gig in Berlin on 21 September, where the boys talked about having spent hours on a particular website that had loads of pictures of the band, on and off duty, that they'd never seen before. The guys were certainly starting to understand the peculiar nature of fame and its attendant fanatics among the crowds, although Jack added that it was fun to check out such websites in order to learn about themselves. As for the European gigs, one real bonus was the quality of the food. 'In the US on tour, we'll have hamburgers and fried stuff,' said Rian. He and Jack both called the architecture of their European adventures beautiful and historical. As for the fans, there was a real sense of energy at the shows and they were a little bit more touchy feely when asking for autographs, pictures or even kisses – which wasn't quite the same experience as in the United States. As for the fan base in general, there was a family feel about it, with fans knowing lots about their favourite band member.

The conversation got a bit esoteric after that with talk of Area 51, UFOs, religion and whether anyone had ever felt close to leaving the band. Jack said he never had, but Rian confessed that after All Time Low had just signed their Hopeless Records deal, there was a moment when the thought of going to college instead had crossed his mind. It was a life decision, he revealed. 'You are basically betting your entire life on this band succeeding. But I talked it over with my parents and my girlfriend and I decided [to carry on with] the band.' An excellent decision, as it turned out. Not many people were aware of that fact, said the drummer; Jack himself stated that the first time he heard it himself was during that interview.

Another revelation was that the band would definitely be looking to release a DVD sometime in the relatively near future. The lads had recorded a video for 'Damned If I Do Ya (Damned if I Don't)', again directed by Matthew Stawski, which premiered on 11 September. In the short movie, Alex is distracted from class and rehearsals due to an affair with his teacher. A brawl ensues, Alex beats everyone up and he gets the girl in the end. As you do. Still, it was another nice piece of video for a song that'd reached the dizzy(ish) heights of Number 67 in the Billboard Charts.

The next stop after the three German gigs was the legendary Melkweg (Milky Way) club in Amsterdam, Holland, one of the world's party cities (not to mention the art galleries and the canals and architecture and flowers and yes, coffee shops). The local support was Destine, who said they had 'the privilege to open for one of our favourite bands.' Alex was showing his linguistic 'skills' off again, asking in Dutch something along the lines of *toon ons je tieten*, to roars from the crowd. While not entirely the best Dutch anyone's ever spoken, it explained a little bit why there are so many bras thrown onstage during the group's set. Given the high standard of English spoken by a great deal of young Netherlanders, his efforts weren't strictly necessary, but they were certainly welcomed, as a smattering of the local language always is from any visitor. The gig was another great one, even if for the foursome it was still something like midday according to their body clocks.

They would get time to adjust as the tour returned to the UK and Newcastle's O2 Academy on 25 September. The gig at the Academy 2 in Birmingham was attended by *The Daily Dust*, who noticed a high proportion of teenage girls in attendance and that they were noisy and positive, as had become the case at most All Time Low gigs. Underwear was thrown – some of which had names and mobile phone numbers cunningly sewn in (presumably these weren't pre-worn pants). 'On this showing they are clearly deserving of the headline slot,' the writer said. 'While the other two bands were both very good, ATL just have the edge over them, both in terms of their songs and their performance. Singer/guitarist Alex Gaskarth charms the crowd with ease and has them screaming back to him almost all of his own words.' The band played excellently, continued the reviewer, who also noted that Andrew Goldstein, the singer with the first band on the bill, The Friday Night Boys, joined the headliners onstage to add his vocals. 'Weightless', 'Damned...' and 'Dear Maria...' gave the crowd what they wanted and the reviewer summed it up by saying that All Time Low's charisma and musical chops were likely to help them step up yet again in their career.

The band completed its short UK stint in the Electric Ballroom London, after which there were rumours that they had got into trouble with the local police while on their way to DJ at an event in Kingston. Initially, Punktastic put an update online: 'Punktastic understands members of All Time Low have been arrested by police for alleged drugs offences in Kingston. More as we get it.' Later, this was expanded to say that the boys had been kicked out of their hotel because too many people were in their room. The website repeated its understanding that drugs were involved – without stating its source at any point – and added: 'Band tell venue they aren't arriving at the venue because "they've passed out after a big meal".' We shall leave this episode merely by saying that the Internet has many voices and anyone can write anything they like – fiction is everywhere. Also, on the Net you'll find a famous quote attributed to Alex, which is something along the lines of 'I don't even do drugs – I'm just weird.' Given the gents' love for liquid al-kay-hol at this point, why would they need to get themselves into strife? The whole thing makes no sense, and it's safe to say we can take it with a massive pinch of salt.

Back to the music. Patrick Stump's remix of 'Damned If I Do Ya (Damned If I Don't)' was released and the bandwagon zoomed in early October back over the Atlantic as the cultural leanings of the Glamour Kills charabanc continued on their merry way towards the U S and A. Is nice, I like. Jagshemash! High Five!

CHAPTER 12

MAJOR NEWS

Alex smiled, a little mischievously.

'I don't know if I'm actually supposed to announce this,'
he told an unsuspecting interviewer for RockTheWalls, 'but
we do actually have a deal signed with Interscope Records.'
Founded in 1989, over the years the label has been home
to Eminem, Snoop Dogg, Dr. Dre, U2, and the huge debut
by Lady Gaga, *The Fame*. It was also the home of two very
pertinent names: The All-American Rejects and Blink-182.
Alex's almost throwaway announcement put the seal on
rumours that had been circulating around the group for much
of 2009, rumours that had gone into overdrive after the huge
showing of *Nothing Personal* in the charts. So those earlier
comments at the Grammys had in fact had some unwitting
truth to them. Interscope's ability to put almost unlimited
financial resources behind its acts was set to send the band's

careers interstellar; its international partners and experience in dealing with musicians, promoters, media and industry in general were unparalleled. Alex went on to explain that the next record would be coming out on Interscope, but *Nothing Personal* would remain with Hopeless Records rather than being taken over as back catalogue by the new label. The major label's team, however, would now also be on board to give the current album another push.

He added that the deal was a cool one, with Hopeless, Interscope and All Time Low all benefiting. That didn't just mean the financial side of things, he explained. The first fruits in terms of the music would come a little down the line. In an interview with a blogger, Alex said that the group had never been pushed to do anything they didn't want to do. 'We've been fortunate to have signed to Hopeless Records and now to Interscope Records, we've been surrounded by people who love what we're doing as a band, so we've never had to deal with anybody threatening to not put out our record,' he said. This is essentially the oft-cited Creative Control, which basically means that the groups take care of the music and the business people take care of the business. It might seem a no-brainer, but there have been countless stories of the boundaries being blurred in both directions by meddling parties who believe they can do better than those qualified for their particular jobs. It never ends well. Ever. Never. Nope.

That bombshell landed, it was back down to business. A reviewer from Patriot Press, a site for the journalism school at Owings, Maryland, saw the gents at the 9:30 club in nearby Washington, DC. The venue was packed, and with a 'Phenomenal blend of Alternative Rock showcasing unleashed talent in the form of guitar strings and drum sticks, All Time Low knocked the crowd out.' The reviewer did, however, call *Nothing Personal* the band's 'sophomore album'. Back to school for someone methinks. (Nothing Personal, obvs.) Still, for a near-homecoming gig it was a damned good one. Talking of Damned, the group was also interested in what would be the third single from their third album and to that end crowd-sourced the answer from its fan base with a poll on the site *SodaHead.com*. 'Lost in Stereo' was the result, due for release in the New Year.

Another bit of movie-related info came out in November, with the intriguing fact that the group would be writing a new track for the forthcoming movie, *Alice*. A retelling of/sequel to the *Alice's Adventures in Wonderland* novel by Lewis Carroll, the director would be gothic genius Tim Burton. No ideas as to what the band was planning to record were forthcoming just yet, but to be attached to such a high-profile movie itself certainly did the boys no harm whatsoever, even if the likelihood of hot lesbian vampires snogging was probably on the low side. Undaunted, the Baltimore blasters put out a live EP on 17 November. The iTunes-only release was taken from a live session for the Internet and technology company, with the tracklisting of 'Weightless', 'Stella', 'Break Your Little Heart', 'Damned If I Do Ya (Damned If I Don't)', 'Lost in Stereo' and 'Dear Maria, Count Me In'. Current label Hopeless said that it demonstrated 'the patented All Time Low energy and enthusiasm', and they were blimmin' right too, an' all, guv.

December 2009 was taken up with more gigs – of course – plus an interview with *Seventeen*, in which the intrepid hard news reporter asked the band what their dream date would be. Zack said that he'd love to meet a girl on the beach who'd been surfing and make a date to meet at 8am by the beach. Alex, meanwhile, reckoned he'd hire out the Baltimore Aquarium just for him and his gal. Rian revealed that Alex and he were housemates, and the band in general put it on record that the singer was a constant present-giver plus an animal lover. The most revealing part of the interview, perhaps, was Rian's explanation of meeting fans after gigs. 'There's this weird thing when people meet bands where they don't really talk, they just stand there and you're like, "Hey how are you?" and they're like, "Eh." It's nice to be able to have a real conversation,' said the drummer.

Things in MTV-land were also going great with pre-orders announced for the release of their *Unplugged* session DVD and CD, which was to come out on 12 January 2010, plus a band appearance on Alexa Chung's show *It's On*, which was aired on 17 December.

One notable gig as the band prepared to say goodbye to a quite spectacularly successful year was on 6 December at the Electric Factory in Philadelphia. The unhinged, homophobic, supposedly Christian nutjobs that call themselves the Westboro Baptist Church had for some reason decided that All Time Low were some kind of anti-American force for evil in society. They therefore decided to picket at a gig. According to their amazingly offensive website *Godhatesfags.com*:

WBC cares about these losers – so let me break it down for you. How do you know how far gone a society is? You look at their social icons. When you look at these gender-confused, haphazard freakazoids then you can plainly see that america is DOOMED, for real! This is the final generation, and a little concussion is the least of their worries [this refers to a report that Alex had suffered concussion while in action]. Here is what they have to look forward to when this once great nation finally falls – for her fall is already started.

Tread carefully, Jedi, the hate is strong in this one.

Alex received a text saying that God hated 'fag enablers'. To which the frontman replied succinctly that the protestors should stay at home because intolerance was firmly unwelcome at an All Time Low concert. Even at the gig, as reported on that church's website *Godhatesthemedia.com* and verified on YouTube footage of the gig, Alex felt moved to talk about the protestors outside: 'Before we start this next song ['Jasey Rae'], I do wanna say something on said public forum, and it's gonna be short, simple, and that's all I'm gonna say about it ever. Some church group is outside our show today and picketing. I'm not gonna mention their name, 'cause I really don't want anyone to know who doesn't already know about them to know about them, 'cause it's frankly not worth your time. However, they happen to be a bunch of bigots and a bunch of intolerant assholes. If you know who they are, then you know what I'm talking about. And I think people should be able to love whoever the fuck they wanna love, and that no matter what you believe, you should be allowed to live your life the way you wanna live it. That's all I'm gonna say about it.' In the name of balanced reporting, your humble author reprints the response to this speech from that same website:

In ATL's estimation, anyone who faithfully preaches the standards of God are 'bigots' and 'assholes.' In ATL's estimation, what God calls 'abomination' is 'love.' In God's estimation? ATL is doomed. These silly boys have horribly miscalculated in thinking that the Living God won't fulfill [sic] His promise to repay them to their faces for their treachery and hatred of Him and their fellow man (Deut. 7:10). 'Thou givest thy mouth to evil, and thy tongue frameth deceit ... but I will reprove thee, and set them in order before thine eyes. Now consider this, ye that forget God, lest I tear you in pieces, and there be none to deliver' (Psa. 50:19, 21–22). This faithless foursome and their fans have two options: (1) put away your filthy manner of life, repent, and obey God; or (2) face the real All Time Low: Hell.

Altpress.com later reported that the band would make no official comment.

One of the truisms about free speech is that it is predicated on the fact that by nature it means allowing voices to be heard even when they are saying things with which you fundamentally disagree. In the United States this is enshrined in the First Amendment. *A propos* of nothing in particular, a study published in the *Journal of Personality and Social Psychology* proved that homophobes were actually more likely to be gay. Co-author of the study, Richard Ryan, explained it to *Livescience.com*: 'Sometimes people are threatened by gays and lesbians because they are fearing their own impulses, in a sense they "doth protest too much". In addition, it appears that sometimes those who would oppress others have been oppressed themselves, and we can have some compassion for them too; they may be unaccepting of others because they cannot be accepting of themselves.' *Livescience* also reported on another study by Gordon Hodson and Michael Busseri that prejudices such as racism and homophobia were linked to low intelligence. Free speech is great, isn't it?

Jeepers creepers, things have got a bit heavy in here! Let's step out into the lighter air of Chapter 13, shall we?

CHAPTER 13

AND SO THE INSANITY BEGINS

With a couple of weeks off at the start of 2010, Alex Gaskarth headed to his Baltimore house to catch up with his squeeze, Lisa Ruocco. The two had known each other since high school – before the madness truly began. After months of touring the reunion was inevitably an intimate one. But here, one of the perils of fame comes in. While All Time Low always made and make an effort to accommodate fans with pictures, autographs, chats and giving their time to interact with their fan base, there are also limits. One of those limits is when fans buy your address from a shady Internet site, piece together your likely movements from your and your girlfriend's Twitter feeds, and turn up at your house. This happened in January 2010 when a fan of the group and some of her friends knocked on Alex's door and asked for photos with the singer. While he was as accommodating as ever, this intrusion into his home life was widely condemned by most of the band's fan base as having crossed the line between true fandom and something a tad more sinister. *Alternative Press* ran a brilliant story about it in which the magazine explored the phenomenon of uber-fandom through the words of bands, fans and psychologists. It's well worth seeking it out.

Alex was a little spooked by the incident, to the extent that he half-joked that he would be building a moat and castle wall round his home complete with archers to fire arrows at people without a password. It was a creepy thing to do, he said on Twitter, particularly as the fan in question had waited outside his darkened house for three hours. As a user called *crying stars* said on *AP* magazine's message boards, 'This was the creepiest thing ever.' Another pertinent comment was from ABoyUnderOath90 who said, 'Poor bastard. I guess being famous isn't as great as people try to make it out to be all the time.' In this case, the fan in question also expressed great regret after the event. Let's put it down to youthful exuberance and hope all have learnt their lesson from it.

Alex did later speak about the incident to Alter the Press! 'It definitely crossed the line, freaked me a little bit, but kids do foolish things. I think she learned from the mistake, based on the bashing that she got from her peers online. It's more of an eye-opening hint of what's to possibly come, if the band continues to grow and have the same kind of success. But again, you can't live your life behind walls. It's a risk, but it's not going to affect my life, I'm not going to live my life like a hermit.' There's one further irony: after the 28 December gig at the Ram's Head in Baltimore the band had invited forty lucky ticket holders to participate in a very special meet 'n' greet Secret Santa, showing that ATL's link to their fans was hugely important on a personal level.

A tribute of a rather more musical kind was revealed in January too and this one was a stone-cold doozy: a tribute to the heroes of our piece in the form of a nine-track cover album by Brazilian bands. The downloadable tunes were put online courtesy of a Brazilian fan site. So for fans of Skore, Poppin, Supercombo, Under Line, Quarter, Believe, Triz, Upset Kids and 2OIS, and fans of a host of classic ATL songs, your dream had come true.

Rumours of varying believability abounded at this time. Patrick Stump, for example, was supposedly ready to collaborate with the group on new material – which was reasonable given the friendship between the bands – and, a little sillier, a forthcoming UK tour was reportedly cancelled. The latter had of course been fuelled by Internet rumours.

Come 14 January and it was time to release the band's latest slab of vinyl (OK, polyurethane substrate readable by laser, if you want to get picky) in the shape of the long-awaited *MTV Unplugged*. The CD and DVD set was received very warmly by fans and Alex spoke to *J-14* at length about it. Echoing his words of 2009 he told the interviewer that the *Unplugged* sessions were of great note: 'Nirvana's played it, and all kinds of amazing bands that I consider legendary. So to even get the invite to come and do it was very cool,' he explained, before revealing that the process of stripping the songs down in an intimate gig made for a great time that the audience appreciated. Because by nature there was a limited audience actually present at the performance, the band had decided to release it on DVD. He added that 'Jasey Rae' worked really well and praised Kate Voegele of One Tree Hill for her singing with him on 'Remembering Sunday'. Turning to the *Alice* soundtrack, the singer delved into the story behind the band's contributed track, confirmed as 'Painting Flowers'. He said it was all about self-realisation, questioning what you believed and finally accepting yourself and your beliefs. As a fan of the work of the director, Tim Burton, he was chuffed that his band was involved.

The vocalist did however deny rumours that the band was imminently to work with Demi Lovato, the singer–songwriter, model and actress. While Lovato and Alex had hung out once or twice, no music was on the table. What *was* on the table was a return to the UK and Ireland, this time as headliners for the prestigious 2010 *Kerrang!* Relentless Tour. Supports for the dates were The Blackout, Young Guns and My Passion for a series of gigs that are often considered one of the launchpads for (relatively) new bands. The reviewer at *Bring the Noise* was impressed by All Time Low's stage entry – at which the screams were 'deafening' and the amount of undercrackers being chucked stagewards was humongous. The group however were definitely worthy as headliners as they owned the stage and the reviewer liked the fact that the high-octane pop-punk was also able to find another gear with an acoustic track ('Remembering Sunday'). 'Using the space in the stage to their benefit,' the writer concluded, 'they seem to jump about and dance and interact with the audience as much as they sing their hearts out to the hits that have make them as big as they are.'

Another music fan, one Dane Wright, was moved to write at length about the gig in Leeds, noting that the cheerfulness and bounciness was fully on show as 'Lost in Stereo', 'Stella' and 'Break Your Little Heart' brought the energy levels up to a standard you'd normally associate with post-energy drink swigging. Of course, the Blink-182 influence on the band and the show was obvious, and the banter was also in full flow between Jack and Alex. 'Weightless' closed the set before the boys returned for 'Damned...' and 'Dear Maria', to which the packed crowd sang every word. To sum up, the reviewer felt, 'If All Time Low manages to put in performances like this on every night of the tour surely arenas await on their next trip across the Atlantic.' Time would tell ...

As ever with the guys, no opportunity was wasted to get close to the fans and a series of in-store appearances was set up at which the lads signed copies of *Nothing Personal* and performed short, acoustic sets. At one performance, at Banquet Records in Kingston upon Thames, one of the highlights was the short rendition of 'All the Small Things'. The Blink-182 classic duly upped the singalong energy towards the rafters, which was no doubt a real buzz for Alex as it was as close as it got to a birth-town gig. He told stalwarts Alter the Press! of his regret that the tour had been so short, because reaction from audiences and radio had been great. Alex confirmed that he had been born in nearby Harlow then lived in Toot Hill, a small village in Essex situated in Epping Forest. He said that while he'd been back to visit family, most of them were now living in the North and in Wales. Of course, they'd come out in force to catch the Manchester and Newcastle gigs on the latest tour. He also revealed that the next single would be 'Lost in Stereo', which had already been played on Radio 1, and for which a video was in production.

Even while work was being done on promoting the current record, as ever the hungry maw of the music business was making voracious rumblings and to that end new songs were been sketched out, said the singer, and while they were similar to those on *Nothing Personal* the likelihood was that the new songs were going to be a bit more rock. In the interview, which took place in early February, he also mentioned the working titles for two new songs that were in the planning: 'Jennifer' and 'Where I Belong'. But for the time being, he noted, *Nothing Personal* was the main priority, with plenty of touring still to be done for at least the rest of 2010. As the band wended its merry way across la Manche towards the continent, the track from *Alice* was put online for all to enjoy.

'Painting Flowers' draws on the strange logic of the words of Lewis Carroll's creations, with dreamy imagery, love and coming home. The song is one of the group's more laid-back, but intense efforts, and while not without its own poppy chops, it's quite a serious-feeling part of All Time Low's oeuvre. In an interview with Buzznet, Alex said that the concept of 'Painting Flowers' brought to mind the bright colours of the film, plus the huge mushrooms and the hair of Johnny Depp. As for the most magical dream he'd had of late, Alex referred back to his band's continued career. 'Honestly I think the dream ride we are on right now has been pretty magical,' he told the interviewer, 'that and the first time I went to Disney World as a kid, boy, was I stoked. Jack has a lot of dreams, but I wouldn't call them magical, just disturbing (ha ha).' As ever, he couldn't go too long without being playful, which is one of the characteristics which makes him such an endearing personality.

Also in the interview Alex named his top Tim Burton movies

as *Pee Wee's Big Adventure* and *Beetlejuice*, also referencing the character Jack Skellington from *The Nightmare Before Christmas* and *Edward Scissorhands*. Keeping with the theme of the book, he said that if he had a tea party he would invite Vince Vaughn, John Lennon and Lady Gaga. That's a pretty fascinating set of characters.

Rumours, rumours and more rumours continued while the guys were in Europe, the latest being that they would be joining the Bamboozle Roadshow with Boys Like Girls and Good Charlotte for gigs during May and June (which turned out to be true, of which more later) and that they would be headlining European festivals later in the year. The boys subsequently confirmed they would be at the Leeds and Reading Fests on August Bank Holiday weekend, 2010 – although not as headliners. The show would be somewhat stolen by another band coming out of hiatus ...

The February Euro dates wound up with appearances in Germany, Australia, Italy, Switzerland and France before it was time once more to go fully long haul and get stuck into those crazy Aussies once again. The Soundwave Festival, somewhat like Lollapalooza or the VANS Warped Tour, is a travelling roadshow that heads around the major cities of Australia and is generally a blend of punk, metal and alternative rock. The 2010 show was headlined by Faith No More, Jane's Addiction and Jimmy Eat World, with a clutch of other famous names including thrash legends Anthrax, Eagles of Death Metal and You Me at Six. One intriguing act on the bill was the oddball magnificence of The Aquabats, whose irresistible deranged sonics once featured the top-class drum chops of one Travis Barker.

A reviewer from the AU Review caught the gig at Eastern Creek Raceway, Sydney, on 21 February and amid the madness managed to rush between stages in order to see how All Time Low were getting on. The band quickly got the crowd singing along with the mighty 'Weightless', while Jack and Alex were on top banter form, wrote the music fan: 'Throughout the set, singer Alex Gaskarth and guitarist Jack Barakat continued making vulgar dick and titty jokes, which the crowd absolutely loved; I must admit, I did too. Pop punk is making a comeback and its [sic] bands like All Time Low that are leading the revolution.'

The lads were enjoying themselves, too, finding time to play a couple of Soundwave Sideshows – gigs outside of the main stages – with appearances at The Metro in Sydney and Melbourne's Hi-Fi on 23 and 24 February respectively. Other bands were The Almost, featuring old mate Aaron Gillespie of Underoath, and Dance Gavin Dance. The Australian dates came to an end on 1 March, after which the boys headed back to the United States for a very quick break. Soon, though, it was time to get back into the studio once more and start working on new material.

CHAPTER 14

DEMOS AND DVDS

Mike Green's career as engineer and producer was a long time in the making. The multi-instrumentalist always had an appreciation of what it took technically to put records together, and as a performer as well as recording maestro had been involved in a number of minor records. In a sense his career as a producer had begun in 2004 with his work on the breakthrough album by The Marches, which led on to producing and engineering for Paramore's 2005 and 2006 records *All We Know is Falling* and *The Summer Tic*. He was fast becoming one of the most in-demand creative producers in the United States by the 2010s having been behind the controls for records by Pierce the Veil, Anarbor and Set Your Goals.

It was a good fit, then, when All Time Low began work on demo recordings with Green in late March 2010. With the band as a whole having just joined Twitter, it was another way for the group to show the fans updates of what was going on, à la *Nothing Personal*. Ideas were duly put down quickly, ready for the group to head into the studio on 24 March to begin recording with Matt Squire and John Fields. The latter had a huge reputation following works with the likes of The Commodores, Pink, Jonas Brothers, Jimmy Eat World and Andrew W.K. over the previous decade, and had also been responsible for LPs by The Rembrandts (who, uh, recorded the theme music to *Friends*, without whom ...), mate of the Low, Demi Lovato, Miley 'sister of Trace Metro Station' Cyrus and even the Goo Goo Dolls. The line-up of talent for what would be the boys' major-label debut was beginning to look scarily good, in other words. At around the same time, long-time mate and tech Danny K left the All Time Low camp to pursue a full-time career, with the full blessing of the band.

With demos going well and tracks being knocked into shape, things outside of the studio were also moving apace. *Nothing Personal* was still selling well but new material was a few months away from hitting the shelves, so a documentary and live performance album and DVD set were being edited together. Footage had been shot throughout the band's autumn 2009 tour both on and offstage in order to provide once more an insight into what it was like to experience a gig as a fan as well as to offer unique behind-the-scenes access. The debut of the forthcoming movie, to be entitled *Straight to DVD*, was set for 10 May at Music Box, Hollywood. The feature movie that comprises the story of the band is an excellent one, and includes some really bad haircuts from the early days and interviews with the group about how things came together over the years. For the first time, maybe, fans got a chance to see how hot the respective parents really were … and how incredibly enthusiastic all the boys and their families were from the outset. In true *Spinal Tap* style, the boys are even interviewed in a hot tub. What comes across really firmly is the fact that first and foremost it's about friendship as well as the growing musicianship of the guys. It's a treasure trove of memories and includes the rehearsal basement where the very first practices took place.

The songs, of course, come thick and fast, with 'Lost in Stereo' never having sounded better than under the high production values of the concert, which was culled from a gig at Hammerstein Ballroom, New York. With plenty of shots of and from the crowd, sweeping cameras and amazing lighting, this is a seriously good piece of production that very much shows a band looking for all the world as though they are on the cusp of a massive breakthrough to mega status. The parents then give their reaction to the group's plans to pursue the band rather than go straight to college, which ranged from surprise to huge support subsequently as the extremely cool older folks collectively realise that in fact this band is more than a passing fad. Again, the love is palpable as the lads talk about sharing hotel rooms with their parents – while on a pop-punk tour. The mind boggles.

'Jasey Rae' kicks in with a mighty sustained chord and as the lights spit out golden flashes the boys kick it up another notch. Sleep, sweat and silliness follow in the next, on-the-road excerpt, as the band shows the importance of keeping busy and messing about on tour buses to the extent of having after-show parties involving friends old, new and frankly weird. Oh and there's lots of semi-nudity – and nudity –

involved in this section. Alex explains how it's one big happy family, before the irrepressible Matt Flyzik gives his own view on the difficulties and triumphs of getting everyone together in the same place at the same time. Not that there aren't silly fights on tour – but like brothers, these boys can shout at each other one minute and make it all OK again just a minute or two later. A cliché it may be, but the truth is that the band that plays together, stays together. And long may it be thus.

Alex's rendition of 'Remembering Sunday', featuring Juliet Simms from Automatic Loveletter, is as good as it had ever been, with a hint of Britpop about it in the Oasis-esque chords and melody – but Simms' performance is universes away from any vocal the Manc brothers could ever hope to offer, as for the matter is Alex's. Flyzik explains what it's like to be part of the crew, taking care of each other, and other crew members agree that it's about working hard, playing hard and the fact that everyone really does form extremely strong bonds with each other whether there's a gig on that day or it's a day off. While some bands treat crew members as employees and chop and change their backstage crew, All Time Low stick with what works – and that is the extended tour family, even to the extent of the 2009 Thanksgiving, when twenty-five people came together to celebrate. Be it crew, band members, other bands or fans, everyone was part of it.

Staying in contact with loved ones, the band explained, is also vitally important. In these days of texting, Skype and the rest, this is easier, but even so being on the road around three hundred days a year means that times spent together in person are all the sweeter.

'Damned If I Do Ya (Damned If I Don't)' features one of

the most splendid singalongs of all time – on this DVD, the fans are truly the fifth member of the band. The next backstage section is full of cross-dressing, dressing up, 1980s neon, wigs and silly dancing – with a fair amount of tour fever kicking in as the band variously kick over water coolers, throw laundry bins downstairs and hang from rafters. There's plenty of bread-based shenanigans on show too, including a unique way to make toast that is frankly not recommended and Jack wanting to do something to a burrito that really is not advised. Matt Flyzik undergoes more ribbing for his perceived Mickey Mouse obsession, with a giant Mickey greeting him, and in one of many hilarious juxtapositions, Jack's mum explains how good a kid he's always been while her son (and bandmates) proceed to get naked and wave their (censored) wangs around. There's also a lengthy edit of farting at this point. Some offstage fun follows, with the band out and about between gigs: Jesus shows up (or is that The Big Lebowski?) with coffee in hand – at which point Jack asks if it's in fact Chad Kroeger from Nickelback, and then the guitarist and the singer do some *faux* street magic à la David Blaine or Dynamo. Normal people wouldn't be able to keep a straight face at this point, but we are talking about Alex and Jack here so that kinda doesn't apply.

The group talks about how they give everything onstage, and that's shown by their high-energy performances and plenty of footage of them ripping it up in their natural habitat, including the onstage banter that's such a part of the band's appeal. And there's plenty about the bras, too: lots, and lots, and lots, of brassières. Useful for any band of four lads touring around. Maybe they're looking to make quilt covers out of them one day? It'd certainly be a unique product even for All Time Low. Again, though, it's all about being onstage and as Rian says, that's by far the best part of every day – those couple of hours playing live to the fans.

As the documentary comes towards its conclusion, a faultless, fabulous rendition of 'Weightless' demonstrates the absolute joy in the moment that is the mark of the band's approach – when everything else is stripped away, the fucking about stops and Zack, Rian, Jack and Alex are quite frankly one of the best live bands of the last twenty years. They might like dick jokes, pranks, playing about and designing daft T-shirts, but without songs and performances like this, there would be no All Time Low and there certainly wouldn't be millions of fans worldwide loving them so fervently.

Finally, there's talk about playing gridiron (American) Football and golf, something the band took up according to Alex in order that they could keep drinking. In fact, as they smack the golf balls around, it seems a secondary activity to jumping in golf karts and crashing them into each other, into bushes, down slopes and so forth. There's also a paintballing session with typical silliness, which the All Time Low crew win against their rivals – definitely a way to overcome frustrations while on tour, Alex reckons. Another funtime activity is a skate/ basketball/biking session at DC Shoes Fantasy Factory, with the boys jumping into pools of foam, faceplanting and finally doing an acoustic show. Alex also undergoes an appointment with an audiologist in order to fit some specialist earplugs to save his hearing – sensible given the huge amount of gigs and the high volumes on stage.

As for the fans – the band are very appreciative of them, and this is honest rather than some kind of set-up for the sake of looking good. It is the fans who buy the tickets and the records, and the band themselves love and respect them in return. Whether that's signing autographs, posing for selfies, webchats, playing darts or just hanging out, it's something central to the All Time Low world and always will be. Gifts that the band had received to that point include a strippers' pole (which got broken due to the weight of the band) and a unique book with a hole in it – the intent being that the reader (or a friend) put their penis through the hole and said band member, literally, becomes the star of the story. As ever, 'Dear Maria, Count Me In' ends the encore, and the documentary too. The boys talk among themselves about the brotherhood and the fact that it really is a dream come true from those daft-barnetted earliest videos to the sleek, massive production of the DVD – and they hadn't even reached their major label debut yet.

The documentary is a great insight into what might be termed the first half of the group's career, and really does capture the spirit, skill and sheer hard work of All Time Low. For fans there's also an outtakes reel of drooling, gambling, joking and pretend-sleeping with hands on dicks. Oh, and by the way, Jack doesn't do what he originally said he wanted to, to the burrito, but it's still quite a mess. And even when the lads are messing about with Tom DeLonge masks, the harmonies still stand up, dammit. There's also the full gig from which the documentary songs were culled, and it's as close as you're gonna get to an All Time Low live experience outside of actually being there.

The DVD/CD was released by Hopeless on 25 May 2015 and also featured an appearance by Travis Clark of We the Kings on the song 'Coffee Shop Soundtrack'. An added bonus for some fans was that their names were printed in the booklet: all members of the All Time Low *Hustlers* Club (their fan club) up to March 2010 were given that honour for posterity.

The launch of the DVD was full of fun. The band's parents were in attendance, as were Benji Madden and Joel Madden of Good Charlotte, Fall Out Boy's Pete Wentz, Jon and Nick from Runner Runner, plus the one and only Mark Hoppus. At a Q&A after the event, the band were in fine form, singing excerpts from 'Mmmbop' by Hanson, bantering with each other and even taking a couple of questions along the way. Rian labelled it 'one of the most memorable nights of my life.' The evening also benefited *Invisible Children*, the charity set up to stop the abduction of Ugandan kids to be used as child soldiers in that war-torn country, which was a typically sensitive note the band struck quietly and without fanfare. A short movie about the charity had been shown prior to the main documentary feature. The after-party was an excellent way to spend downtime from the studio, while also putting something of a line under ATL's career as an independent artist just before the move to the next level under the wing of multinational record company.

Reviews began to come in, too, and they were pretty positive, as you'd expect. A writer on Wattpad said it was one of the funniest DVDs anyone could view, and that it would have fans in peals of laughter. 'Armed with instruments, a tour bus, alcohol and hordes of fans All Time Low talk about the importance of fans to them and how they came together in the first place to perform as a band today' was the summary.

Elsewhere, 411Mania began by dismissing the documentary in favour of concentrating on the live CD, meaning that they were reviewing a DVD of a live performance as a live performance in effect, which gave the group little wiggle room. The slightly cynical attitude is explained by the writer having experienced the auto-tuned, processed versions of music that made up certain records, only to be disappointed when the live experience was technically nowhere near. Luckily, though, 'either someone out there has found a way to transport studio trickery to the Hammerstein Ballroom, or All Time Low can actually put on a tight, solid show. Alexander Gaskarth and Jack Barakat are perfectly capable live vocalists, with Zachary Merrick and Rian Dawson providing a solid back line.' Songs that stood out were 'Stella', 'Six Feet Under the Stars', 'Jasey Rae' and 'Dear Maria, Count Me In'. The reviewer also commented on the large amount of crowd noise that was relatively high in the mix, which made the Hammerstein venue sound massive, although on occasion the banter between the boys got a little too much. Giving the record eight out of ten, the writer said that the band was great live, which put them way ahead of other pretenders to the throne.

A guilty pleasure was the verdict of Punkrocktheory as regards the band in general but the release of the CD/DVD was puzzling. 'I guess if you're a diehard fan, you might want to pick this up,' the reviewer wrote. 'Everyone else is better off with the studio albums where at least you don't have to endure the seemingly endless screaming of teenage girls in between songs.'

Talking of live performances, it was time to head out on the Bamboozle Road Show, which would prove to be eventful – and not always for the right reasons.

CHAPTER 15

ROADWORKS AHEAD

Early dates of the roadshow passed without massive incident, albeit that, typically, the weather tried its best to derail the show on 25 May at the Cruzan Amphitheatre in West Palm Beach, Florida (sounds familiar, eh?). It was clearly a sign that things weren't gonna go completely smoothly – All Time Low's set was massively curtailed due to a couple of blown speaker-heads suffered by the band. The techs zoomed into action and borrowed spare stacks, but this meant that the lads could only play for twenty minutes such is the tightness of the schedules in these situations. Nonetheless, as *Spin* wrote: 'Frontman Alex Gaskarth and company tried their best to cram as much as possible into about 20 minutes. There were plenty of poses atop risers, ribald jokes, spurts of smoke, and countless F-bombs uttered to drive the point home that the band was all grown up.' The songs played, the writer recalled, were 'Damned...', 'Lost in Stereo', 'Weightless', 'This is How We Do' – and there wasn't much time for anything else. Still, the screaming fans loved the songs they did get, even if it wasn't the full gun.

Spin awarded the band the title of Best Comeback from Technical Difficulties, which would be an awesome actual gong to win and would look miles better on your grandmother's shelf than one of those second-rate Grammy or Oscar awards, right? Joel and Benji Madden joined the band on stage for 'Dear Maria, Count Me In' while Alex and Jack dove into the crowd.

That technical hiccup, however, was to prove a relatively benign one in light of events at the concert in Six Flags Over Texas at Arlington, Texas, on 29 May. During the performance of the Baltimore boys, the usual excitement from the crowd was high and noisy. So far, so normal. But, according to a fan at the gig, Tanner Holland, as reported on NBCDFW: 'One of the band members [Jack] took off their shirt and threw it to the audience [...] A group of girls who were about 15 or 16 began to fight over the shirt. Security was already on edge from all the fans running up on stage to hug the band members.' The in-house security at the venue, trying to keep fans offstage, couldn't calm the situation down, reported the news outlet, which noted Sharon Parker, media spokesperson for Six Flags Over Texas, had told them that a call was put through to a local police officer to help. The result was that the crowd was sprayed with pepper spray in an effort to get them to disperse. Tanner Holland said that one of his friends unconnected with the scuffle over the shirt had to be taken to paramedics as a result of a reaction to the mace-ing.

Alternative Press, as ever, was the definitive source for further details, with updates on the incident as they occurred. The first post on the subject on the website was timed at 10.34pm, the night of the gig. In it, the magazine reported that the onstage fans had been maced and the band immediately walked off. The music publication quoted tweets from Alex that said he could not care less how rowdy the audience had been, there was no excuse at all for police to pepper spray fans. 'That kind of protocol is insane for an all-ages show at a theme park. A girl who looked to be about 15 walked up to me and said she was removed from the crowd after being maced. Are you fucking kidding me? That being said, you were an absolutely incredible crowd, and that may have been one of the best shows we've ever had the chance to play,' the mag quoted him as writing.

Zack also took to Twitter to express his disgust, noting the safety of the kids was paramount and compromising that was not on. The singer of Boys Like Girls, meanwhile, was even more strident, tweeting with heart firmly on his sleeve: 'you mace our fans you fucking die. bands locked on busses for defending helpless fans getting MACED for having a great time at a rock show. i dare security to come backstage,' he wrote, and apparently named the officer he thought was responsible for the over-the-top response.

The next day, it was revealed that the band would not perform at the San Antonio Six Flags show that night. Alex again wrote a series of tweets and said that they would not be playing despite having showed up to the gig because they had been 'banned because I stood up for our fans who were victimized by security last night. And now they're telling the public that –WE – dropped off the show? Unbelievable. We were told that we "aren't allowed to perform". So to all the folks coming to see us tonight, I'm deeply, deeply sorry; this was not our call.'

Alternative Press went on to say that Alex had tweeted his deep dissatisfaction with the decision and the events of the previous night, too, reported verbatim as: 'It's disgusting to see that a family oriented theme park covers up their flubs by shifting the blame and hiding behind shoddy excuses. Big thanks to the park for not only condoning the macing of kids at an all-ages show, but also for fabricating stories in order to ban us. I sincerely hope that karma catches up to these degenerate liars,' thundered the vocalist, who repeated the band would not be playing that night and sent his sincere apologies to anyone who had been hoping to watch them perform. Subsequently, All Time Low were not allowed to play any of the other remaining Six Flags venues on the roadshow. In order to partially make up for the loss of their 13 June set at Six Flags, St Louis, Eureka, Missouri, the boys did what came naturally and played an acoustic set in the car park late that night to a small but delighted group of fans.

All of that avoidable and seriously out of order stuff couldn't, however, dampen ATL's enthusiasm for being on tour with a set of bands that they admired, not least Good Charlotte. Jack told a Buzznet interviewer that, in the past, Charlotte were one of the groups that the boys would go and see, hanging around outside to get autographs and all the rest of it. Alex said that the hysteria of some fans left him a bit uncomfortable when they were freaking out in front of him, and his bandmate added that fans were always asking him to be the recipient of a piggyback. He said he was scared that they'd drop him – and that his balls would drop out. Typical Jack, in other words. Alex added that he'd stopped playing in bare feet because all the jumping around was hurting and that he'd almost broken his heel once in a particularly energetic performance.

Key in the interview, however, was the tease about the new album, which was still in the process of being tinkered with. Alex slipped into *Spinal Tap*'s David St. Hubbins mode, reckoning that it wasn't like any music anyone else would play. 'It's not notes,' he drawled, drawing on his English background for an accent. 'It's more like …' at which point he and Jack pretended to drop off to sleep. It would be finished following the Bamboozle Roadshow, the lads confirmed. A date was set for a possible release in January 2011, it was also reported.

The Bamboozle bus bludgeoned on through the north of America, with more rain – Minneapolis was soggy – and a few more technical difficulties, such as the stop-start set at Chicago's Soldier Field. Conditions were even worse at the Pittsburgh date, with water absolutely sheeting from the sky. Good Charlotte's Benji Madden told Idobi that the stage had to be shut down because things were being blown around so much. However, 'the bands decided to play acoustic instead … All the bands went up on stage and played 4–5 songs each, and then played some together. Most of the crowd stayed, and it turned out to be my favorite show of the tour. It felt really special, like one of those rock 'n' roll moments nobody will forget.'

His brother Joel referred to the camaraderie of the tour, saying that everyone would hang out together; as an example of the friendship involved, the bands would all buy food and cook together, sometimes on the Good Charlotte tour bus. He said it had the vibe of a family. Likewise, when he and Benji went to DJ gigs along the tour, they would be joined by a large crew of fellow musicians, techs and other crew. 'And we're talking like 20 guys that are all 22 or 23, who all want to rage. So we'll go and set it up and then they'll have the whole club at their disposal. They party their faces off,' he said.

Gigs came thick and fast, with the Molson Canadian Amphitheatre in Toronto on 16 June hosting a concert at which of course our lads reigned supreme. According to one report, however, 'ATL made sure they got an OK from the venue's security before inviting people who didn't get general admission tickets into the half-filled pit.'

In an interview with AbsolutePunk Alex spoke about the new record, and said that around eight songs were completed. This newest record had been a longer-gestated affair than previous LPs, which was an approach that really appealed to the boys. 'It's nice to have such a long time to really work on the whole thing,' explained the singer. 'In the past we've had to cram it in between tours a lot of the time. This time we took some time off to write and made sure the songs were there first and then started tracking. Then take a break, step away from it, look at the songs for a minute. Then go back and make sure everything's perfect.'

He went on to say that the new album would be more of a mixture of sounds in comparison to the previous LP, in which some of his lyrics were a little tongue-in-cheek and designed to fit in with the general atmosphere and feel of the album. By contrast, he said, there would be more 'genuine' lyrics this time around, plus making sure that the music, while still fun and upbeat, would have interesting arrangements, more riffs, and thoughtful approaches. The main issue, he said, was that they had no idea what to call the album. At this stage some of the songs didn't even have names but as the year went on, no doubt something would emerge.

That gnarly question about 'selling out' reappeared, too, but the fact that the band sounded more poppy was much more to do with the fact that they were listening to more pop music. 'I legitimately listen to like Justin Timberlake, Britney Spears and Lady Gaga for songwriting influence,' he told the interviewer. 'I feel like pop songs have something about them [...] they're so simple but they are so able to connect with such a wide audience, I think there's something genius about that.' The singer also revealed that the hotly awaited song that he and Mark Hoppus had written together would not be appearing on the new All Time Low record. That said, the Blink-182 man had another project under way called *City (Comma) State* for which that track plus another song that Alex and Mark had written together might be used. That said, he wasn't sure on any further details of the Blink dude's latest musical foray but it would be something cool, for sure.

Jack celebrated turning twenty-two on 18 June with another energetic gig, this time in Cleveland, Ohio. He was also the unwitting subject of a *Boston.com* story that dealt with the increasingly risqué behaviour that the writer felt was the nature of modern rock concerts. Jack, according to the writer, wasn't pleased with what he was seeing from the crowd, so he demanded more 'bras from the female fans in the squealing crowd at the recent Bamboozle Roadshow tour. By the end of All Time Low's set, at least seven brassieres dangled from Barakat's microphone.'

The article went on to discuss the appropriateness of That Kind of Thing and noted that a lot of the girls were in fact being chaperoned by Mum and Dad. One of those parents was quoted as saying that they'd brought their daughter because they didn't want her ending up alone in the backstage area. Aside from that, though, 'I don't know that it's that much different from when I was growing up. Women used to throw their panties at Tom Jones.' However, the same parent wasn't too keen on the X-rated language from All Time Low, saying their kids were Catholic school pupils ... and as everyone knows, these are naïve little angels, right? Educational psychologist and parenting specialist – whatever that means – Michele Borba said that it was up to parents to do a little research on the bands that their kids were wanting to go and see. 'Get a CD and listen to it,' she said, instantly upping sales figures in the key 35–50 Parents of Kids Who Go To Catholic Schools And Listen To All Time Low demographic.

With the dates coming to an end, studio work was back on the menu, and by 27 July, recording was complete. As ever with the band, that wasn't the whole story – they'd also managed to put together a quick downloadable cover of Lady Gaga's 'Alejandro' plus an acoustic session for Alter the Press! for fans to enjoy. There was even a new demo online, called 'Actors'. The mid-paced beginning framed Alex's lyrics, which talked about being safe at home, with friends, with your thoughts, putting barriers up to keep secure in the face of the bad old world. The song then kicked in, very Blink-ish, to a tuneful chorus highlighting the ultimate insincerity of that approach – hence the 'actors' of the title. It's a very well-considered meditation on being honest with yourself. As Shakespeare put it, 'All the world's a stage, and the men and women merely players; they have their exits and their entrances; and one man in his time plays many parts ...'

All of which goes to prove that Willy-boy would have been a fan of the Baltimore blasters, without doubt. We are still firmly in our salad days, however, so it's time, once more, to hit Hawaii and the Far East before Europe beckons again.

CHAPTER 16

IF IT AIN'T DIRTY, IT AIN'T WORTH A ...

In February 2009, news came to gladden the hearts of many pop-punk fans from around the world. Mark Hoppus, Tom DeLonge and Travis Barker came onstage at the Grammy Awards after four years since the band had split. Travis had his arm in a sling, a knock-on effect of nerve damage after a terrible plane crash that had claimed the lives of two of his closest friends, and in which he'd suffered about 65 per cent burns. The trio was onstage ostensibly to give the award for Best Rock Album, and after a quick Mark Hoppus joke, Travis took to the mic to say, simply: 'We used to play music together, and we've decided we're going to play music together again.' Cue great cheers from the audience. Mark announced that 'Blink-182 is back', and the noise only increased further. Later, Tom told the interviewer that people in bands had a kind of unspoken bond, that the band was more like family.

The plane crash had brought the trio closer together than they had been over the past half a decade, although their bond would inevitably have reunited them in due course. It just needed something to break the ice, he added.

Blink toured extensively in the United States and Canada during September and October 2009 and picked up the pace a year later by heading to Europe. The day finally came – on 24 August 2010 – for All Time Low to do something they'd only dreamt of for so long. They were to support their heroes and inspirations for the first time ever, with the concert taking place at the Trabrennbahn Bahrenfeld, Hamburg, Germany. An interviewer from Trident Perpetual Festival caught up with Alex after the famous Rock en Seine Festival a couple of days later (where power was lost due to rain at certain stages), and the singer was relaxed and excited to answer some questions that fans had posted on Twitter. He began by saying one of the best things about being in a group was meeting people and seeing places he may not have done otherwise, due to the large amount of travel involved. He also recounted the story of an over-enthusiastic fan who'd literally cornered him on the bus to confess her undying love in an intense moment; quickly the two Matts (Flyzik and Colussy) stepped in to escort the young lady back outside. But there was one revealing answer indeed. When asked what he would change the band name to if all the merchandise and material could also instantaneously change, he replied, 'Dirty Work' – in a variety of accents.

The boys were also on the bill with Blink-182 at the Leeds and Reading Festivals. Alex and Jack spoke to *Kerrang!* after their performance in the latter fest. Although the weather was dry when the band stepped onstage, an immediate downpour added to the drama of their set, with crowd surfing, mud and an additional frisson to the performance. Jack said it was like something out of the movie *300*. 'It felt like a war,' Alex added, referring to the surrealistic scenario. A bit of rain was OK, Jack said, albeit lightning might be a slightly different matter given the whole stage was constructed (literally) from heavy metal. That said it would be a hell of a way to go out. 'I'd go down a legend,' Alex said, smiling.

He confirmed that the album was as near as dammit done although some songs were still left to mix. The goal, he said, was to get the new record out by January 2011. He added that as it was a first record for a major label there was some pressure, but as the label understood what the band was all about there was no pressure actually to change anything or do things in a certain way. Of course, the band was now experienced and on album number five, Jack pointed out. Alex added that while *Nothing Personal* was great, he had higher ambitions, and in this new record the group pushed at the boundaries ever more. There would also be surprises for fans, but the new album would still sound like a record by All Time Low.

The United Kingdom, Jack said, was the only place at that stage where they'd enjoyed success in terms of a radio single, even including their home country, although there had been bits and bobs of radio over there. The band was more about touring than radio, though, Alex added. The boys had three days off following the Reading Festival, so Alex was enjoying a nice 2005 Cabernet Sauvignon and making plans to watch a host of groups, including You Me At Six, Limp Bizkit, Paramore and Blink-182.

The *Manchester Evening News* caught up with the pair, with Alex in very mischievous mode, saying that their set had been the best to date, 'even better than Blink-182', with Jack adding, 'even though they haven't played yet'. The boys also noticed that there had been a lot of boobs flashed during their set, as they skanked to some reggae playing in the background during the interview. The boys, I mean. Not the boobs. Referring to their heroes again, Jack joked that his mic stand was positioned where Mark Hoppus would be standing later that night. The two added that they'd be looking to find future wives (or a husband, for Jack, as he said) in London – or India – during their time off.

One thing that can definitely be derived from these upbeat interviews is that the guys were certainly enjoying their job. The only downside to Reading – weather aside – was the delayed set by Guns N' Roses (at least, the Axl Rose plus members-for-hire version). The plugs had to be pulled as the band came onstage an hour late, meaning the legal curfew to end the music at midnight was in danger of being exceeded. Axl wasn't happy, to say the least, ending up onstage leading a singalong of 'Paradise City' through a megaphone rather than the full-band extravaganza it should have been. He's a complex character, that chap!

After the short break, the band decamped once more to mainland Europe, passing through Germany, Austria and Italy before a couple of dates in Spain again, a country where Alex had said he'd consider living. Then it was back to the States for more wrapping up on the album during September and then another set of gigs that would bring the United States back into the fold. It was during October that MTV tracked the band down and the lads explained why they had finally given the album the title of *Dirty Work*. Rian joked that it was a nod to the Rolling Stones' record of the same name, plus a movie also sharing that moniker. Jack, meanwhile, laughed that All Time Low fans had no idea who the Rolling Stones were, so that wouldn't be a problem. Alex brought it back to serious-land (for a change) when he spoke of the album process in some way reflecting the anxiety of moving to a new label, plus experiencing difficulties in his own personal relationships due to not having enough time to spend with the ones (outside of the band) with whom he was closest. He said he felt like 'an island stuck in the middle of the ocean', and went on to say that the title was a nod to that subject matter. It was, he said, a juxtaposition of being cocooned in that bubble of fun, good times and the band, which also sometimes meant that life's problems were being ignored due to being preoccupied with living in the moment. 'You have these songs about the good times, and then there are also these songs about "Wow, because of these good times, everything else is completely burning." And "dirty work" was the first [...] set of words that came to mind to define what I had been doing for the past two years. It was "dirty work".' Rian concluded that fans were unlikely to mistake the new album for one by Kings of Leon, for example, but that they would hopefully say, 'Wow, that's a better song than they've ever written!'

The Internet was awash with rumours; the latest being that the release date would be 17 January, with the tracklisting: 'Overtime'; 'Dirty Work'; 'Never Coming Home'; 'I Think I've Had Enough'; 'Freakout'; 'After All'; 'Grab Whatever

You Can'; 'I'm Not Gonna Save You This Time'; 'Leaving So Soon?'; 'Tomorrow'; 'Don't Make Me Do This'; 'Actors; Highlight of My Life' and 'Better Days'. However, by 28 October, Alter the Press! was already running a story that these rumours were simply untrue. This was confirmed by an interview Jack gave to Review Rinse Repeat in early November, while the band were out on their latest set of gigs, the Small Package Tour, also featuring A Rocket to the Moon and City (Comma) State. '[W]e're probably looking at an early spring release,' he said. 'I think it's better for All Time Low because we're a summer band, and I feel uncomfortable, among other reasons, releasing an album in winter.' He confirmed that recording while on the road was pretty much impossible so it had been a case of getting in and out of the studio when they could. It was an album focused on Alex's writing rather than that of the band, he said. '[Because of the band's schedule] a lot of the writing process was Alex writing songs and us going into the studio to put in our two cents and changing a couple things around.'

That schedule showed no signs of slowing down either, with early gigs in 2011 set to see the chaps heading to Brazil and then going back to Europe. Jack rightly said that his group was now a global band and that the UK in particular had a good fan base. As far as Brazil was concerned, it was something new and – tongue-in-cheek – he envisaged some tricky times there. 'From a country standpoint, as far as stability, I think we're kind of nervous because we really don't know much about South America and we've never been there,' he offered. 'We'll probably have some sort of security with us just to make sure we're not going into dark alleys and buying crack from hookers, or getting shot, stabbed, raped, or kidnapped.' Spoiler alert: none of this happened, obviously, otherwise this would be an entirely different kind of book.

Nonetheless, the rest of the year was not misspent. The album was reported to have been completed on 9 December, which was also the date that – briefly – a special Christmas song was put on SoundCloud by a user named 'tygbistheyeahhh' under the title 'shittyatlxmassong-mp3'. And the track in question? A lovely non-album ditty entitled 'Merry Christmas, Kiss My Ass'. This was a song firmly in the tradition of Blink-182's notorious 'Happy Holidays, You Bastard' – one of Blink's dafter numbers, hailing from 2001 – in which the protagonist talks about a whole host of unsavoury activities including fellatio with the dad of the person the song's addressed to, manual hand relief from the same person's mum, and the fact that his grandfather always poops in his pants. The All Time Low song 'Merry Christmas, Kiss My Ass' was co-produced by U4L, whose Scott Stallone recounted exclusively for this book his thoughts on how it came together.

'Well, ATL was always one of my favourite bands,' he told the author.

I produced and co-wrote a couple records for another Baltimore band called Voodoo Blue on DCide Records. We spent a lot of time digging on ATL. They defined the genre in my opinion and because I spent a lot of time in their hometown their music was omnipresent and they were always around. The collaboration on 'Merry Christmas, Kiss My Ass' happened over the Thanksgiving weekend in 2010. I was in NY when I got the invite from Dan Book to come write a Christmas song with Alex in Baltimore.

Scott wasn't present at the actual recording session, but the group did email him their rough ideas one night, which the producer rated as 'obviously awesome'. The song title, he said, came from the Chevy Chase *Christmas Vacation* movie, where the lead character says those words, plus 'Happy Hanukkah', to the 'assholes in his office'. Alex, said Scott, was

into the Pink song 'So What' and the swing feel was the jumping off point. The song was written that night and Alex cut all the demo vocals too. When I got the session files of the demo I replaced a lot of the electronic drum sounds with better ones and added rock samples in the heavy sections knowing that Rian would eventually re-play the fuck out of it! I added the synths and created some transitions and dynamics. Then I mixed it and sent it to Alex and Rian a couple days later. They were making *Dirty Work* with [producer] Mike Green at that time. I was told what happened after that was that they recut all the guitars and live drums and new vocals but kept a lot of the sounds I added. Mike Green rocked it, of course!

As far as working with the band in writing and pre-production sessions is concerned, Scott says although he has only worked closely with Rian and Alex, they were both 'total pros'. 'Alex will write an entire song complete with lyrics that'll blow you away in twenty minutes,' says the producer and musician. 'And as far as Rian goes, by the time he gets in the studio he's already written and rehearsed every single sick drum part and could play it backwards if he was suspended upside down. I had added some cool shit in the demo of 'Merry Christmas, Kiss My Ass' but with the parts that Rian wrote and played I was like, why did I ever even bother! HA!'

The track's tongue-in-cheek vitriol was a great way to say goodbye to another year that had had many ups, a few downs, and quite a few knockers (in all senses). What would 2011 bring?

CHAPTER 17

A NEW LP

The UK was the first port of call as the band headed to their second home. *Rock Sound* caught up with Alex, who predicted the year ahead would be a chance to boost the group's career to another level. At the moment, he said, the venues that the boys were playing were around two to four thousand in capacity but the goal was to try and reach five to ten thousand fans per gig. He said he really wanted All Time Low to be a name on everybody's lips, 'like the Green Days of my generation. I think that's what we've all been striving for all this time: that's the ultimate goal.' He also updated fans on the status of the new album and explained that the finishing touches on the songs and overriding theme were being undertaken. Because the band wanted to get everything completely right before hitting the streets with the record, it would now come out some time between January and March.

He reiterated that they were pushing themselves on it, saying they had taken chances and tried to write stuff that hadn't previously been in the All Time Low sonic canon. It was exciting, he noted, to play fresh stuff and to see how it went down with the fans.

The two UK gigs – in Newport and Belfast – were a quick stop-off before heading down to South America, followed by a UK return during March alongside Yellowcard. That band were in the headlines for putting a Facebook update out on 11 January that stated their Philadelphia gig on 22 March would be the same day as records were released both by themselves and by All Time Low. As it turned out, the news snippet was quickly retracted. Still, there was some definite news, Alex writing on his Twitter account that a recording of a new track especially for the interactive game *The Sims* was to be scheduled. Exciting times!

It was also very exciting to have visited Brazil, as Jack told AbsolutePunk during a March 2011 interview. A huge crowd had watched the band at the Via Funchal concert in São Paolo, he explained, although it wasn't quite the biggest audience they'd played to so far – that accolade went to the European festivals with Blink-182. The guitarist did clarify that 'it was the largest headlining crowd we have ever played to. It was our first time in Brazil and the entire country treated us like their own. Pretty eye-opening experience.' No kidnapping, kneecapping, toecapping, or nastiness, then, thankfully.

A clip of a new song, 'Art of the State', was briefly uploaded but the release date of the LP was once more pushed back, as Alex explained to *Cambio*. 'We never actually gave an official release date; it's all been left to speculation and stretching of the fact,' he said in the article, which ran in mid-February. 'At this point, it's looking more like the record will come out a bit later than March, but I think folks can still expect to hear some new material in the coming weeks.' With the advent of social media, he observed, rumours and news spread incredibly quickly. As for 'Art of the State', he said that he was pleased with the reaction that putting it online had garnered. He told the interviewer that there was a lot of interest about the new album and that people were looking forward to hearing new stuff. As regards social media, he compared the likes of Tumblr and Twitter to forest fires. Leaking that track in its entirety was like fuelling the flames, and while people may have thought it was an introduction to the new record, in fact it was more like an ending to a story. He also reiterated that the Interscope deal was no reflection on the excellent relationship with previous label Hopeless; it was more that the major label enabled access to a much wider market. 'Partnering with Interscope simply introduced us to a larger team, with global reach and resources, essentially opening new doors for what we can achieve as a band,' mused the ambitious young musician.

New material was also making it into the band's set; in Brussels on 15 February, the lads introduced an unfamiliar number to the crowd. It was confirmed on social media thereafter that the track in question was called 'Time-Bomb' and Alex's words about the near-instantaneous propagation of information on the web were confirmed when a mere hour after the concert finished, a video of the track taken from the crowd was already online. Ten days later, the studio version of 'Time-Bomb' was put online for fans to listen to. Alex even participated in an online thread in which he thanked people for listening to the track and said he was pleased that some people were into it. However, it wasn't a song that represented the album as a whole.

'Time-Bomb' was one of the more dancey songs from the forthcoming opus, but he reckoned it felt like a good way to link the new stuff with *Nothing Personal*. He also noted there was no plan to release it as a single but the group were keen that people had a quick taste of the material. As Jack said, 'We thought it was the perfect song to bridge the gap between our transition from *Nothing Personal* to *Dirty Work*. It's not a single, just a track to get fans pumped on the album. There is a good mix of faster-type typical ATL songs and also some slow ballad type songs.' A tracklisting was imminent, added the guitarist.

Another song that might be in the running for a single was 'I Feel Like Dancin'', a track the band had written with none other than Rivers Cuomo of Weezer. That band had influenced All Time Low significantly for some time and the chance to work together was obviously super-cool. Alex said that when the collaboration was first mooted it was something of a shock but when the logistics of this were discussed it became something that was actually going to happen, schedules permitting. 'We're such big fans,' he told *AP*, 'so it's been very rad. He's such a good dude; he's very down-to-earth. There are a lot of stories about him being such a character and to be honest, he's actually a pretty straightforward dude.'

Another unlikely celebrity link-up was when All Time Low were rendered characters in a new iPhone game called *Mike Tyson: Main Event*. The game was an update of, or tribute to, an ancient 1980s arcade fighting game, and the band members all had signature moves included, such as Rian using his sticks and the singer swinging his microphone. Which is all fun until someone loses their teeth, or bites someone's ear off!

The older material was still selling well; 'Dear Maria, Count Me In' was officially certified Gold in the United States in early March, having sold a whopping 500,000 copies according to the Recording Industry Association of America. The band's cover of Lady Gaga's 'Alejandro' was also imminently to be released, as part of Hopeless/Sub City's latest charity compilation, *Take Action Volume 10*. The double CD was made available at gigs, Hot Topic stores and other retailers from 26 April and also featured such rarities as a Skrillex remix of Twin Atlantic's 'What is Light? What is Laughter?', Ryan Key of Yellowcard guesting on Silverstein's track 'Stay Posi', an acoustic version of 'Lights Out' by We Are The In Crowd and of course the delicate classical ballad by Veara, 'Getting Kicked in the Face Has Never Been So Much Fun'.

Jack's clothing company was expanding all the while and a hook-up with the group I Call Fives during March meant that the band's new EP, a split with Rust Belt Lights, would be available, along with a special T-shirt through JAGK.

Back on the road, though, and while the album wasn't available on 22 March as previously mooted – there had been some restructuring within Interscope – a new song was debuted at that Philadelphia gig. The name? 'Under a Paper Moon'. 'I want to play you guys a song from the new record,' Alex said. 'And I hope you've got your cameras ready, because I want this shit all over YouTube.' He added that he wanted people to learn it and love it, and that it was one of his favourite tracks from the forthcoming record.

Management were busy, too, revealing the artwork to *Dirty Work* on *AP* and also noting that 'I Feel Like Dancin' would indeed be the first single from the album. The reaction to the gigs on both sides of the pond had so far been excellent. A reviewer who'd caught the band at Glasgow's famous Barrowlands venue noted not only that Jack had guested with Yellowcard on a song but also the venue was absolutely buzzing. 'You only need two things for a dance party,' they quoted Alex as saying. 'People and dancing.' And so the crowd jumped up and down – without any music playing. Bizarre. But when the music did start, it was awesome. At one stage a chant of 'Charlie Sheen' grew for no particular reason, which Alex videoed for posterity before coming onstage with merely an acoustic in hand to treat the crowd to his version of 'Teenage Dream' by Katy Perry. On a high the lads came back out to hammer the encore. The writer was happy, it's safe to say: 'They're an incredible live band, they're fun and sure, the elaborate light show adds a certain je ne sais quoi to their shows but there's such an energetic vibe that emanates at their shows it's hard to find fault.' Indeed so.

A month later and the bandwagon had descended on Minneapolis, where the bras were in full flow. 'To say the least, they make the night interesting,' wrote The Sound Alarm. 'Asking fans to get rowdy, crazy, and sexual, they have everyone's attention all the way through their set list and multiple encores.'

At the gig on 1 April at Orlando's House of Blues, Cassadee Pope joined the lads for 'Remembering Sunday'. The Internet was awash with talk that a sequel to *Straight to DVD* was possibly being filmed on the current tour, albeit said footage might simply end up as part of the *Dirty Work* package. Talking of that album, the release date was announced for 7 June, although the timing could have been better as the news came out on April Fools' Day. No doubt the irony was not lost on our protagonists.

That same day Alex's interview with *OC Weekly* was published, in which he professed his love for pop music, saying that he was a fan of Maroon 5, Lady Gaga, Madonna and Nicki Minaj. He noted that pop music was intended to be catchy and to hook you in immediately. 'I think there's something to be said for music that can connect to the masses in such a quick way,' he offered. 'It's sort of like you're doing something right. Because music is such an internal thing, that if there's a song that catches your ear and immediately you're hooked and remembering the words, that's genius.' That said, the Internet sensation *du jour*, one Rebecca Black, had released a widely derided track called 'Friday', which he felt was terrible. He did however give her props for getting out there and doing it. In contrast to Perry's 'Teenage Dream', though, it made him want to throw up. Simplicity was one thing, and 'Teenage Dream' was beautiful as a result, but the simplicity of 'Friday' was entirely the opposite, he believed.

During May, a video of the group's cover of the Britney Spears' track 'Hold it Against Me' was released – ATL had performed it at a special Radio 1 Live Lounge session. Around this time, too, Alex spoke to old friends AbsolutePunk, discussing the differences between being on a major label and being on an indie. The singer noted the transition hadn't been too difficult as the band had of course been with Hopeless for quite a while, building up a big fan base and lots of momentum – it wasn't the case that they were a new act trying to lift off from nothing. That said, while they were with Hopeless Records, All Time Low were one of the larger groups and a priority for the label, meaning that resources of time and expertise could be dedicated to them in a way that a label like Interscope, with its huge acts, could not match. 'There's a lot going on, it takes a little bit longer to get things done and get things moving,' he said. 'At the same time, the ability and resources that they have to push those things, even though it takes a little longer, we kind of come out better because of that.' Time would tell.

Alex also discussed how Blink-182 had developed their sound between *Take Off Your Pants and Jacket* and the more complex and serious *blink-182* albums. He reckoned that while his band was obviously linked with and compared to the San Diego trio, they were very different entities. Specifically, he noted you could in retrospect hear the tension of the band's deteriorating interpersonal and musical relationships in the second of those two mentioned Blink albums, which resulted in the group taking time off. He said that in the case of his own band, he couldn't predict what might happen – these things tended to come out in the writing of the new material. That said he was aware that a very important part of being in a band was not putting a spanner in the works of the relationship with their fan base. They weren't about to change overnight into a country-rock band, that was for sure, but of course it was about writing the music that was inside while being aware that there were fans out there who loved

Above: A very young looking All Time Low attend the pre-taping of the 2009 MTV New Year's Eve program at the MTV studios on 15 December (Left to right: Rian Dawson, Alex Gaskarth, Jack Barakat and Zack Merrick).

© *Bryan Bedder/Getty Images*

Below left: The band on the red carpet at the RedZone Entertainment & Radio Killa Records Pre-Grammy Party, February 2009. © *Beck Starr/WireImage*

Below right: Enjoying some down-time, playing beer pong back stage at the mtvU Woodie awards, 2008. © *Roger Kisby/Getty Images*

Above: One of the band's many signings, this time for their album *Dirty Work*, 2011.
© *Rachel Murray/WireImage*

Below: All Time Low completely fill the HMV store in Manchester with their eager fans, as they perform and sign copies of their new album *Future Hearts* in 2015.
© *Shirlaine Forrest/WireImage*

Right: Alex Gaskarth entertains the crowd as the band performs on the main stage at Leeds festival in 2015.

© Andrew Benge/ Redferns

Below: Again, Alex owns the stage as he plays in front of thousands of fans at Wembley Arena, 2015.

© Gus Stewart/ Redferns via Getty Images

Above: The guys scoop their most recent award at the Kerrang Awards 2016, winning Best Track for their song, 'Missing You'. © *Jo Hale/Getty Images*

Below: Don't they scrub up well! The band at the Blink 182-Karaoke Summer Tour Announcement, 2016. © *Brian Gove/WireImage*

what you did. Somewhat prophetic words from the singer: All Time Low's new album was about to be put to the test, as it contained some slightly unexpected twists and turns.

Busy as ever, the band joined the Red Bull Bedroom Jam on 4 April, which brought upcoming bands to the attention of a wider audience. The boys talked with Katie P, host of the show, about their touring experiences and gave advice on dealing with press and fans. The significance of this type of interview beginning to come through for the band should not be underestimated: such interviews mark a rite of passage of sorts; the moving of the group from young hopefuls to the status of experienced and truly established acts with experience and stories to share.

There was just time for Alex to appear on 'Freakin' Me Out', a Simple Plan record, before all eyes finally turned towards that magic, long-awaited, much-moved date: Album Release Day. Or 7 June 2011, if you want to be pedantic about it. Sheesh!

CHAPTER 18

IS IT REALLY
COMING OUT NOW?

After all of the speculation and many delays fans were finally treated to some ninety-second clips of the new album on 17 May 2011. A week later, a very limited edition of 900 copies of the new album was made available for pre-order in the unusual format of white spattered vinyl, which looked as beautiful as the album sounded blasting. The week that *Dirty Work* hit the charts, Hits Daily Double estimated that the band would sell around 55,000 copies, which would be a pretty good result as the quartet was in direct competition with new records from Adele and Lady Gaga. Other names in that site's chart predictions included Eddie Vedder, Arctic Monkeys, Mumford & Sons, and Katy Perry, whose own LP was still selling at a rate of around 20,000 copies a week.

Dirty Work's cover features the four lads wearing suits, with Alex spraying – or should that be poppin' – champagne, while the other three play it cool. The art in the CD booklet portrays what looks like a pretty rockin' party with plenty of girls, booze and laughter. Alex is also shown topless, lying on the floor and stuffing his cakehole with what looks like a burger from a fast-food outlet. The back cover is a tad more sinister, maybe, with blow-up guitars that literally say rock 'n' roll on them plus the disembodied legs of a blow-up doll. If you were to take two copies of the album, remove the back cover and put them side by side – one upside down – it would look like Alex has blow-up doll legs. Try it – it's funny as hell!

To the music, however, and the album begins with 'Do You Want Me (Dead?)', which is credited to Alex Gaskarth and Mike Green. It kicks off with a rolling guitar figure, some huge chords and some pad-like synth songs, before hammering in to a track that is pop in the vein of L7 or Pixies at their more melodic moments. The pre-chorus and its relatively simple chords are followed by the high production whistles and FX that do indeed show that the band is pushing at the possibilities of the studio. The song's many layers of tracks are both a wall of sound and a canvas within which ideas come thick and fast: when Alex sings that he's looking to get away, the vocals move through the stereo field boldly.

Next up is the superior 'I Feel Like Dancin', which, as mentioned earlier, was a co-write between Alex and Rivers Cuomo of Weezer. As you might expect, it has the feel of the latter's band melded with All Time Low in party mode, plus is that a hint of a Def Leppard influence? Well, not one anybody would admit to anyway. So, two songs into the album and two big party songs with a real message: I'm gonna get out there and do it, no matter what others might say. As to the writing sessions with Cuomo, Jack had some interesting memories that he shared with Punknews about the surroundings in which they'd taken place. 'One of the coolest things I remember about the Rivers session was what he had in his house,' the guitarist revealed. 'He had a bunch of books from Harvard and a couple of those skeletons you see in science class [...] Luckily we had spent a couple years writing with producers like Matt Squire. So by the time Alex was in the room with Rivers, he was prepared.' The evidence is in the song's quality.

Third track on the album is 'Forget about It', which is credited to Alex and producer John Fields. The song is one of the vocalist's meditations on whether he is in the right relationship or not and it has one of the catchiest little synth riffs that the band had produced to date. It's also one of the poppiest songs on an All Time Low record to date, with a great little solo from Jack just before the breakdown and a spoken-word conversation between Alex and the unnamed other party in the relationship.

'Guts' comes next, another collab with Green and featuring the not-inconsiderable talents of Maja Ivarsson, the strikingly beautiful lead singer with Swedish indie rockers The Sounds. Her vocals offset Alex's nicely in one of the most emo songs that the lads had provided up to this point.

The fabulous 'Time-Bomb' is up next and this one's a collaboration between Alex and Mike Green, plus singer Pierre Bouvier and Chuck Comeau, who are respectively the singer and drummer with Canadian pop-punks Simple Plan. The song is about a relationship of two daft kids who have no fear of the explosions that are bound to come along in the future. On record it's a very controlled slice of pop-punk but also includes within it the dynamic changes, riff-heavy choruses and singalong vocal lines that would set it going crazy in the live arena.

'Just the Way I'm Not', credited to Alex and Butch Walker, has stadium-sized snare sounds and damped barre chords before setting itself free into a call-and-response chorus absolutely made for audience interaction.

'Under a Paper Moon' is another Gaskarth–Green co-write. Alex told PropertyofZack that Mike Green had become something of a star in the process, 'He did production on most of the songs and he absolutely killed it. He hit it out of the park and delivered us a record that sounds phenomenal. He kind of brought the best out of us. I've never sang like I have on this record,' the singer said. It's another track that sounds nothing like what has preceded it; it's got an offbeat blend of pop-punk choruses and skew-whiff verses that showcase some great performances from the ever-solid Rian and Zack, whose basslines are fluid and drive the whole thing along.

'Return the Favour', which was co-written by Jacob and Daniel Luttrel, has a dramatic minor-chord feel about it, nodding more towards a more metal type of sound while still keeping things within the framework of All Time Low. Alex said that while the main influences of the band had been Blink-182, New Found Glory and Green Day, as things moved on the lads were also listening to Third Eye Blind and Eve 6, bands they had grown up with and that had an influence on their work almost without them noticing it. The neo-classical piano intro and outro to 'Return the Favour' were certainly realms away from songs about grandfathers and their nocturnal scatological adventures, for sure.

The huge talent of Christopher 'Tricky' Stuart was brought in to work with Alex on 'No Idea'. Tricky's credits over the years are numerous but some of the production credits include Britney's 'Me Against the Music' and a co-write of none other than 'Umbrella' by Rihanna – which of course All Time Low had gleefully performed many times over the years. The other writer credited is Terrius Nash, also known as The Dream, who'd worked with Tricky on both Rihanna and Britney's LPs, as well as their huge hit 'Single Ladies (Put a Ring On It)' for Beyoncé. Quite a team to have on board for a song about an unreciprocated love affair, but one in which the cheeky repeat of 'dea' at the end of the song is a definite echo of 'ella-ella-ella' from that mega Rihanna song.

'A Daydream Away' is an acoustic-led number written by Alex with Mike Green, featuring a rather lovely cello line marking another of Alex's sensitive tracks about wishing someone would stay one more night, wanting to head out to have a drink and watch the rest of the world go by in its manic way. On one level this is about a failed love affair stymied by the fast pace of the rest of the world out there, but on another there is a reading that nods once more to the loss of Alex's half-brother, Tom. All interpretations of course are pertinent and this track really does show Alex has the skill as a lyricist to deliver a song that can feel personal to each individual's own experiences. The track is beautifully delivered and is an underrated high point of the album.

Green and Gaskarth's next co-write is 'That Girl', which David Kahne produced. When I asked him, he gave a real insight into the recording process. '[There wasn't] a lot of preproduction,' he said. 'Tracking went smoothly, and the comments back and forth were easy. I work on whole albums, so sometimes it's a little strange for me to just do a track, as I learn about the group through different tracks and realize based off of working on one track what can help another one. I would have liked to have done a little more, but that wasn't the plan for this work.' He said that prior to working with All Time Low he'd only heard the albums but definitely liked the vibe. 'They were very strong creatively,' confirms the producer. 'They got their momentum up quickly and went right to work.' The result in this case is a catchy, singalong typical All Time Low track.

Next up is 'Heroes', which was written with John Feldmann, with whom Alex had long wanted to work for his skills in writing and production. Here Rian gets the chance to show off some absolutely speedy double bass drum work, which requires stamina and precision. His tom-tom fills are also really interesting throughout and again the group breaks down into a metal-tinged middle eight that in another band's hands could be cheesy but here is a gang vocals-led interlude between the first half of the song and the second, in which the villain of the piece is described in no uncertain terms as a liar, vampire, train wreck and more.

That's it for the original album, but there are four bonus tracks on the UK edition. The Green–Gaskarth axis is back in action on 'Get Down On Your Knees and Tell Me You Love Me'. Here the singer spits more vitriol to or at someone who has cheated on the protagonist. Sonically, it blends electronica with pop-punk and emo, with handclaps and guitar stabs punctuating the action.

Matt Squire is back in the writing team for 'My Only One'.

Alex had praised the producer's development saying that Squire had reached a new place and way of thinking, making it cool to work together. It's a love song for someone who isn't necessarily of the same mind.

There's just time for the notorious 'Merry Christmas, Kiss My Ass' – hardly a classic summer song given its content but a lot of fun nonetheless, bringing the fourth All Time Low album to an end with some daftness.

A bonus track is an acoustic run-through of 'Time-Bomb', which is actually a very different version with plenty of arrangement on show, including loads of backing vocals, triangle tings and bongo drums plus percussion. Scott 'A4L' Stallone recalls his involvement with that track, as well as with 'I Feel Like Dancin' (for the United States deluxe edition). 'Dan and I got the a capellas for 'Time-Bomb' and 'I Feel Like Dancin',' he told the author. 'And we were asked to produce the acoustic versions that showed up on the *Dirty Work Deluxe* edition based on the work we did on 'Merry Christmas, Kiss My Ass'. We did them here at my studio in Philadelphia, one right after the other and had complete control. We went kinda nuts with orchestral fills and strings and shit … we thought they'd tell us to rein it in a bit but they let them go on the record exactly as I delivered them.' That intriguing little extra added to the bumper set of songs on a record that was more than worth the wait.

Reviewers agreed in general about the new territories aimed at by All Time Low as their career continued apace. *Rolling Stone* paid tribute to 'Time-Bomb', calling it 'a tightly wound anthem that sounds like a real panic at the disco', although the venerable mag did say that the band had been somewhat caught between 'bratty snot-rock and witty power-pop'. In the United Kingdom the album went down pretty well with *Rock Sound*, which opened by saying that the music of the group had attracted a fan base of some import but that hadn't meant the group had forgotten what the key parts of their approach were. The reviewer said that the album was 'still super-catchy, but has enough of a rock edge to differentiate it from radio-friendly pop'. Although the band sometimes get criticism for the subject matter of girls, the writer felt, they wrote music that was relatable, blunt and honest, which Alex's spoken-word elements in 'Forget about It' showed. The one misstep was 'I Feel Like Dancin', which to the reviewer felt like it was a throwaway effort, but in general the album showed that All Time Low had kicked things up a notch in terms of how well put together and poppy the new sound was.

The boys hadn't gone totally Green Day-esque on the album, referring to that trio's new ventures into rock operas and the like, but maturity was in evidence. That was the verdict of *Entertainment Weekly*, which also highlighted the poignancy of 'Guts' and 'Time-Bomb', where there were sparkly choruses to punctuate the shouty bits. '*Dirty Work* proves you can grow up and still act like a kid—just as long as your songs are this head-rushingly catchy,' the mag offered.

There had been pressure on the band with the continued wait for release, thought *Kerrang!*, which said that even though the group had told the magazine of their intent to get down to work rather than partying their way through the album, there wasn't all that much evidence of it on the final work. Worst of all, it felt 'like a ramshackle collection of outtakes borrowed from their peers'. New Found Glory and Sum 41 were invoked in the mag's interpretation of the inspiration for 'Do You Want Me (Dead?)', and 'Return the Favour' was overproduced, sounding like a b-side of the band Panic! At the Disco. 'Time-Bomb' was also felt by the mag to be substandard. That said, 'Under a Paper Moon' and 'Heroes' were punchy and definitely showed they had stepped up. In conclusion, the mag gave the record three K ratings out of five and said that *Dirty Work* wasn't a great album, just a good one.

One of the best reviews the album got in the UK was from *Big Cheese*, a rock magazine. The anticipation had been high, said the reviewer, but All Time Low were 'back, bigger, bolder than ever before'. The opening song's production and pop-rock really did show that the Baltimore boys were now on a major label and the Rivers Cuomo collaboration was a 'pure party pop hit' that had humour all the way through it. The Motion City Soundtrack-esque 'Forget about It' was praised for its massive chorus, which was something the band was good at throughout the album. The reviewer gave it five out of five, concluding that '[the album is] pure pop rock and it's sure to be all over the radio and the soundtrack to the summer. Fall Out Boy may be about to be usurped ...'

Other reviewers weren't quite so convinced, with an intriguing metaphor coming into play in a middling Under the Gun review, in which the writer felt 'whelmed' and said, 'The sheer lack of any sort of words to describe the album is fantastic. I'm not extolling it, nor am I trashing it, I just feel vaguely lost in a generic netherworld where the entire album feels like one prolonged episode of *One Tree Hill*.' The lengthy review did go into plenty of detail about the tracks, showing that the reviewer had given it a good chance albeit that it only gained six out of ten in the end. The reviewer admitted she'd interrupted her reviewing to watch a new trailer for *Breaking Dawn*, and also invoked *Sex in the City II* as an example of something that was aimed squarely at its target audience and unlikely to be of much interest to anyone else.

A site called Mind Equals Blown felt that this album was one that would divide fans. There were, the writer felt, those who were once drawn towards the early days of the back catalogue, who were disappointed by *Nothing Personal*, the type of fans who'd reckon the band had sold out to a major label; and by contrast the supporters who'd be happy to go along with the continued musical development of the group. 'Change, for lack of a better word, is good,' wrote the reviewer. 'Bands can't rewrite the same songs time and again and expect to be praised for it.' The album did straddle two camps – the top 40, poppy lot and also the pop-punks eager for a summer album. 'Time-Bomb' and 'Guts' were both praised, as was 'Just the Way I'm Not', and the reviewer liked the idea that the band had spread their wings a little rather than playing it genre-safe.

The album was a game of two halves, reckoned Alter the Press! The gloss of the production on the opening track was irresistibly catchy, but 'Forget about It' and 'That Girl' were forgettable. 'Time-Bomb' showed off mass appeal and 'Guts' was great in terms of vocal harmonies. Giving the album two and a half out of five, the website said that sometimes it felt flat and that the band hadn't given itself the space to expand, rather they provided a bunch of guitar-based pop-rock targeted at the younger fans. 'Understandably you don't expect to widen their appeal, but compared to their early potential (see 'Coffee Shop Soundtrack') *Dirty Work* seems a bit empty and at times lifeless,' concluded the site.

One of the more insightful reviews, arguably, was from AbsolutePunk, long-time supporters of the band. After a lengthy analysis of the songs in general the writer concluded it had been obvious for a while that this catchy pop rock sound was what the boys had been aiming for. There were haters of the group for it, but ultimately the band were a guilty pleasure for many. 'At the end of the day, All Time Low made the catchiest record possible and have their fingers crossed for airplay in the upcoming months,' said the writer. 'For those who accept it, *Dirty Work* will be a staple in their summer playlist. As for everyone else, they'll bump it in their rooms when no one is around like Tom Cruise in *Risky Business*. And who can blame them?' Who indeed?

The album debuted at Number 6 in the Billboard 200 and at Number 20 in the UK's official Top 40. It also hit No. 1 in Billboard's Alternative Album and Rock Album charts, peaking at Number 10 in Japan, Number 13 in Australia and Canada, and Number 83 in Sweden. Well, you can't win 'em all, can ya? Still, there was also the bonus of a Cash Cash remix of 'I Feel Like Dancin'' to keep things rockin' along, and also the rather excellent news that All Time Low were nominated for an award by *Kerrang!* magazine in the category of Best Live Act and Best International Band. The boys duly walked away with the gong for the live award – a splendid trophy and testament once again to the sheer energetic party quality of the live experience. They just missed out to Thirty Seconds to Mars in the other category.

Alex and Jack talked to *Kerrang!*'s podcast about the experience a little later. 'It was one of those things where we read the [names of] the other bands in for it [and thought] there's no fucking way [we would win],' Alex said. Jack said that he thought there had been some huge mistake. Alex countered that he was waiting for Thirty Seconds to Mars or My Chemical Romance to appear somewhere and take the award, but that he gave full props to the fans as it was a fan-voted award. Jack meanwhile said that he was waiting for Jared Leto to kick All Time Low offstage and grab the award. The Thirty Seconds to Mars table, in fact, had given ATL a standing ovation and Alex reckoned that Leto was one heck of a cool dude.

Hooking up again with Mark Hoppus was also on the cards, this time to perform a couple of tracks on the Blink bassist's TV show, *Hoppus on Music*. The lads duly romped through 'Do You Want Me (Dead?)' and 'I Feel Like Dancin', which was also announced as the next single. An acoustic version of that was on the latest *Another Hopeless Summer* compilation, which was again available through iTunes and at VANS Warped Tour gigs. Alex, however, got himself in a tad of trouble for some throwaway comments regarding Big Time Rush, specifically that band's cover of 'No Idea', which ended up on their latest record. The singer said that during a previous interview he'd compared the Rush to 1960s manufactured pop band The Monkees, who were formed in order to provide a sort of clean-living alternative to The Beatles, perceived by some folks in the United States at the time as being a bad influence on the youth, for some reason.

Big Time Rush was a Nickelodeon series that followed

the lives of four people who had been selected to form a boy band, hence Alex's comparison of them with the 1960s band, who also had their own telly series. Alex wrote on his blog, Earth To Alex, that certain parts of the band were in the hands of the Nickelodeon powers-that-be and that the music and band were formed due to the television show, which was a simple fact. That said he wasn't having a go at what defines a 'real band', because that is subjective. Alex added that his remarks could have been taken as condescending when taken out of context, which was not his intention when he gave the interview in question. In conclusion, he wrote on his Tumblr blog, 'Those guys are homies, and they're doing what they do very well—I certainly wasn't tryna hate.' Having clarified that one, it was back to Europe to continue to support the new album on the road before returning to North America for the cheesily named Gimme Summer Ya Love tour.

CHAPTER 19

AFTERMATH, NEW MATERIAL, OLD FRIENDS

*T*he hard-touring band's experiences in Europe coincided with a bunch of festival appearances, which meant a lot of country hopping, as well as seeing some brilliant bands. That could mean a line-up one day with Blondie and Foo Fighters and the next with Weezer and All Time Low. Unfortunately, Alex didn't get the chance to meet up with Dave Grohl because of scheduling, but Taylor Hawkins, well-respected drummer for the Foos, did tell him that he'd wanted to catch All Time Low's set but hadn't managed to do so amid all the madness. Speaking to *Alternative Press*, Alex said that, 'I was so pissed, because we're all such big Foo fans. That was a cool moment, to know that they actually know who our band is.' Rivers Cuomo also joined up with the lads onstage at the T in the Park festival in Kinross, Scotland, a nice moment for the band and the fans alike.

Speaking of the album, Alex said that the record's sales numbers had looked really bad but in context with other artists' weekly sales it was actually normal that there should be something of a drop-off after strong first-week figures. It was hard to see what was actually happening, he added, but if you looked at the pre-sales for the upcoming tours outside of the United States they were very strong. As ever, added the frontman, he'd been checking out the Internet and gauging the reaction to the new material, which seemed to be pretty positive in general. Alex also revealed that the band was now boosted onstage by a third guitar player – none other than Matt Colussy, assistant tour manager and ex-member of The Morning Light. That was down to the fact that the new record's arrangements often involved more than two guitar parts happening at the same time so Colussy would be an unofficial touring member. Many bands do this, including Green Day, for example, in order to provide the best experience possible for the fans. With the group now ready to tour North America once more, the lads would soon see exactly what the Stateside fans thought of the new record.

While in Toronto, the group appeared on *New Music Live* to support their Give Me Summer Ya Love tour and what ensued was a typical interview that ranged between the silly and the definitely insightful. The interviewer quizzed the band over a growing All Time Low phenomenon: the increased incidence of fans – of the female variety – throwing their underwear at the band. Jack reckoned it started when he told a particular crowd of his intention to establish a lingerie shop some three years earlier, to the amusement of all. The record amount of bras onstage at one show was over a hundred, apparently.

Some even came prepared with extra bras while others were 'floppers'. Fans would write their names, numbers and social media addresses on said underwear. Alex produced a pair of neon yellow Y-fronts signed by the band and presented them to the interviewer.

Alex also explained how 'Time-Bomb' came together. The story goes that he was working in the studio with producer Matt Squire. Simple Plan were also working with Squire and they had an unfinished track that they sent over for Alex to try ideas out on. He did just that, the end result being the song actually worked better as an All Time Low track. 'When they caught wind of it, they said that their record was almost done and said I should finish the song,' he told TheyWillRockYou, 'because it seemed to fit the vibe of our album more than it did theirs and we could just all collaborate on it together. So that is what ended up happening, I finished writing the song with Matt in the studio and we tracked it the next day. It was a good time.'

One track that was ruffling a few feathers was 'I Feel Like Dancin', the results of that Rivers Cuomo collaboration and the single that took the lads through the summer months. As usual it had a great video to accompany it – this time a satirical take on the music industry itself. It's very postmodern in its approach, too, with the band playing versions of themselves in a fictional recreation of what might actually be happening elsewhere in the music industry. We see the lads talking with a record label about their ideas for a new video, only to be rebuffed by The Man, who proceeds to tell them how it's done. First off, get some cool products in there – Rockstar is the chosen one in this case – then use sex to sell the band. They are dressed in a style that calls to mind popular shows such as the inexplicably successful *Jersey Shore* and surrounded by girls in bikinis (aside from Jack, whose new friends are a couple of hunky dudes). Referencing other bands or artists is also a way to get the attention of the audience, reckons the executive, so the group are dressed up in a way similar to Justin Bieber, Lady Gaga and old mate Katy Perry. That's the last straw for our boys, who make their excuses and leave. As a comment on the plastic nature of fame and the processes sometimes used cynically to manipulate the audience, it's a pretty powerful one even while being a fun, entertaining and somewhat daft piece of film. More evidence that there's a lot more to the Baltimore chaps than a summery chorus and a goddamn sharp haircut.

Alex explained that the band had chosen 'I Feel Like Dancin' as a single specifically to try and crack the tricky US radio situation. The label, he said, had ideas as to what the single should be but it felt good to get the song out there. 'It felt like it was something that was interesting to throw out there because I think it threw a lot of people for a loop,' he explained to *Confront Magazine*. 'It was obviously a song [stylistically] that we had never done before.' Jack agreed, adding that it was a happy, fun vibe as a track and that the video was extremely well executed by director Matt Stawski. 'A lot of the time, when you're with a director for a music video, they have this awesome idea but then it goes on paper and you see it and it sucks,' the guitarist noted. 'Every time he has an idea and he makes it in real life, it's awesome.'

Stawski's colours as ever were bright and arresting, making for a memorable piece of work. Under the Gun liked the single, noting the record certainly was suitable for daytime radio in the summer, and that it would fit nicely between tracks by, say, Katy Perry (her again?!) and Taio Cruz. 'I personally find my foot tapping along to the song as I write this,' was the conclusion, 'so in the end I will say that it isn't that bad. With pop punk, you should take it for what it is: Pop punk. It's fun and it's catchy so buy it and sing along.' The mark was eight out of ten.

The next single to hit the streets was 'Forget about It', a video for which was released on 6 July. Again it starts with a colourful intro before cutting to the lads pre-gig getting ready, then shots of them onstage or preparing for gigs, with regular interspersions of interactions with fans, backstage bits and bobs and lyrics to colourful backgrounds. It's basically an insight into what the band experienced on tour that year, with loads of sell-out gigs, trying to make some sense of the madness, and Jack bending over in front of the camera – thankfully fully clothed for a change. Nakedness does happen later, obviously. The slightly cheesy ending features lingering close-ups of each individual member, showing him in full heart-throb/simmering mode. The song clocked in at just under three minutes and kept things ticking along nicely in terms of keeping the album in the minds of the music biz.

The lads were touring hard throughout the summer and managed to nip to Virginia Beach for a guest appearance at that leg of the VANS Warped Tour, the day before they kicked off the US tour proper in nearby Richmond. The tour went well, with reviewers noting that the pop sound had evolved and the entertainment factor was still as present as it always had been. MusicNeverSleeps caught the concert at Wallingford,

Connecticut, on 3 August and reported that the room was 'filled with screams of excitement' as the band hammered into 'Do You Want Me (Dead?)'. The set was peppered with the usual banter between the lads and contained some old classics like 'Jasey Rae' and 'The Party Scene' plus several from *Dirty Work*, including 'Forget about It' and 'Time-Bomb'. 'All Time Low does not disappoint on this tour and delivers a quality show sure to any fan' was the verdict. Similarly, The Sound Alarm went to the Des Moines, Iowa, gig on 22 August and were blown away by the four bands they saw, with We Are The In Crowd, The Cab and Mayday Parade the supports that night. More screaming, more jumping and more stunts from Jack were central to the set, with the guitarist prowling across the stage and getting straight into the security gap between the stage and the front row. Alex provided some flawless vocals, the webmag wrote, and was full of smiles. The crowd took the Juliet Simms' part for 'Remembering Sunday' and the encore showed the quality and togetherness inherent in the group.

'During the finale, the band came off as a united front even more so than ever before,' the reviewer wrote. 'Barakat ran around everywhere from the right amps all the way to the left, while drummer Rian Dawson stood up with pride. After the song ended, Barakat stood on speakers to hit one of Rian's cymbals and eventually grabbed Gaskarth and threw him into piggyback ride position, where the band all ran off waving as one.' The writer concluded that the band's success was down to a mix of banter and the strong bond between them and their fans. A gig by All Time Low was like going to hang out with mates, with all its attendant silliness and unexpected moments.

The chaps posted a tour update during August which, in a

more lo-fi way, echoed the approach of the 'Forget about It' video, with actual behind-the-scenes footage including Alex becoming extremely frustrated with his phones, but quickly smiling as the rest of the band cheers him up. It's a small and easily missed cutaway of the short video, but it encapsulates All Time Low's essence: friendship and the magic created between lads whose career was based on a brotherhood that cannot be created, only forged by shared experiences and creativity – and, by the looks of it, a lot of swearing too.

North America and Europe duly done, it was time to head east once again, with a quick stop-off in Honolulu before three gigs in Japan. On 22 September there followed a Philippines gig at which the *Philippine Daily Enquirer* noted that teenage girls had turned up with spare bras and panties – some with messages written on them – to chuck at the band. The paper also said that there was a lot of profanity on show and the audience, some of whom were twelve or thirteen years old – were more than used to that kind of language. The writer felt that maybe the girls were too busy checking out the good-looking lads to notice. The review went on to say that while the tunes were catchy and delivered in a frenzied punk style, the lyrics weren't what you'd associate with that original late seventies movement. 'The lyrics, however, were devoid of the no-future howls and bring-down-the-establishment political rants that turned British bands like The Sex Pistols and The Clash into overnight celebrities in the late 1970s,' mused the writer. However, while some bands of that era were largely political, there were others, including the Ramones, who sang more about what was happening to them personally. That included having a good time, something the Baltimoreans were excellent at. Alex delivered a touching acoustic version of 'Therapy' amid the songs about having fun and chasing down a good time, the writer added. Ultimately, if there were any worried mothers and fathers accompanying their kids to the gig, their youngsters could respond that basically it was just rock 'n' roll. And every generation, of course, has its own version of that fabulous and somewhat indefinable cultural/musical force. It's *meant* to make the parent worry/hate it/not understand it. That's the point.

Well, so much for cultural theory: it was time to head to Australia for the Soundwave Revolution shows. Or, rather, to find out that the shows had been cancelled. The huge bill for the travelling festival was to have included Van Halen (featuring David Lee Roth), Bad Religion, Alice Cooper, Machine Head, Hole, Sisters of Mercy and Danzig – a mighty line-up indeed. However, just a couple of weeks before it was due to kick off at Brisbane, the whole thing was pulled. A statement from organiser AJ Maddah released on 9 August said that a co-headliner should have been announced on 1 August, but the band had been forced to pull out because of personal circumstances. 'Unfortunately we don't have enough time to replace them and we didn't really want to go ahead with an incomplete line-up. We could have taken the option of linking through with the line-up as we have now – it would have obviously still been a much better financial outcome for us than to go through the road we have – but we just didn't want to put an inferior product on the market.' Offering a glimmer of hope, however, the Soundwave website carried another statement that confirmed the cancellation of the concerts, but also said that a lot of the planned line-up would be in Australia regardless and that mini-festivals or multi-band bills would definitely happen in three of the tour cities – Brisbane, Sydney and Melbourne. Three years later, Maddah gave an interview to Full Metal Lockdown in which he revealed the name of the band that had pulled out. 'Soundwave Revolution was actually created for a specific band. It was actually specifically put together for Rage against the Machine,' he said. Apparently there had been eight months of uncertainty about whether RATM would be involved or not and in the event frontman Zack de la Rocha had not signed on to participate.

The major line-up may not have happened as planned but a series of gigs entitled, with some irony, Counter Revolution, did go ahead. The Melbourne gig on 30 September was testament to the difference between a true festival and a day-long gig inside a hall. The AU Review reckoned that the choice of venue let the event down but the performances were great regardless. Problems included long lines for food and drink (the venue did not allow even water inside) and a bar downstairs that had no line of sight to the stage. Both those factors combined to dull the experience in comparison to the main events of the past. The crowd was younger than for normal Soundwave events, said the reviewer, but All Time Low even won the writer over. 'As much as I hate to admit it, pop rockers and fangirl favourites All Time Low really did play a great set, and were quite impressive live,' conceded the reviewer. 'Through hits like 'Weightless' and 'Coffee Shop Soundtrack', front man Alex Gaskarth had the room alive with screaming teenage girls, and the atmosphere in the mosh was great.' As usual.

After Australia – via a quick stop-off in Singapore and Kuala Lumpur, Malaysia – the band benefited from a quick couple of weeks off. During this time, Alex teased fans in the best way by tweeting that he was busy watching American football, going to see bands ... and recording vocals on a brand-new demo track.

CHAPTER 20

GIGS, GIGS, GIGS ... AND A NEW LP ON THE HORIZON?

*S*erious as ever, the lads went back out on the road with the philosophically titled The Rise and Fall of My Pants tour. They said that they'd been asked by the manager to find a name for the new dates, but admitted they were notoriously bad at coming up with that kind of thing. The name came about following discussions on the bus. As it was taking place in the autumn – called the Fall in the States – Alex suggested that it could be The Rise and Fall of ... and Jack chipped in with 'my pants-tent', referring to a state of gentlemanly excitement experienced by all healthy young chaps at one time or another. OK, OK, he means a boner. That was then shortened briefly to Pants Tent tour and then, finally, The Rise and Fall of My Pants seemed perfect.

The gigs included supports from The Ready Set, He Is We and Paradise Fears. The latter had found themselves invited to tour with All Time Low after an unusual but certainly productive plan. Paradise Fears had previously followed the Low's tours across the country, driving themselves around, and had sold their own music and merch to fans of the Baltimore band. Cheeky, but definitely impactful, and it resulted in an invitation that could not be refused. Alex said that the band were looking forward to returning to some smaller cities that they hadn't played for a while. 'We've spent a lot of time in the major cities and the major markets,' he told Clevver Music, 'so this is for the kids who haven't necessarily had the chance to see us, or who have had to drive three hours to get to us.' Jack added that although the band had toured the United States around fifteen times there were still some cities that they hadn't yet managed to get to. There would also be a return to the United Kingdom as of January 2012, somewhere that the band loved to play. 'I guess they really love their rock 'n' roll,' Jack observed.

The dates would begin on 23 October and were preceded by a stunning appearance by All Time Low on the extremely influential Conan O'Brien show. The lads performed there what was to be the next single, 'Time-Bomb', which Alex described in an interview with *Muen Magazine* as being a super-cool experience. 'I was super nervous and I wasn't super excited about my performance when I watched it later,' he super-said. 'I thought I could have done a little better, but it is hard to do when your nerves are going. You get one shot and it is live. It's pretty nerve-wracking, but we had fun. We had a great time and everybody there is just so nice. The staff is really cool and Conan is really cool. It was rad!' Super-rad, no doubt.

Alex noted that it was tricky to gauge how a record was doing on album sales in these days of Internet distribution but that ticket sales told a story of their own. Overseas, crowds had grown, he said. In terms of fame itself, he continued, things could get a bit crazy if the band headed out and about at home over the weekend. That said, he didn't take it too seriously and was happy to take photos with fans because looking after the fan base was always important. He also revealed that after the North American leg of the Pants tour, the band would try to have some time off with their families over the holidays. All Time Low had been on the road for almost three hundred days, he said, so the year had flown by. As ever, though, they had loved being on tour as well as putting out *Dirty Work* at last. He also referenced the band's Hustler Club, an online fan community for the real diehards who wanted to become members of the fan club. Signing up for that meant early access to pre-orders and pre-sales, possible meet-and-greets with the group, which was pretty much every day on tour, and things like random video chats, message boards and more. It was a case of building the community around the group, he said, and it was a very positive thing. Indeed, he got a big thrill when he heard that people had met new friends or hooked up with old mates because of the fan club.

As indicated, the next single to be released was 'Time-Bomb' and again it had a clever video, this time directed by K. Asher Levin. Levin had written and directed the 2009 short *Adventures in Online Dating*, then moved on to the full-length *Cougars, Inc.*, which featured a boy expelled from school, who went on to form an escort agency. Classy stuff, but his video for All Time Low was a great one. There are plenty of live shots, the lads playing Beatles-style on a rooftop. There's also a dude in his workshop working on something that turns out to be an artificial heart he's created in order to save his girlfriend. The heart in question is very much like that invented by Tony Stark as Iron Man, as depicted by Robert Downey, Jr. A SWAT team chases the hero of the piece through suitably gritty Bourne-like cityscapes until he does indeed find his comatose girlfriend. He works his magic and the heart kicks in – the two initially escape across those same Los Angeles rooftops before being caught by the guys with guns. However, the girl's glowing heart seems to strike some kind of confusion in the eyes of their pursuers and the video ends on this unresolved note. It's basically a small movie, with Malese Jow of *The Vampire Diaries* putting in a great shift as one of the lead characters.

Clevver Music attended the shoot, which was at a warehouse in LA. As the main part of the performance is on the rooftop and the venue had no internal staircases, the band had to load their gear up there with a huge forklift truck. The people had to climb up via a ladder – not for the faint-hearted. Jack explained that the song had been selected as a single after it'd gone down so well with the fans in the gigs over the past few months. The video, Alex said, was created with the idea that the song was a focus on the struggles of love and a breaking relationship in mind. 'We created a little analogy for that,' he told the interviewer, 'by having them being chased by people with guns.' As you do. The lads also revealed that it was the first time that Alex had written the entire script for a video – in a five-minute spell of creative fire. The guys both agreed that it was the most intense video that the band had shot so far and that Bourne and Bond had been inspirations. The 2009 sci-fi film *District 9*, with handheld cameras and kinetic action shots, had also had an influence.

Noting that the band were showing a more serious side, which was great, Malese Jow said that the video was cinematic and reminiscent of the *Bourne Identity* movie and that appearing in it did indeed feel like being in a *Bourne* film. She'd been a fan for a while, and it was exciting to be a part of a music video, which was on her bucket list.

Alex re-recorded the vocals of the track for use in the video game *The Sims*, in which the player controls virtual characters throughout their virtual lives. It is a curiously addictive game based on mundane day-to-day actions such as sending them to work, making sure the house is clean, cooking, meeting other Sims, having babies and all the rest of it. The language the Sims use is called Simlish, so Alex had to re-record the vocals in that made-up language. 'It was funny as hell,' he told Common Revolt. 'I had no idea that they had an actual language ... [they] created a whole dialect for this video game.' He had initially thought that he'd just be singing gibberish but in fact there was a translated lyric sheet to work from. It was a hilarious, weird opportunity to do something unique, he said.

Intriguing news came in early November with the report that the boys had begun writing again, with a new album on the cards. In the meantime, 'Painting Flowers' was re-released and Alex played an acoustic set at the pop-up shop of 'Glamour Kills' (or as they put it, GLMRKLLS) in New York City. Alex and Mike Green put in some serious work as December began with three days of intense demo recording, during which five songs were put down. One of those, revealed Alex in a tweet, featured the excellent harmonies of Hey Monday vocalist and long-time friend of the band, Cassadee Pope. He said that the approach for the new record was to do everything with producers that the band admired and worked well with, getting back to what the All Time Low sound was all about and letting things happen naturally.

The boys may have showed off their serious side with that all-action 'Time-Bomb' video, but balance was restored to the Force with the release of the entirely silly video for the entirely silly 'Merry Christmas, Kiss My Ass'. This time Jon Danovic was in the director's seat and he delivered a puppet-based piece of work that is as memorable as it is hilarious. It begins with the central character, Stuart, an office drone, talking to his workmate. The workmate lets slip that everyone is getting a bonus – aside from Stuart. Cupcakes appear with the gorgeous Molly, who is definitely someone that the character fancies but finds it difficult to talk to. And all this is before the actual song kicks in.

Stuart, of course, sings the song to Molly but is jealous when she talks to other people in the office. He becomes very upset as Molly flirts with his workmate and he imagines that she straddles him. Stuart is a bit twisted up about the whole thing as he imagines Molly getting into all sorts of sexy situations with everyone apart from him. He simply can't bear it and starts knocking decorations onto the floor and pulling them off the walls. At the Christmas party he completely loses his mind as he imagines his love doing all sorts of stuff including giving rather more than a chaste kiss on the lips to a colleague. Her focus, according to the viewpoint of Stuart anyway, is rather lower on that lucky guy's body. Finally, Stuart does manage to talk to Molly and she even asks him what he's doing after the party. The dude, however, has had enough and tells her to kiss his ass. Good to see the Christmas spirit is strong in ATL-land, at least.

Alex took the opportunity to catch a breather and look back at 2011 in an interview with Common Revolt. He said that there hadn't really been anything bad to report about the year, which had been pretty crazy-busy but also successful. There had been, he recalled, tons of gigs and the album had come out at last, so it had been great. As for the 'Merry Christmas…' video, he noted that Stuart was in fact a revived character that the band had '[put out in a viral video … for 'I Feel Like Dancin'. This time, though, Stuart was at work. 'He's having a little bit of relationship trouble and also may be crazy,' explained the singer. He revealed that the opportunity to work with Before You Exit was cool, being the first time he'd really written with another band. The younger group reminded Alex of the earlier days of his own band and he rated them as super-talented, having of course seen them in action numerous times as they were one of the support acts on the 2010 My Small Package tour and the spring dates of the Dirty Work tour. The year ahead, he added, was an opportunity to get back to the heart of what All Time Low as a band was all about, and a few surprises were in store for fans.

CHAPTER 21

SMALL SHOCKS AND BIG SURPRISES

Alex was clearly feeling left out. Zack had a clothing line; Jack had a clothing line. Rian had ... actually Rian didn't have a clothing line, but that was still half the band who were budding Tommy Hilfigers. So he hooked up with Glamour Kills, that vowel-averse company, and announced in early January that he was to launch his own clothing line, to be titled A.W.G. Hey, that's his initials – what a coincidence! He began his announcement of the fact with an apology for having grown a beard, saying that he'd clearly been at home for too long. That important vignette dealt with, he added he was excited 'from the bottom of my heart and the depths of my testicles' to announce that the clothing line was a reality. 'Me and Marky [Mark Capicotto, founder of Glamour Kills] have been working for a while on this and we're going full on, balls to the wall, nuts to the face ...' The clothes were available from 10 January and, the singer assured, would not cause chafing or rashes. Alex's dog agreed and contributed some woofs and yowls of its own. 'Let's do it ... let's do this together,' Alex said, before adding a tongue-in-cheek, 'stay in school.'

It was back to work quickly, however, with the UK tour having dates added to it because of the huge demand. The gigs were going down as well as ever and included some unusual choices of cover songs. At Newcastle's O2 Academy, the lads played 'A Whole New World' from the *Aladdin* soundtrack, in Birmingham the *Top Gun* theme, and at the Cardiff gig they manfully tackled Adele's smash-hit torch song, 'Someone Like You'. Clearly having fun, Alex also joined We Are The In Crowd onstage in Glasgow for their own, soon-to-be-single, 'Kiss Me Again'.

A reviewer from Lights Go Out caught the concert in Manchester's gorgeous Apollo Theatre, on 21 January. Admitting a soft spot for All Time Low, the writer said that one good thing about their gigs was that the bar was always empty during their set, so it was easier to get a drink of highly priced lager. The bras were in full flow, he added, and the floor was in danger of needing an architect to fix it, such was the energy of the crowd. 'As hits rolled out it became apparent that a venue the size of the Apollo is more than adequate for a band with All Time Low's natural talent for pure pop hooks. The band quite clearly love what they do, and judging from the consistently ecstatic crowd reaction for the entire 90 minutes, they aren't alone,' he concluded.

The Guildhall, Southampton, was another gig that was reviewed, this time by The Edge. The reviewer said that there had been at least a hundred young fans in onesies and duvets outside the venue – some of them had been camping out since 7am that day, such was the dedication. The fan base, felt the writer, was on average around fourteen years old on that evidence. As to the gig, each member was screamed at loudly by the fans on their appearance onstage. The reviewer contrasted the show with a previous appearance in Yeovil, at the 350-capacity Orange Box, back in 2008. Since then, things had ramped up to a whole new level.

The set was going down really well but Alex was unwell so had to cut the show short. The crowd, of course, had helped out on 'Remembering Sunday', a performance the writer said was 'spine-tingling'. The writer quoted Alex as later tweeting that he was bummed out about his voice and that it was a horrible feeling to feel helpless like that onstage. He also thanked the fans for singing so loudly. 'Overall, despite the shortening of the show, they were great,' the mag wrote. 'Nothing about the show was half-hearted. I'm pretty sure all the fans felt that waiting in the cold for 12 hours was sincerely worth it.'

Things were back to normal for the Forum gig, but during that same heart-rending song support band We are the In Crowd thought they'd have a little fun, coming onstage and joining in with rather a unique performance before smashing up a poor unsuspecting acoustic guitar.

Get to the Front caught up with Jack and Alex at the Birmingham date and Jack joked that the new album was going to be called *Crazy Horny Panda*, which would have been awesome had it been even remotely true. The interviewer asked the boys what they thought of the dubstep genre and

Alex reckoned it sounded like 'robots fucking'. Jack felt it was more like 'robots throwing up'. *Transformers*, said the guitarist, was the original dubstep. The interview was notable too for the revelation that *Straight to DVD* had been a lot of fun and that the second DVD, according to Jack, would be called *Cockumentary*, a play on words with 'Rockumentary'. Joking aside, Alex stated, straight off, 'Are we doing a second one? Yes.'

Chemical Magazine also talked to Alex, who spoke of how strange the transition between indie and major labels had been. They had learnt, he said, how to promote a record in a different way, but the band stayed true to making music and going out on the road. 'Pop-punk is what we do,' he said. '*Dirty Work* was us trying to get out of that box a little bit.' He confirmed that the band had a very busy year ahead, with new music being worked on immediately after the Canadian dates that ran through February. 'We would like to have a record out this year or early next year,' explained the singer.

He also spoke to *NME* about everything, saying that the record had taken a life of its own and the songs had gone over very well live. 'I am, I would say, about halfway through the writing process for the next record,' he explained, noting that he had realised he had a lot to say and that so far there were around nine songs done with a plan to work on another ten or eleven. The songs were honest to himself and that honesty always got a good response from the fans.

'Our audience is smarter than a lot of people give [them] credit for,' said the singer. 'They don't just want to be placated by fucking noise and repetition. They want something real.' The honesty therefore hit home. He also mused on the piecemeal way in which the previous couple of albums had come together, working at various times with different producers and then fitting those pieces together as an album. That was a cool way to work and to learn but it also had disadvantages, including losing sight of the album as a whole because you're working on a song rather than an overriding concept or aesthetic. This time, one producer and one timescale was the approach, and making sure everything was correct before contemplating a release. Previously it had sometimes been the case that songs had been completed in order to chase down deadlines but making a coherent record was now the priority.

The band returned to the States briefly in early February, during which time Alex appeared in the video being shot for We Are The In Crowd's song, 'Kiss Me Again'. Another couple of video snippets were put online – 'The Beach' and that 'Umbrella' cover – and reports came in that the band would appear at the Reading/Leeds festivals during August Bank Holiday.

While in Kitchener, Ontario, Rian went on the popular website Reddit for a chat with fans, during which he appeared to confirm that All Time Low would once more be playing the VANS Warped Tour in 2012. He also said that he had dreamt of becoming an electrical engineer but there was always still time to do that. His career and life, however, were pretty darn good: 'I'm rarely discouraged. I get to play drums all over the world for a living, and it makes me the happiest dude alive. If people don't enjoy it, that's their choice. There are plenty of artists that I don't enjoy, I just don't find the need to be spite-filled towards them! To each their own.'

The sticksman also revealed that he'd love to play in China, New Zealand and South Africa, plus be the first group to play Antarctica, and that he and Jack were keen on seeing the sights while on tour, taking cabs to tourist attractions and going for a walk whenever possible. In terms of drum heroes, he named Travis Barker, Dave Grohl, Taylor Hawkins, John Bonham and Neil Peart as inspirations. He also revealed that he was dating Cassadee Pope. Tellingly, he skirted around a question about the Interscope experience. '[The transition to Interscope] was pretty smooth actually, but it was a little awkward floatin' around on a major,' he wrote. 'I can't get into too much detail about this quite yet, but definitely will revisit this questions [sic] a few weeks/months from now.' Note the past tense: *it was a little awkward*. Intriguing stuff, but no official word on that would emerge for some months.

In the meantime, writing the new record was still ongoing. A Facebook update on the group's page showed a bank of amps and pedals with the simple caption 'And so it begins', and four days later Alex tweeted that Patrick Stump had been in the studio working on a new song with the band. Recording for the new album officially began on 18 April, with Rian completing his own tracking a day later. On 23 April the boys shot a video for an as yet unnamed new song, Alex joined Cassadee Pope for a quick appearance on the song 'Apologize' in San Diego a week later and Rian added his drums to his squeeze's new EP in early May.

Jack and Alex appeared on MTV's *Punk'd* on 3 May, freaking out Demi Lovato. The segment started with some weird sounds appearing on one of the new tracks they were recording. Underneath the studio, said the engineer, was a swimming pool that had been forced to shut down due to 'incidents'. Some deaths had occurred but those incidents were downplayed due to the studio not wanting to have negative energy in the room. The track was played again, with more spooky noises and a lady speaking Spanish. One of the victims, went the story, was an Argentinean. The spookiness continued with the manifestation of an apparition in the studio becoming visible ... eek! Some kind of blue light, which was supposed to be a blonde woman in a dress. Another apparition appeared, but this time it was the hosts of the show shouting, 'You Got Punk'd!' Lovato later said that Nick Cannon was behind the prank. 'I'm a sucker for, like, ghosts and aliens and stuff like that, so they got me pretty good,' the singer told Stay Strong.

Recording was completed on 16 May and All Time Low announced that a single would be released on 1 June, entitled 'The Reckless and the Brave'. But there was a bigger announcement than that yet to come ...

CHAPTER 22

WHEN THINGS LOOK HOPELESS, THINGS ARE LOOKING GOOD

It was AbsolutePunk that broke the news during an interview with Alex Gaskarth, published on 1 June 2012. 'We are unsigned,' the frontman confirmed, putting to rest rumours that had circulated around the subject for some time. 'After we parted ways with Interscope/DGC, at the end of 2011, *Dirty Work* was kind of dead in the water, which is why we started working on the new album so soon. We haven't made any decisions as far as to what label the next record will be released on.' He added that the idea was to make the album for themselves and the fans without anyone from the outside 'diluting or influencing' the vision that the band had.

Alex also revealed that a lot of the new album would be about topics associated with the experience of being signed to Interscope. The very scenario that the group hadn't wanted to happen had in fact come to pass, he said. Basically, that the team that initially was set to push *Dirty Work* was moved to another department and/or lost their jobs, which led to the many delays of the album and the subsequent loss of momentum that led to All Time Low deciding to part ways with the record label. He said that the people who worked with the band were great and had totally bought into the band and the project, but with a very large restructuring within that business things had got snarled up. Alex mused that Interscope were amenable to letting the band out of their contract because they understood the reasons the musicians were citing.

Another theme of the new album would be self-discovery and confidence, about acknowledging that uncertainties exist, so facing them is important and indeed valuable for one as a person. Ambitions of course are always there and the key is to avoid people mucking you around when it comes to realising them.

Amid the rush for the band's signature that followed there was of course a record label particularly suited to working with them. That was the team at Hopeless, which had been such a successful partnership until the lads tried their luck with a major. Alex confirmed that after having recorded much of the new album while unsigned they put feelers out towards various companies to see who suited the project. The band were philosophical about their position and happy to take the chance collectively to think about what would be the absolute best thing to do. While signed to a deal, Alex told *Alternative Press*, there was always the prospect of having to compromise in order to get music out there, but in their current position they could effectively make a checklist of what they wanted from a label and see who came closest to fulfilling those requirements.

There were a lot of good labels and people out there, so a lot of talk was going on until Hopeless came along with what Alex termed a 'really cool and forward-thinking deal'. It was, he said, 'a very equal opportunity and beneficial situation for everyone, which I think is sort of the wave of the future, especially with independent labels. Not to mention, we just love everybody there. We know they love us and we know that they love the band – that's really the biggest selling point at the end of the day.' It did feel like coming home, albeit that it was a different way of working, but the team at that label was essentially unchanged, plus they knew how to work with the Baltimore band. In contrast to the essentially stillborn *Dirty Work*, said the vocalist, he wanted to put down a marker that the group was in it for the long game. Some people, he acknowledged, had perceived that the previous album's difficulties might indicate a full stop in the band's career. However, the experience had brought them to a more self-sufficient place, having learnt from the experience. As ever being out on the road was going to be key and the group were excited to think of the possibilities that the future entailed.

Later that year, *Rock Sound* interviewed Jack and Alex about various matters. The vocalist said that there had never been a conversation about breaking the band up. Jack summed it up: 'None of us want to do anything else. From four dudes in ninth grade, it was always this band, we have nothing else.' While there were sometimes moments of conflict in the high-pressure situation of touring, it was never the case that anyone was even close to being out of the band, Alex added. 'This band could not exist without the four of us,' he reckoned. 'One member of Blink can't quit. If one of us was gone it wouldn't be the same, playing the songs would feel like a covers band. We knew we were going to get on each other's nerves but we are family, you don't split the family up.'

Having only been away from Hopeless for eighteen months it felt natural to go back to work with the people who had been so instrumental in the group's rising fan base. The climb, Alex said, might be slower, but it had no end point. Rian added in an interview with Gigwise that it had felt like a completely different label after the departure of a lot of the people who'd been there when the band first signed. He said that the split was pretty amicable. 'We were like, look, this isn't the same label we signed with, you don't really have much interest in our band, let's just split ways. Let's not make it all lawsuit and all that. And they were like, alright! And it was truly that easy. It was much worse on the outside than it was actually on the inside, everyone was like, "what the fuck, they're done", and for us it was just the right choice.'

It was hardly a coincidence then that the first single to come from the new recordings was the somewhat pertinently titled 'The Reckless and the Brave'. It was made available for download on 1 June and a special studio-based video came through the pipes on 6 June. Alex, Rian and Jack talked about the record in the interview that came with that video (Zack was busy tracking bass at the time). High-resolution shots of the lads working on the new record were intercut with comments from the boys, who said that the process had been very cool. It was, Rian said, about getting back to the band's roots, or as he put it, 'Getting back to All Time Low being All Time Low'.

Speaking of the single, Alex explained that the title

was central, thematically, to the LP. It was all about not necessarily following the well-trodden path. Jack – serious despite wearing a T-shirt emblazoned with BONER – said that the group were directing the sentiment towards a fan base who were in middle school, high school, college and other situations in which they were trying to find their place in the world. Alex, wearing a trademark beanie hat, said that there were people who followed the leader in terms of doing the things that they felt were expected from them but taking risks and being true to yourself was important. The song is an autobiographical one in the sense that All Time Low did not take the option of school-college-work but instead followed their dreams. Rian said that although he'd loved all that the band had done to date, 'The Reckless and the Brave' resonated hugely, summing up the group's ethos in one short(ish) track. It also set a tone for the album in general. The band was developing, Alex said, and maybe there was actually a message they was putting across, in contrast to what he'd previously thought. That message was to have self-belief in who you are and what you do.

The whole album, Rian confirmed, was done with Mike Green, in contrast to the scattergun producer-fest of *Dirty Work*. Green knew the band inside out and Alex on many occasions had praised the relationship that had developed. Although the quartet were keen to get back to being themselves, that didn't mean they were ever interested in replicating their previous work, Alex added. All that the band had gone through over the years was reflected in the new album, which he reckoned was the best stuff they'd ever done. Things felt good and it had seemed natural as a progression, he said.

The lyric video featured a cartoon version of the band playing the track while in the background, alien spaceships basically started to blow everything up. A giant octopus was attacked by helicopters as Alex talked about not fitting in, not wanting to be saved and the fact that his song has not yet been sung. Placards of doom and disaster are held up by a crowd, fireballs raining down, but long live us, Alex sings. Robots, giant green monsters and all sorts of destruction continue apace, zombies stagger about, but the band are untouched: they're too busy watching the spectacle while eating pizza, reading books, and enjoying a tasty beverage, and are entirely nonplussed by the naysayers and negative ones. While the background is all greys, greens, browns and pastel colours, the group is rendered in colour. It's an absolute cracker of a video and a track that has the kind of instantly powerful belief in the future and rejection of suburban dreariness that so marked out the band's most effervescent moments of *So Wrong, It's Right* and *Nothing Personal*. A fine choice for a first single, indeed.

Another return for the lads was the 2012 VANS Warped Tour, running from 16 June through to the start of August. As ever, the gigs were a lot of fun and featured this time veterans New Found Glory, Yellowcard, Four Year Strong, Taking Back Sunday and We the Kings. As usual it was the rolling funtime party of music, skating, silliness and friends old and new. However, tragedy struck on 15 July with a young woman collapsing and dying at the Toronto concert. The nineteen-year-old had collapsed during the set of Chelsea Grin. She was later identified as Taylor Nesseth of Ontario. Alex was reported as tweeting his and the band's devastation at the news. 'Taylor: A comrade, a friend, a hustler, an enthusiast, a dreamer, a sweetheart – I didn't know her well, but I'm hit hard by her passing,' he wrote. 'Per today's very tragic events, take a minute to really appreciate all that you have as a human being. Grow. Live. Respect. Love.'

A tribute from a friend, Donald D'Haene, later appeared on The Huffington Post. He contrasted the passing of Taylor with the passing of another friend who had been in terminal pain and for whom the final goodbye was a relief and a rest: 'But beautiful, vibrant, ebullient Taylor? This young girl radiated an energy and happiness that was truly like experiencing a force of nature, an inextinguishable light. It's true, as Proust wrote, death could – indeed did – arrive on an afternoon after our visit. But the reels that play in all the minds and hearts of those who knew her will keep the flame that is Taylor eternal.'

CHAPTER 23

AUTUMN MAY FALL, BUT WE WILL STAND TALL

The reviews of the tour often noted the energy of All Time Low as at an all-time high. An early review came from the Pomona, California, concert on 22 June. The lengthy write-up talked about the tour's ins and outs as a rock, fashion, charity and punk bonanza that included free condoms, energy drinks and even people like Bayside band members teaching youngsters the basics of various instruments. Pop-punk, reckoned the reviewer from mxdwn, was the order of the day, with Bayside only one of the groups that fitted the bill, playing 'all of their up-tempo fan favorites with one or two newer songs peppered in. This seemed to be the time honored trend of many of the bands with a larger repertoire such as pop-punk legends Taking Back Sunday, All Time Low, New Found Glory, Mayday Parade, Yellowcard; all of whom gave over-the-top performances in which they left everything on the stage.'

The lads' performance at First Midwest Bank Amphitheatre, on the outskirts of Chicago, was attended by a reviewer from the Examiner, who spent a good deal of their time running around the various stages to catch as much as possible. The writer described the band as Warped Tour veterans and said that while the day had been blazing hot, by the time the guys got onstage the temperatures had subsided. The set was full of 'emo pop songs,' said the reviewer, who then revealed that the chaps were also joking around. 'Their guitar player had a shirt that said "boner" on the front and he would regularly flip up his guitar to reveal a sign he taped to the back of it that said "tits", both of which were probably a big hit with those in the crowd just entering puberty,' was the write-up, although the dude did also say that the songs were very well received. The same website also ran a story by a writer from the *Hartford Music Examiner*, this time regarding the 22 July gig at the Connecticut capital. There was a buzz around the stage when All Time Low were about to hit it, proving that the band was still surfing high on the wave of success. 'Great pop-rock and dedicated fans had them running on "high" about mid-set' was the succinct summary there.

The band hit Columbia, Maryland, two days later, and the home-state show was videoed by Tom Falcone for a live video to accompany 'The Reckless and the Brave'. Jack and Alex spoke to Stage Right Secrets about a whole bunch of things while at the Ohio gig and the resulting interview was posted on 27 July. They talked about things that had been chucked on stage recently, including sex toys, blow-up dolls and bras. They added that they'd been hanging out with Taking Back Sunday, chilling out backstage as their vans were parked close to each other. As ever the pair were in tongue-in-cheek mode, which did get them into a little bit of strife. When asked about the camaraderie on the tour, Jack said, 'The one thing I've learned from Warped Tour is that music genres kind of don't even matter. It's like everyone's just kind of hanging out and chilling with each other.' Alex, clearly joking, then mugged to the camera, 'Unless you're Blood on the Dance Floor, then everyone hates you. It's a bummer.' Everyone laughed. However, BotDF took it a little to heart, tweeting all manner of weird stuff including some homophobic ranting. Alex responded that he didn't hate the band at all but his joke had come off worse than he'd really meant it to; he did, though, call the strange response a little unnecessary. The video is at *https://www.youtube.com/watch?v=IY97SAvGz6s* and it's pretty obvious that the singer is indeed just joking. But this being Internet-land, things can always escalate way out of proportion almost instantly, can't they?

Alex joined Yellowcard onstage on 1 August, adding guitar to the track 'Chasing Rainbows' by No Use for a Name as the groups paid tribute to the music and life of Tony Sly; the vocalist and lead guitarist of that band had died in his sleep on 31 July at the age of just forty-one. Fat Mike of Fat Wreck Chords posted his tribute to the songwriter, saying, 'One of my dearest friends and favorite songwriters has gone way too soon. Tony, you will be greatly missed.' The influence of the musician lives on through all those he and his band influenced, including of course All Time Low.

As the Warped dates came to a close, Alex seemed to confirm in a tweet that there would be another *Straight to DVD* around this time, although again no further info on when, where and how were forthcoming. The group was also busy recording some acoustic versions of tracks from the new album, with Alex saying that he enjoyed stripping the rock songs down to a naked form. No doubt the songs enjoyed it just as much. On 12 August, a new video was being shot and the next day the group revealed that there would be an autumn tour of the United States along with The Summer Set, The Downtown Fiction, Hit the Lights and some dates with The Early November. The tour was to be titled The Rockshow at the End of the World. A short thirty-second preview of the dates, released by sponsors Rockstar, also exhorted people to check out the new CD by the band, which would be available as of 8 October, with dates beginning four days later. Just enough time for the ever-enthusiastic fans to learn the words inside out.

The band headed back to Europe for a clutch of dates. This included the longest set in their career to date at the Melkweg in Amsterdam with a whopping nineteen songs, including the live debut of new track 'For Baltimore'. The group then returned to the UK for the Leeds and Reading Festivals. The dates were headlined by Kasabian, The Cure and Foo Fighters, whose mighty sets left people with an intense feeling. Tom DeLonge's new project, Angels & Airwaves, also put on exuberant performances. One of the biggest surprises was provided by a secret 11am set on the Saturday at Reading by none other than Green Day, another huge influence on the boys. Of course, Blink-182 still loomed high on that score and All Time Low played 'Damnit' onstage at Reading.

In the sister festival in Leeds, the chaps said that the growth in their career at the festivals had been amazing, climbing from smaller to larger stages and inching ever closer to the top of the bill. 'We've gone from a small tent to the entire world in the open air,' said Jack. Playing in front of 30,000 people was awesome, Alex added, and the shorter, forty-five-minute sets meant that basically every track was going to be a crowd-pleaser. This was honed by their headlining gigs in which the band were very aware of the reaction that different songs got and could therefore design a set accordingly. Having just put out 'For Baltimore' online, Alex said that the reaction had been excellent. 'The Reckless and the Brave' had previously also gone down well. 'I'm proud of it,' he added, 'I'm really stoked.' He revealed that there were some dates imminent with Green Day, which was very exciting for all concerned. Also at Reading, Jack said that while there had been a slight technical difficulty the crowd had still been super-amazing. Alex added that he'd forgotten how massive the stages were at the festival. 'I have so much room to run around that I get lost,' he told an *NME* video crew. 'I go over to have a drink of water and then have to go and start the next song and sometimes I miss my cues.' Jack added that it was a weird time for music with so much competition and so many bands, and that it was important for the band to continue to release music and videos so people didn't forget about them.

Alex also explained some of the reasons why the album was called *Don't Panic*. 'The theme behind the title is that we were in a very transitional period when we made this record, so it's kind of a reminder to ourselves to just get through it and press on,' he explained. Jack said that the new album would be something like a mixture of the previous three LPs, and Alex noted that as the album had been written when the group was technically unsigned it was all about making it as much of an All Time Low record as they could, with the entire album being produced by Mike Green rather than spreading it out among many people as had previously been the case. Indeed, on the final product Alex himself gets a co-production credit and Rian is also there, listed as having added Additional Engineering, meaning that the technical side of the recordings was also something the band was getting more hands-on with as time went on.

The lyric video to 'For Baltimore' was released on 29 August; the words are written in cursive over the top of some black and white footage of the boys looking pensive during the self-searching acoustic intro, before things kick in with some live footage at the aforementioned festival as well as other gigs. There's a return of some animations of monsters and explosions from the previous video for 'The Reckless and the Brave'. The song's one of Alex's more upbeat paeans, this one a real tribute to the dual excitements of his hometown and a relationship at the same time. Don't say goodnight is the message because the city only comes alive when the protagonist and his squeeze are together. Sonically, there's a huge difference between this one and some of *Dirty Work*, which was replete with synths, twinkles and studio explorations. 'For Baltimore' is simply a straight-up pop-punk track written and performed with absolute energy by a band that has proved over and over again that it's at the top of the genre.

It didn't trouble the charts – that wasn't really the point – but the UK's Rock Chart did have it peaking at Number 3. Alex later said that it had been a bit unlikely that 'For Baltimore' would appear on *Don't Panic*, because initially it had a different chorus which wasn't quite working out but as time went on, he decided to try a rewrite. 'There was something endearing about the song,' he explained. So the lads went back to basics and put a new chorus in there – and it ended up being one of the most loved tracks within the band. Yes, it's about a relationship, but it's also about love of a hometown that you return to again and again, he said.

After a couple of weeks off from touring, the boys returned with a special free gig at MLB Fan Cave in New York City on 26 September. The next thing to come out of the All Time Low camp was another single, 'Somewhere in Neverland', which did hit Number 1 in the official UK Rock Charts and would later peak at 26 in the Billboard Rock Digital Songs. Another behind-the-scenes-type video with the lyrics on top, with shots of signings in Manchester, England's famous Arndale shopping centre and plenty of live stuff as ever, put the new/old All Time Low sound back into the consciousness. The lyrics reference Wendy, lost boys, attempting to feel young forever and Neverland – the home of Peter Pan, rather than Michael Jackson, of course.

Another track came out on 8 October, called 'Outlines', featuring the vocals of Acceptance's Jason Vena. The destruction-cartoon video was the same for the video that introduced the lyrics to the world.

Talking of introducing things to the world, the band arranged a special *Don't Panic* Triptacular – three shows in three days, to take place in Tokyo, London and New York City on 7, 8 and 9 October. This global release event was a typically crazy idea and involved crossing thirteen time zones and travelling over ten thousand miles, but certainly one that the band hadn't done before so obviously worth doing, as Alex told *Teen Vogue*. 'We're doing three shows that span two days in three different countries: Tokyo, Japan; London, England; and New York. So by the time we hit New York, the record is officially out. I think that's going to be a really cool experience for us to do that kind of intensive touring in such a small amount of time.' Gigwise was at the London leg of the triple-dipple and said that, as ever, the boys were quick with the banter. The energy, as usual, was huge and the fans lucky enough to attend the 600-capacity gig were hit right between the eyes with a set full of old and new classics. The writer also tackled the difference between *Dirty Work* and what was shortly to come.

After 'Dirty Work' fell short of expectations, due to major label drama and a slightly too mainstream slant, there's a certain sense of relief that so far 'Don't Panic' seems to be the band getting back to what they're good at – and they're really good at this, no doubt about it. 'For Baltimore' has the entire room singing along and hits every great pop song button, and 'The Reckless and the Brave' makes sure that the fun doesn't let up for one minute.

The lads stayed onstage for the twin blasts of 'Weightless' and 'Dear Maria, Count Me In', then headed straight to the airport for the New York show, at which they threw in covers including Limp Bizkit's 'Break Stuff' and 'Tell the Mick He Just Made My List of Things to Do Today', the snappily titled track by Fall Out Boy. Hopeless Records streamed images of the adventure, and the New York event at The Studio, Webster Hall, was also filmed by HD cameras. Unfortunately technical problems meant that the live stream wasn't available, but the show was broadcast later over the Internet for the many fans who couldn't get there, so there was no need to panic. Speaking of which ...

CHAPTER 24

DON'T PANIK

*T*he new All Time Low album's artwork was familiar to anyone who'd watched their previous lyric videos, being the colourful and cartoonish stills from those animations. As for the title itself, it's a reference to the fabulous book *The Hitchhiker's Guide to the Galaxy*, a sci-fi comedy by the late Douglas Adams in which an ordinary bloke, Arthur Dent, finds his life turned upside down by the realisation that his best friend – Ford Prefect – is in fact an alien from a small planet near Betelgeuse. Without giving away too much of the plot, the pair escape an earth scheduled for demolition by hitching a ride on a passing star destroyer. Their adventures are punctuated and driven somewhat by information gleaned from the eponymous handheld electronic guide, for which Ford was on earth as a researcher.

As lovers of sci-fi, All Time Low would have been well

aware of the trilogy of books (of which there are five, plus a sixth written by Eoin Colfer after Adams passed away). On the *Hitchhiker's Guide* is emblazoned, in big friendly letters, DON'T PANIC – which many travellers felt comforted by. Alex and Jack spoke about the album, Douglas Adams and their continuing career to Watch Mojo. Alex began by saying that the band had always looked to grow and evolve and that music ought to be a growth process, both creatively and as people. He felt that the execution of *Don't Panic* was great. The title of the record was inspired by the Adams book, he said, but not necessarily the content. 'It was really just about admitting the fact that a lot of things are out of control and you really just have to roll with it,' he mused. 'Which I think is the overall sentiment of the book.' It was about making the most of what you had while you can, he and Jack agreed. Alex also said that the upcoming tour, The Rock Show at the End of the World, was a reference to the second book in the *Hitchhiker's* series, *The Restaurant at the End of the Universe*. He told TheMusic that he felt that a fitting sentiment to the band's 2011/12 was, indeed, not to panic, 'because the entire cycle of us leaving our last major label, Interscope, and then making this record and resigning with Hopeless and stuff, there were a lot of times where we could have freaked out. It was sort of one of those things where we held it together, we made it through, so it's kind of a testament to not panicking and keeping your cool.'

Don't Panic begins with 'The Reckless and the Brave', that aforementioned statement track about not wanting to be 'saved' and saluting those who went their own path and eschewed the dubious seductions of a mainstream or mapped-out life. It is a vicious, precious world that other people want everyone to adhere to, but by gum there's so much more out there for those who prefer to explore and adventure on their own terms. In sentiment, it's one of the most pure punk rock songs that perhaps the band had ever released; it is in many ways a grandson of the fabulous 1980 Stiff Little Fingers song 'At the Edge', which deals with very similar concepts.

'Backseat Serenade' is next up, with an almost Beatles-y backward pumping guitar framework while Alex sings of being lonely, particularly at night. Cassadee Pope adds her ace backing vocals to this, making for a nice contrast between his tenor register and her sky-soaring vocals. It's got a lot of AOR chops: as well as it clearly being an All Time Low track there's a hint of the likes of Free about the aesthetic and some more of those epic, 1980s-ish drum sounds too. Nowt wrong with that, of course.

Third track, 'If these Sheets were States', begins with a highly processed statement that the protagonist was lost in pillow talk once more, and empty pillow talk at that. The song goes on to use the metaphor of the United States to bring home the reality of the distance between the protagonist and his love. If those sheets could only be folded and scrunched up, he could bring his squeeze closer to him – he can't sleep on his own and he misses her. The middle-eight breakdown here foreshadows a final couple of choruses that are based round simple chords that allow the band to play with dynamic, rhythm and arrangement.

'Somewhere in Neverland' is next up, the pop-punk back in full effect with a song that is in one way a sort of set of advice sent back to a younger All Time Low through the years as well as a comfort to listeners who might be going through moments of insecurity or unsure of where to head next. Alex is also in good lyrical form here, one particularly resonant line talking about laughing at mates who have wine-stained teeth.

There's more reaching to the past with 'So Long Soldier', which also features Pope plus Anthony Ranieri of Bayside. This one's got the lads' slight penchant for the nearly metal stamped over it; the guitars and double-kick drums push it into hyperspace as Alex sings about a boy who hails from near London taking a trip across the ocean. Wonder who he could mean? This boy has noise in his bones and by 2005 has got a bunch of mates with crazy plans, who drive to the west and see what happens – they need six more years, he reckons, and while they may be dreamers the trajectory can send them on a place of thought from which they can come down to become the voice of a generation. More sci-fi, of course, and in contrast to other space-metaphor tracks like David Bowie's 'Space Oddity', or 'Rocket Man' by Elton John, the dude does actually make it back home intact and ready to once more take on the world.

'The Irony of Choking on a Lifesaver' is a splendidly titled track that talks about a particular individual who seems to have it in for the protagonist, looking to sabotage his life (or career?) at every turn. This poisonous person talks a lot, laughs and thinks their opinions are somehow special – but they should let it ride and be happy for him. The catchy *na-na* section and the contrapuntal backing vocals are both typical in that they're instantly catchy slices of Baltimorean pop-punk that reference the influence of Blink-182.

The *whoa-ohs* of 'To Live and Let Go' herald another epic

about burning through cities and maybe regretting wasting time and energy on the unnamed individual to whom the song is directed. While they are a cut above others the main character cannot be trusted to live and then to let go again. The band has never sounded so together and on this excellent track there's a brilliant blend of soul-searching and defiance, which is delivered by Alex with a skilful honesty of vocal.

The Patrick Stump collaboration of 'Outlines' is next. Again it's all about looking at the past or past places and homes, and contrasting that with living in the moment. Jason Vena's vocals here throw the song into a wider context; this could be about anybody who's ever loved, been depressed, wanted to get away and start again. Though the lads were only around twenty-three and twenty-four at this point, it's an astonishingly mature outlook on life, which speaks loudly to their near-decade as a touring band, doing their growing up on the road and still searching for meaning and answers.

'Thanks to You' is another song about trying to move on, turning a new page in the book but still being haunted by someone who continues to give them nightmares. The protagonist is stressed and unable to sleep a quiet night through without medication; they have lost their touch and are having trouble making sense of it all, let alone having strong feelings about it. Of course, this could be about a relationship gone wrong, but sometimes contracts and commitments to things that have turned out contrary to what was initially hoped or promised can have the same effect too.

The magnificent optimism of 'For Baltimore' is next, proving there ain't nobody or nothing that can keep a good Marylander down for too long.

As the album begins to wind up towards its denouement, 'Paint You Wings' talks of a princess who can't quite work out that she isn't worth being saved. The protagonist was never really more than a short-term fix.

The title of final track, 'So Long and Thanks for All the Booze', is a direct reference to Adams' fourth book in the *Hitchhiker* trilogy, *So Long, and Thanks for All the Fish*, and Alex told Billboard that it was 'obviously a send-off and a farewell and a big "f-k you" to some of the people from our past that tried to steer us in the wrong direction'. It begins with a real Nirvana-ish intro, with lyrics about being too good to be held down to the ground by people who don't understand who you are and what you want to do. Dreams, motivation, revelation and the scene are being recovered and those who lie behind their smiles are simply never going to win. It's a perfect ending to an album beginning with the equally rampant 'The Reckless and the Brave', with the two sentiments dovetailing excellently.

In a later interview with Uniter about the band's experience with Interscope, Alex summed it up succinctly: 'I can't speak for how every major label operates, but I think what we benefit from is having a team that totally understands this band and understands what we're trying to achieve,' he began. 'In the end I think the problem was basically being a small fish in a big pond.'

After a quick 2 October stream by Hopeless in order to get people ready to rock, the album dropped on 8 October 2012 and the reviews poured in. *Alternative Press* discussed the time the band had spent on Interscope and said that while there had been too many people involved with the previous album it didn't always mean that the spark was missing. 'Guts', 'Under a Paper Moon' and 'Heroes', felt the mag, were all great but now that All Time Low were back in the driving seat, 'They've created *Don't Panic*, an album that drops any of the pandering pop-radio bait and rightly focuses on the band's strong suit—upbeat, catchy pop-punk indebted to Blink-182, New Found Glory and Jimmy Eat World with lyrics that actually mean something.' Further, the mag reckoned that it even felt somewhat like a greatest hits album, because it showcased all the stylistic elements the Baltimore boys had visited over their career. 'So Long Soldier' reminded the reviewer of early Yellowcard, 'Backseat Serenade' had some kind of connection with the build-ups Blink-182 were prone to, for example in 'Adam's Song', and 'Outlines', featuring Patrick Stump, could have been from the Fall Out Boy album *Folie à Deux*, although the writer bemoaned the fact that Stump didn't sing the Vena vocal.

For an idea of what All Time Low sounded like in 2012, 'Thanks to You', said the review, was the ideal example, blending musical chops, vocal earworms and a passionate lyric that was evident in the earlier work. That said, 'The Irony of Choking on a Lifesaver' and 'So Long, and Thanks for All the Booze' weren't up to those standards. The reviewer concluded that it was the band's best work up to that point and given the group's development since 2007 they looked forward to hearing what the band would be like in 2017. Where's Marty McFly when you need him?

Rock Sound were also fans of the record, saying that the new album returned the band to their old label and old sound. 'Without the hands of major label henchmen edging them into the most marketable direction, there's an overwhelming feeling that consumes you when listening to 'Don't Panic' that they've had more time, more room to breathe, and more fun this time around,' read the review. The writer reckoned that the lyrics to 'The Reckless and the Brave' and 'So Long...' were significant and said more about the band than they would ever really let slip in interviews about their previous year and a half. The album, though, was 'crunchy, sharp and totally, wonderfully reinvigorated'.

But *Kerrang!* remained unconvinced, saying that 'while 'For Baltimore' proves they can still write a grade A banger when they put their mind to it, too many songs are destined to have "must try harder" stamped on their report card.'

Over at Alter the Press! they mused about the easy road being to place the boys in a good-looking, generic pop-punk category, but in fact the album would show that they had way more to offer than that. The writer explained that it was a case of back to the band's roots and 'trademark catchiness' right from the start, in what seemed to be an autobiographical set of songs about where the band had come from, their hopes and their passion. Going through the tracks, 'The Irony' was simple but punchy and angsty, 'Somewhere in Neverland' was full of memory, regrets and nostalgia, and 'So Long Soldier' was 'heart-warming yet attitude-ridden' as it talked about Alex's experiences and dreams. Again, the fact that Stump didn't sing on 'Outlines' was bemoaned but the track was well received, particularly its dark edge, which was shared with the aesthetic of 'Thanks to You'. 'For Baltimore' was 'brilliantly energetic' and 'So Long...' was 'catchy as hell'. In summary, the writer felt that *Don't Panic* would appeal to new and old fans as well as somewhat rubbing out the disappointment some had felt concerning *Dirty Work*. The band was back in a good place and getting stronger and stronger. 'Pop-punk isn't dead,' concluded the writer. 'In fact, it may have just raised the stakes.'

A writer for Under the Gun this time began by noting that there was possibly no band that polarised the scene more. The early records made them essential for many and as the group continued to throw out records to secure ever more recognition, it culminated in the 'overproduced, shallow, and a tarnish on the band's catalog' that was *Dirty Work*. But all that said, 'returning to its original indie powerhouse home, Hopeless Records, has helped All Time Low release as good a bounce-back record as you'll hear all year in *Don't Panic*'. The writer did manage to mistake one of the track names as 'The Irony of Choking on a Lightsaber', which he said was unique in being the only track that may not have been worth putting on the album, but he concluded the record delivered in spades and that the lads couldn't have released a more appropriate and splendid record, giving it eight out of ten.

In the interests of balance, we must note that Punknews took the opportunity to aim a few kicks at a band that never really fitted with its own idea of what punk was all about in the first place. 'Hopeless isn't just the label; it's also a description for the record,' read the review. 'As for the album title, I'd have panicked had the album been decent because that would have been fucking unexpected.' The rest is worth reading for its absolute trashing of the record and the band – sometimes the bad reviews are the most entertaining and of course, as with all reviews, it's only one person's reaction.

Slightly better was a lengthy analysis from AbsolutePunk, whose writer gave the record every chance. 'It's clear these four guys have a knack for writing a catchy song,' mused the writer. 'While the lyrics may be weak at some points, the instrumentation is great. Some of these songs are insanely catchy, and could get stuck in your head if you're not careful. Also, vocalist Alex Gaskarth does have a nice voice. He may not have the best voice I've ever heard, but he does shine on the record as well.' In general, it was a pop-punk and pop-rock record with a fantastic middle section and while the writer wasn't a fan before hearing it, the experience had somewhat won them over – cheesy lyrics aside. Fans, however, would love it.

Finally, down under, the AU Review identified it as 'a perfect example of the saying "if it ain't broke, don't fix it". Since their breakout sophomore album *So Wrong, It's Right*, they've managed to stick to their core pop-punk sound while at the same time keeping things fresh and, well, fun.' References included Fall Out Boy, New Found Glory and Blink-182, and intriguingly the writer reckoned 'For Baltimore' was reminiscent of 'Coffee Shop Soundtrack'. '*Don't Panic* is a solid record, and a good entry to All Time Low's discography,' was the verdict, and the review score was 7.6 out of 10.

With 48,000 sales, the record debuted at Number 6 in the Billboard chart. It also hit Number 9 in the UK, peaked at 18 in Canada, 14 in Japan and eventually hit Number 1 in Billboard's Independent Albums and the Top Internet Albums chart. As comebacks go, it was beyond doubt a triumphant one.

CHAPTER 25

THE END OF
THE ROCK SHOW

The autumn tour began on 12 October at Starland Ballroom in Sayreville, New Jersey. The set-list was a mighty one of some twenty songs gathered from the band's career up to date, kicking off with 'The Reckless and the Brave' and, as ever, ending with the twin encore blasters of 'Weightless' and 'Dear Maria, Count Me In'. Cover versions were also getting an airing, with the latest foray being a version of Cyndi Lauper's magnificent torch song 'True Colors', which was part of the Chevy Cover the World Music Sponsorship in conjunction with MTV Iggy. Needless to say, the boys turned it into a proper pop-punk track with some glee.

Also out was the full video for 'For Baltimore', which continued the cartoon theme and was directed by Brett Jubinville and produced by Morghan Fortier, both of Tinman Creative Studios. It begins with pages from a high-school yearbook, with Alex's character exchanging glances with a girl called Zoey Morgan from their respective places in the book. However, she disappears and the singer goes in search of her by jumping inside the pages of the yearbook. The book is set out in cartoon/graphic novel style, with panels and frames, including moving representations of the school, band members rocking out and Alex searching everywhere for his love. There are jokes aplenty therein. For example, look closely at the twenty-seven-second mark and one M. McFly fades from the yearbook, presumably after having failed to get his dad to smack Biff upside the head in time. That famous BONER T-shirt is in evidence, too, as the song rocks out, jocks chuck footballs at the heads of other students, other kids make out with each other, people get gunged, some smoke, there are skulls, pregnancies and ... hang on, was that an alien? There's some drinking outside a pub called The Bull's Head. A skull on fire, strange eel, fish and wolves take over and Alex heads to a gig, where he's astonished to find he is looking at his slightly older, and more road-hardened, bristle-chinned self. This last revelation makes his brain explode into space. He joins it as the middle eight's laid-back bit kicks in, his eyes closed as he floats in orbit. However, he soon catches fire himself and hits the stage as a fireball, gaining a hand tattoo and once more fronting the band, all of whom are absolutely rocking out. It's a fine piece of work which firmly follows the set-out aesthetic of the album artwork, focus and style. There's also the inevitable comparison to be had with a video directed by Steve Barron way back in 1985 (aka *Back to the Future* year zero) for the Norwegian pop group, A-ha, which had a similar comic book feel. Not a comparison that's obvious musically, of course, but in terms of innovation it's definitely there. Who'd have thunk it?

The gigs were progressing niftily as All Time Low continued to play with the freedom and enthusiasm of a group that had come through some tricky times but were determined to prove they were back in the groove. The weather at the Cincinnati gig was torrential to the point of tornado warnings on the 14 October, but the boys hit it hard regardless. The group's love for playing in the rain has been documented and the ensuing abandon when fans let themselves go is one of their favourite experiences onstage. There was a short wait as the stage was reset for All Time Low, but the charismatic energy shared between Jack, Alex and the fans was turned up to eleven. Jack told the fans that every time the band came to Cincinnati the audience went crazy. He also joked that it was National Handjob Day.

All the joking aside, there was the little matter of an actual concert to play, with a writer from RockOnAnotherLevel reckoning that although it was only the third night of the tour so far the band hadn't really fired up the afterburners. That said, the stage lights were a step up from previous set-ups and there were backing vocalists and a guitarist also playing. 'I know ATL continues to get bigger, but they must realize that their fans love them for them,' said the writer, unwittingly tapping into the zeitgeist of *Don't Panic*'s creation. 'The raw, classic sloppy, hilarious, no-gimmick them. So, the fancy sets, lighting, and musicians aren't really necessary to please their dedicated fans. After all the Cincy crowd went through to enter their show tonight proves just that.'

Highlight Magazine was at the Chicago show on 16 October

and noted that some of the fans were actually crying with excitement. 'This show was overall a reminder of how much music can truly affect people,' wrote the reviewer. 'You know? When you attend a show you're there for the same reason as anybody else. Because whether you can admit it or not – music has done something for you. Most of us aren't afraid to admit it, most of us embrace it to the fullest extent.' The Baltimore boys had one of the strongest fan bases out there alongside bands like Paramore and of course Fall Out Boy and such was their commitment to their careers they had already been to a meet-and-greet, done some interviews, a signing session and then the gig, after which the lads no doubt met up with fans again. That level of bonding between the group and its fan base – Hustlers or not – was remarkable and had created a very strong relationship. As to the gig, the crowd sounded like there were ten times the 1,200 actually in the venue, the writer continued, and played a set that reminded them of 2008, such was the refreshing atmosphere there. The writer continued, somewhat old before their time perhaps, that it was something that took the twenty-year-olds back to feeling fifteen.

By the time the group hit Denver on 24 October they were indeed firing on all cylinders. Tickets were sold out for weeks in advance of the gig at Summit Music Hall and so ticket touts (scalpers in the US) were selling them for $100 on the day. The writer for The Sound Alarm referenced the popular belief that 21 December 2012 would in fact be the end of the world. It was a calculation of an ancient Mayan calendar, which happened to run out on that date. Many did actually believe this would herald doomsday. So the writer reckoned that if they were right, a ton would be a small price to pay for the last time they'd ever see All Time Low. The gig, of course, was ace and full of all the fun, frolics and first-rate tracks that you'd expect. *Dirty Work* wasn't at the forefront, observed the writer: 'Sure, they played 'Time-Bomb', 'Guts', 'Heroes', etc. but one would expect with *Dirty Work* being their only major label release that it would have been greater represented. Not that I'm complaining, as I personally find *Dirty Work* to be their weakest release.' Fair enough.

There was more good news with the chaps being named Number 3 in the 10 November edition of MTV's *10 On Top*. A short interview to coincide had Alex explaining that 'For Baltimore' was an ode to the place where they all grew up and to where they loved to return. He also joked that the more animated stuff they did, the less they actually had to do in person.

One enforced absence, sadly, was the concert scheduled for 14 November at Cat's Cradle, North Carolina, due to what was reported as a 'family emergency'. The gig was subsequently rescheduled for 3 December. The boys put out an update from the tour around 16 November, in which they showed the large crowds both in and out of the venues, to a soundtrack of 'For Baltimore'. There's also bits and bobs of the lads meeting fans, kids getting onstage to hug their favourites, and the gents messing about in various shops. At one point Alex wears a Slash-esque hat, complete with *faux* dreadlocks.

That same day – when the band were in Allentown, Pennsylvania – Alex, Jack and Zack performed some acoustic stuff for B104 Radio, including a splendid run-through of 'The Reckless and the Brave'. All night long Jack was in silly mood and even handed his guitar to a crowd member at one point. The band then started jamming around some of their songs as well as 'Don't Stop Believin' by Journey and 'Back in Black', the AC/DC classic, with the new temporary member.

The next day the group were at the Theatre of Living Arts in Philadelphia but made time to visit the children's hospital there; a charitable act that may not have received headlines but that speaks volumes for the lads' attitudes and humility.

Jack and Alex spoke to Buzznet on Thanksgiving, 22 November that year about what they were thankful for. Alex was in skull makeup and Jack dressed as Batman, as you do. Alex said he was grateful for friends, family and Pierce Brosnan while Jack was happy that Daniel Craig was James Bond. 'I'm thankful that no-one has to listen to Jar-Jar Binks [the widely hated *Star Wars* prequel character] anymore,' added the singer. The same day they recorded some tracks for *Walmart Soundcheck*, which would be streamed from 1 December.

The tour came to an end in Baltimore and was absolutely as exciting as you'd imagine from a group whose current single was a love letter to their home town; a group who'd come back from a relatively low point of losing their identity; a group of gentlemen who'd grown up on the road while always retaining a hankering to head back to the town where they'd first broken out. As usual, there was some near-the-knuckle onstage chat, with Alex joking at one point that Jack was in need of a tampon. Cue the throwing of a dozen or so of that feminine hygiene product – unused ones, of course – onto the stage.

Also hitting the Baltimore streets was an interview Jack gave to the *Baltimore Sun* in which he discussed the label change, the fact he was having flashbacks to schooldays while there, and the news that the band had started to donate a dollar to breast cancer charities from every bra that was thrown on stage. According to the paper, future plans include releasing more DVDs and 'perhaps a few acoustic side projects'. Plus of course continuing to tour. As Jack said, 'It's all we really have. It's how we reach our fans; it's our lives; it's our career at this point. Without it, we are nothing.'

The *Walmart Soundcheck*, which was a special online programme for Billboard, also featured an interview that was available on 17 December, where the guys, shot beautifully it must be said, again talked about the latest single, travelling, the rewards of success, and feeling back home once more. Rian also talked about the collaborations, specifically on 'Outlines'. He said that Jason Vena's Acceptance had made a huge mark on loads of people despite having put out only one record. 'We are still in the middle of our career, hopefully [...],' he said. 'Then you have Patrick [Stump], who's had five or six records and it is cool to see all three artists or bands who have left their mark in some way [collaborating on one song].' Ultimately it was about embracing the moments when they came along, because there was no guarantee that they would come along more than once. The songs the lads played were 'The Reckless and the Brave', 'For Baltimore', 'Somewhere in Neverland', 'Weightless' and 'Dear Maria, Count Me In'.

Rian's girlfriend, Cassadee Pope – who'd lent harmonies to 'Backstreet Serenade' and 'So Long Soldier' – hit the mainstream on 18 December, being named the winner of TV show *The Voice*, under the tutelage of mentor Blake Shelton. She'd sung 'Over You', which Shelton had co-written, in the third round. That song actually hit the top of the iTunes charts – knocking off the phenomenon that is 'Gangnam Style' by Korean hoss-dance-hero Psy. The album associated with the TV show, *The Voice: The Complete Season 3 Collection*, went on to hit Number 1 on the Heatseekers chart with first-week sales of 11,000, and Cassadee went on to perform on Carson Daly's New Year's Eve show before heading to Times Square to sing at those world-famous celebrations.

Back in pop-punkland, in an interview with students at Shippensburg University on 2 December for The Slate, Alex revealed that the majority of 2013 would be spent on the road. 'I think there'll be a couple of exciting releases at some point,' he added, 'but it's too early in the game to talk about now. We have a lot of cool things lined up like music videos and some interesting things.' Intriguingly, in the same interview Jack revealed that one of the producers that the band would have loved to work with was the late Jerry Finn, influential music producer and mentor for Blink-182. Finn had worked with Bad Religion, Rancid, Green Day, The Offspring and, er, Morrissey, and was one of the ultimate pop-punk engineer/ producers up until his untimely death in 2008. Mark Hoppus, said Jack, was behind the idea and had even emailed the producer, but tragic circumstances were to intervene. 'Blink was a huge inspiration for us, so if we'd have got to work with Jerry Finn, that would have been [incredible],' said the guitarist. He added that Blink-182's longevity as a band, hiatuses taken into consideration, meant that he could see that All Time Low also had a long-term future ahead.

It was also true that the boys themselves in turn acted as an inspiration to upcoming young bands, and in mid-December the twosome gave a quick video interview about a UK competition for unsigned artists – founded by a Member of Parliament no less – called Rock the House. The band would be patrons of the contest, and give it their support for the 2013 version, revealed the pair, following in the footsteps of the likes of warp-speed guitar-noodler Yngwie Malmsteen, Deep Purple singer Ian Gillan, shock-rock icon Alice Cooper and – him again – Mark Hoppus. 'We were asked by our homeboys and Members of Parliament [...] to become patrons,' said Alex. The boys explained that there were prizes up for grabs and that any band was able to enter the competition.

Let's just pause there for a minute. We're talking about a bunch of dick-joke-obsessed lads from Baltimore, who like a drink and a good party, who get bras thrown onstage as a matter of course, who regularly curse and swear and do lots of things your mother told you not to do, who tour the world playing music instead of getting 'real' jobs, who sing songs about following your dreams and not taking the easy path. Lads with tattoos, who are not afraid of sexuality and epicurean delights; lads whose teenage years were spent in the company of musicians, techies and assorted beautiful freaks. And these are the role models to whom the UK government is pointing young bands to follow?

The Mayans must have been right: the world was surely coming to an end. And may the Flying Spaghetti Monster have mercy on our souls.

CHAPTER 26

AFTERLIFE

Or, y'know. The world didn't end. (Sorry to report that, but the fact you're reading this book either means that the doomsters were wrong, or that Valhalla has one hell of a cool library. Hi, Odin, how's the beard?)

So it turns out that the Mayan calendar end date was just meant to be the end of one cycle. So said a proper science boffin called E. Wyllys Andrews, speaking back in 2008. 'There will be another cycle,' said the Director of the Tulane Middle American Research Institute. 'We know the Maya thought there was one before this, and that implies they were comfortable with the idea of another one after this.' So if you paid $100 for a ticket … lesson learned.

Meanwhile, in rare moments of time off, the band would be doing their own thing, as reported by Fuse, which interviewed Jack and Alex in December. The guitarist said that it was an important bit of downtime. Rian was taking the opportunity to go on a cruise while Zack was going to Hawaii. Alex said that it was good to plan holidays but equally brilliant not to have to think about doing anything. 'I'm sure I'll eventually make some plans but right now my mindset is, "Just get me home, put me on my couch. I just want to eat mac and cheese and watch a football game in my bed." Just something normal and slow.' Well deserved, sir: we hope you did just that.

And while you kicked back, we hope also that you enjoyed the results of the 2012 *Alternative Press* readers' poll. The VANS Warped Tour was best tour/fest of the year; All Time Low were second in live band of the year (Pierce the Veil won) and Jack's Twitter account was rated second best of the year behind Andy Biersack's of Black Veil Brides. Better still, the cover art for *Don't Panic* was voted second best of the year below Pierce the Veil's *Collide with the Sky* and *Don't Panic* was voted second-best album of the year, er, below Pierce the Veil's *Collide with the Sky*.

Clearly, then, there's only one thing for it: set up a co-headlining tour with All Time Low and Pierce the Veil, and call it The Spring Fever Tour. Other guests would be Mayday Parade and You Me at Six for the dates that were set to span April and May 2013. First things first, however, and the guys were back on the road, starting on 15 January with a gig at Burlington's Higher Ground. Yellowcard were the other main band on this jaunt, making for a package of quality.

The Canadian tour proper kicked off the next day at Metropolis, Montreal, and Yellowcard's hour and fifteen minutes onstage as ever featured the unusual pop-punk instrument the violin. Some of the veteran band's followers headed out into the night after that set, which was a shame as All Time Low, as ever, smashed it – the gig, not the violin. The lads' set was typically entertaining and even felt short, according to *Confront Magazine*. Still, the writer was a fan: 'It's clear that Yellowcard and All Time Low love to tour together, and I can promise that everyone else who will be seeing the bands on the tour are in for a treat!'

While up in the Canuck territories Jack and Alex spoke to 99Scenes about what was coming next. The boys revealed that they were playing five songs from the new record that they were very proud of and that they were looking forward to performing for fans around the world. While they didn't have favourite albums from the back catalogue, the new songs were definitely ripe for airing, not least because the band had taken a rare month off to regroup over the holidays. In any case, after five (not four) albums, there was so much to choose from that it was impossible to play every song that everybody wanted.

Due to the co-headline set, there was less time – the headline tour of 2012 had featured sets of an hour and a half but there just wasn't the scope to be able to do that. The interviewer brought up the fact that All Time Low had now reached the ten-year mark as a band. The lads smiled with pride at this. Jack said that ten years ago people would ask him what he'd like to be doing a decade down the line, and his answer would be, 'I don't know. Still playing music.' Which of course came true in spades.

Alex expanded on how the lads' relationship worked out during an interview with the Examiner. He said that they were basically family, brothers in fact, and though it was tough to live with people all the time they all did understand each other and living in such close proximity was the only option for a successful touring band. 'We all care about each other, and it doesn't matter if there is some bullshit on the table, you figure it out, get through it, and move on. We all remain really close friends,' he added. The singer also revealed that during the *Don't Panic* sessions there had been one more song that had been recorded but hadn't made it to the album. That track, he teased, might yet come out as a bonus on a later date. Again the duo alluded to the plan to make a sequel to *Straight to DVD*, which had given the fans a window into the day-to-day lives of the band. 'That one was about the origins of the band [up to that point],' explained Alex. 'But now there's another chapter to tell.' That next chapter would tell the story of how the group became a worldwide touring behemoth.

After the Canadian tour, Alex added, the lads would stop off in New York to record a video for the next single, 'Somewhere in Neverland'. The singer also mused on the accelerated pace of the music industry and said that the single would be followed in fairly short order by another one in order to keep the story motoring along. On a personal note, Alex responded to rumours about him having dated Taylor Jardine, singer with We are the In Crowd. He laughed and said he didn't really like going into detail about things but that the bands were good friends. Jack jumped in and said that he was dating Mike Ferri, who played the bass for their Hopeless Records stablemates.

A more philosophical question was posed to Jack by Beyond the Watch: 'What do you think life is?' The guitarist paused for a moment to ponder before replying, simply: 'Party. Party rock man is in the house tonight,' and broke into peals of laughter. He ended by saying that when he was growing up, as a really young kid he'd stand in front of the television singing along with the theme tune for *Batman*. His mother, he said, remarked that he was destined to be on stage one day. Very prescient, ma!

Of course, the weather was taking a hand in matters, as usual. This being Canada in January, there was a lot of snow about but shows weren't in danger of being cancelled because the country knew how to handle the white stuff. Talking of which, Jack and Alex said that when they walked out into the fresh air and took a breath their noses froze instantly and the first breath in the open basically hurt, it was so cold. Jack even had to wear thermal shirts onstage, the poor little mite! As for current listening, the axeman reckoned that he was all about the new record by Macklemore, *The Heist*. Alex agreed that it was awesome; it had come out the same week as *Don't Panic*. He also told Stitched Sound about a spot of bother he'd got into again by saying that he hadn't enjoyed a particular song by mega-selling boyband, One Direction. 'I thought I was going to be killed,' he said, tongue halfway in cheek. 'I legitimately thought I was going to be assassinated.' Social media, he said, had been full of 'a lot of elaborate death threats', none of which he was taking seriously because they were also hilarious.

Alex confirmed that the boys wouldn't be playing the Warped Tour 2013, largely because they were going to concentrate on festivals in other parts of the world. After that, Jack joked, the group would be doing a tour of purely Bar and Bat Mitzvahs – the Jewish coming of age ritual. Which would be a really brilliant idea – do it!

Meantime, the Canada dates came to a thumping end with Jack of all people getting behind the drum kit for a few bars of Yellowcard's 'Ocean Avenue' – and doing a pretty solid job of it, too. There was more good news at the end of January with the announcement that *Nothing Personal* had been certified as a silver record by the British Phonographic Industry for sales of more than 60,000 in the UK alone.

The lads also celebrated on 3 February when hometown team the Baltimore Ravens won Superbowl XLVII with a dramatic 34–31 win over the San Francisco 49ers. Controversially, there had been a power failure halfway through the game during a time when the 49ers were largely on top in terms of momentum. When the lights came back on it was the Ravens who soared highest. Even more remarkable was the fact that Jack very nearly called the result, predicting in an MTV interview: 'It's going to be a hard game ... but I'm going to say the final score will be 32–27, Ravens.' Jack was in attendance after having received the offer of a last-minute ticket. Lucky chap!

With the United States thus conquered on the stage and in the sporting arena, it was to the land of Alex's birth that the All Time Low bandwagon moved next. The tour featured sold-out shows all over the place, including the Bristol Academy, where the band were ably supported by Arizoneans The Summer Set and Lower Than Atlantis, the UK group that was beginning to ruffle a few feathers themselves. The crowd was energetic, passionate and bra-chuckingly up for it, as a reviewer from Punktastic commented. 'The show itself is fantastic, and their ATL backdrop, complete with incredible light show, is spectacular,' wrote the journalist. 'Tonight is the ultimate success for all bands involved, but especially All Time Low. Great work.'

Another writer took a different tack, comparing Alex's 'baby-faced looks' to Justin Bieber, and his 'silky smooth moves' to Justin Timberlake, before commenting that most in the crowd looked as though they were largely Year 10 school pupils (age fourteen/fifteen). The light show was again praised for its laser blast although some fans had to be helped out of the venue as a result. Jack's antics this time included putting on a wig, shadowboxing Alex's head and basically running around like a man possessed. At one stage, a girl in the crowd took a fall. The singer stopped the gig and asked the crowd to part so she could get attention. Many bands wouldn't even notice but this is All Time Low and the fans mean everything to them. The stricken lass was given some treatment by a staff member and only then did the group kick back in with the rest of the set, which finished with 'Dear Maria...' 'All Time Low showed why they are endearingly popular nationwide,' concluded the reviewer. 'Of course, Barakat did his own thing, this time getting lifted up by the bouncer so he could get to the crowd before taking a picture of himself with one lucky fan's phone. But that seems to be one of the reasons for this band's continued success: a livewire performance mixed in with real care and compassion for their fans, with a healthy dose of unpredictability to boot.'

The UK gigs ended with a three-night sold-out special at the O2 Shepherd's Bush Empire, which holds 2,000 people. Alex had flu and Jack had a bad back and claimed also to have an ingrowing toenail, but the lads were ebullient in an interview with Gigwise. They revealed that their rider – their requests for sustenance to be provided backstage by the promoter – used to be lots of food and a little alcohol, but now that had been reversed, according to Rian at least. 'We're really not rock star guys, unfortunately,' he said. 'Because I really wanted to have the stories of the heroin and the drugs and the sex and the massive success but we don't have any of that, unfortunately.'

One thing that had caught the imagination of the band was the fact that, come June, they would be supporting Green Day, one of their long-time heroes. Jack said that it had been a long-term dream to play with someone of that stature so it was an honour to have been selected. Rian said that it had come directly from a request from Green Day themselves. Often, he explained, it was the booking agents who would decide which support bands would work the best but he noted that the So-Cal punks had personally asked for All Time Low after having shared stages with them at various 2012 festivals. 'As a band, I'd like to get in tighter with the Green Day guys, I think that's a relationship that could really benefit us, obviously, and it would still be a dream come true to have them take us out on stage or somewhere else in the world,' he added. 'And just to kind of take these shows that we have with Green Day and get new fans. It's tough to get new fans where we are right now and that's the way to do it.' Of course, he couldn't be serious for too long and he immediately joked that Jack and he would be the only two left in the band because Alex and Zack weren't interested in continuing!

Talk went on to the Fall Out Boy comeback after four years apart. Patrick Stump et al. had certainly guided the boys on their way in the earlier days and all agreed within the Baltimore band that it would be brilliant to go on tour together at some stage. As for the gig, a reviewer from Bringthenoise was bowled over, albeit in need of a couple of spelling lessons: 'All Time Low have an arsenal of music ready to blow the roof off an arena. Their polished performance is barely contained in tonight's intimate confines. Sherpards Bush Empire has been truely spoilt,' read the review. There was one last Euro date at Paris's Le Bataclan on 18 February to negotiate, but by this time Alex's cold had transmuted into laryngitis and sadly for all concerned the gig had to be cut short as a result.

Australia beckoned once again and this time the Soundwave shows did go ahead as planned, with a couple of Sidewave shows at Sydney and Brisbane to boot. Alex's illness still wasn't resolved, so at that Factory Theatre, Sydney gig Luke McChesney of Sydney's pop-punkers Forever Ends Here stepped in while the group covered Blink-182's 'Damnit' and 'All the Small Things'.

'Your heart is beating really fast, are you done?' Jack asked him between the two songs, before turning to the crowd thus: 'This guy needs CPR. Are there any girls out there?'

The screams were even louder but the roof was blown off when Jack told the crowd that they would be back later in the year. Alex was fixed enough for him and Rian to give a quick interview to Soundwave TV, in which Rian explained that the temperature change between Canada and Australia had been remarkable – going from -33 to an Aussie summer is quite a shock (the UK was right in the middle of those temperatures). No wonder, really, that the newly bearded Alex had a few issues with his voice.

Switching from the headline gigs to festival appearances necessitated a real change of gear, in terms of playing shorter sets and having to aim to convince new attendees to become fans rather than already being masters of all they surveyed. Alex said that one of the things the band had learnt over the years was not to over-think things or to second-guess themselves. This also applied to songs which had ostensibly been finished but that the band afterwards had continued to work on, so much so that they'd lost all perspective as to whether that track was actually any good at all. 'It sounds great and it sounds polished,' he said of such occasions, 'but it's lost a lot of its [character].' And thus he succinctly summed up one of the main differences between *Dirty Work* and *Don't Panic*, or indeed any other album in the All Time Low oeuvre.

Of the band's ambition, Rian mused that they didn't necessarily want to become a Stadium Rock act and Alex recounted a Dave Grohl quote along the lines of, 'If you've ever had a promotional picture taken of yourself then you can never say you don't want to be famous.' The reason to start a band was to share the music, Rian concluded, and if you can do that in front of 60,000 people then why the hell not?

CHAPTER 27

NEVERLAND SAY NEVERLAND AGAIN

*I*t was time for the eagerly awaited video to hit the streets.
Or to hit the Internet, to be exact. Yes, folks, the moment
everybody had been waiting for finally happened: All Time
Low's dance performance to Harlem Shake. That world
phenomenon also involved Of Mice & Men, Sleeping with
Sirens and Pierce the Veil as part of the ongoing Soundwave
TV silliness. The lads left Australia to head to Singapore in
2013, where there was significant anticipation for their gigs.
As ever the boys kept themselves busy with appearances on
the 987FM studio for an acoustic session, a chat on *Toggle
Talk Show* and plenty of press conferences. One of the
interviews, for MeRadio, had a few moments of insight: Zack
snores very loudly, Alex is always late on the bus, Jack likes to
smell things ('He's a very scent-oriented person,' said Alex),
and if the band were ever to rename itself it would either be

Meatcurd (according to Jack) or Singapore Swingers, which was Alex's contribution.

The gig at the Coliseum, Hard Rock Hotel, on 6 March was reviewed by multiple news agencies, one of which opened with the immortal, tense-mashing words, 'It isn't an All Time Low concert if one didn't have a ballin' good time.' The two thousand in attendance loved it, particularly when Alex claimed that Stella was, in fact, about the beer of the same name. 'All in all, ATL surpassed any and all expectations despite the fact that they were on an arduous touring schedule and that Gaskarth had only recently recovered from an ailment in addition to the fatigue,' concluded the writer for Spinorbinmusic.

According to Poached, Alex said that the band were going to move to Singapore and play gigs at the venue each month, such was the awesome response. The writer this time flagged up the reasons for the group's success. 'All Time Low has some of the wildest fans out there, and this concert certainly bears testament to how far the band has come in the past decade from their high school years,' was the verdict.

Award for eloquence goes to the great writer at More Than Good Hooks, whose prose concluded thus: 'In years to follow, it seems like the importance of chemistry within the band has been strongly raised and has been passed around all too regularly. All Time Low reinstated that and stamped their love onto our hearts. That little piece of intangible possession called passion still holds great importance, too.'

The boys then headed to Japan for gigs in Tokyo, Osaka Shi and Nagoya before a stop-off in Honolulu on the way home. They shared scenes from the Japan trip in a special tour recap on their return to the States, including a few lovely beverages shared, Thug Life T-shirts everywhere, packed out crowds going nuts and set-lists from the gigs. Alex is shown at one stage wearing a lovely kimono and looking rather bemused at the TV show, which is an animation of some people getting into an elevator. The fast pace of the streets and the immensity of the vista is stunning, with Mount Fuji looking incredible. The soundtrack? 'Somewhere in Neverland', of course. The Aussie accents need a little work though, boys.

It was time for the eagerly awaited video to hit the streets. Or, to hit the … hang on, we've done that bit already, haven't we? Suffice it to say that 19 March 2013 was the day that the *Somewhere in Neverland* video was released, directed by Raul Gonzo. It begins with the curtains opening as if in a theatre before a besuited Alex is seen hammering away at a computer in an office cubicle. While someone photocopies their backside, Alex heads for the window along with a blonde girl (presumably the Wendy of the lyrics) and jumps out. Luckily, though, instead of hitting the ground he is picked up by Jack, Rian and Zack in a hot-air balloon that takes them out of the atmosphere and towards a truly magical place where things are all different: cardboard fire, Plasticine chicken legs and a lovely sweater modelled by Zack. The band gets to 'fly' through the clouds, spying dinosaurs squaring up and aliens attacking the planet. Oh, and according to the logic of the video, chickens live on the moon. It's splendid stuff; entertaining and fun even while the lyrics are extremely to the point regarding the rejection of the path well-trodden. To illustrate as much, Alex and Zack played a surprise acoustic show on 31 March back at their old stomping ground of the

Recher Theatre in Towson, one of the key venues a decade previously. Two of the tracks were 'Running with Lions' and the gorgeous, haunting and extremely personal track, 'Lullabies'. There was also a teaser from Alex on Twitter that he had been getting his funk on in the studio – was this the genesis of some new material? Time as ever would tell.

After a short break of a couple of weeks, the lads prepared themselves to head back out on the road on the Spring Fever tour. This time around the additional guitar onstage would be provided by Bryan Donohue, who had previously played bass with The Tower and the Fool and Boys Like Girls. He'd been brought in to replace assistant tour manager, backup vocalist and additional axeman Matt Colussy, who had signed off from his band duties in amicable style, even enjoying a brief guitar solo at the final O2 Shepherd's Bush Empire gig in London on 16 February.

Colussy may have stepped out of the eye of the storm, but the tour with Pierce the Veil made for as packed a schedule as ever. Alluding to the fact that Pierce the Veil had a more hardcore edge, Alex told Poached that 'the coolest thing right now is that 10, 15 years ago all those fan bases were very separate, and they didn't really go to the other shows. Now with the internet and the way the music's distributed, we're at a really cool place where you have fans from both bands coming to the same shows.' There wouldn't be any post-hardcore screams on any All Time Low songs any time soon, he assured the interviewer.

That shared fan base, Vic Fuentes of Pierce the Veil told *Alternative Press* after a week of the tour, seemed to work out because they'd never considered themselves 'super-heavy'.

'We've kind of travelled around in different directions, so we have heavy parts, but we also have a lot of poppy parts,' he explained. He revealed that the tour had come about following a chat between Rian and himself backstage at Warped. It was then a case of asking good mates Mayday Parade to get involved, as well as You Me at Six – all groups that could happily perform as headliners in their own right. Vic's voice was shot though so he was on medication to help him through the shows. Alex added that it felt like a festival, such was the strength and diversity of the bill.

The shows were selling out very fast as crowds flocked towards one of the most irresistible line-ups the United States had ever seen. The Atlanta date was attended by *Substream*, who said that they expected 'organised chaos' due to the fact that all the bands were known as being prone to the odd prank or two. The band was introduced by Vinny Vegas, the merchandise guy for All Time Low, by asking the crowd if they were ready for 'sixty minutes of mediocre rock 'n' roll'. Alex and Jack then came on in boxing robes, shadow boxing as Vinny said 'Let's get ready to rumble', in true over-the-top style. What followed was another awesome gig. 'No-one can come close to predicting the shenanigans of an All Time Low show,' the reviewer wrote, 'and let's be honest, plenty will happen. Alex, Jack, Rian and Zack have blurred the lines and crossed limits, whilst dirty jokes and humour are synonymous with ATL, but they do have a serious side. Their performances never cease to amaze. The crowd sang along to every word so throughout the night, Alex gave them the lead.'

The show on 21 April scheduled outside in Philadelphia's Electric Factory was halted briefly due to a bomb scare. A suspicious package had been spotted in the venue area and the police were called out. Luckily, it was a false alarm. The atmosphere was edgy at the time because on 15 April terrorists had attacked the Boston Marathon, using pressure-cooker bombs that killed three civilians immediately and injured over two hundred and seventy-five others. In all, five people died at the hands of the terrorists, after police deaths in the violent aftermath. Ultimately, one of the bombers died after being run over by his brother, the other perpetrator of the deadly crime. After a manhunt, the surviving brother was caught and sentenced to death. The incident sent shockwaves through society and as a result extra care was being taken with any large gathering of people in terms of security. Gigs, and particularly outdoor ones, certainly fell into that category.

The tour moved on and the venue on 26 April was Lowell, Massachusetts – the closest gig to Boston. One person who had tickets for the gig was Sydney Corocan, a high-school senior. She had, however, attended the Marathon and was standing near where the first of two bombs went off. As a result, her mother Celeste lost both her legs and the eighteen-year-old Sydney suffered severe injuries from flying shrapnel, which nearly cost her her life. She was taken to Boston Medical Center to recover, so could not attend the gig. No problem – All Time Low, Mayday Parade and Cassadee Pope nipped down to the hospital to meet Sydney and share a joke or two.

'It's the absolute most sweetest thing anyone could do for anyone,' Sydney's friend, Sarah Cassella, told the *Boston Herald*. 'She loves them. I'm just so happy she met them. She deserved this. She's been so excited about this concert. This is like the best thing. She's so happy that they even did this. It's unbelievable.'

Derek Sanders of Mayday Parade said that it had been an incredible experience to meet the teenager. 'She's a wonderful person, and her family just showed incredible spirit,' he told the paper. 'To see a family that's been through a life-changing thing like that, you imagine just how devastating it can be,' he continued. 'But to see them laughing, smiling, joking and just having hope was so inspiring.'

The tour continued to plough through the States and although Rian contracted an illness during May, he powered through sets regardless; Detroit's Filmore on 1 May being one such occasion. The Examiner quoted Alex as having a gentle dig at the crowds all filming the gig on their phones rather than letting go and enjoying themselves. 'So I was planning on spending my night staring at beautiful people,' began the vocalist. 'But all I see are cameras and phones. I can respect that you want to capture the memories but can we put 'em down and just live in the moment right now? [...]. I see an orange light, I don't wanna see that! I see a green light up there, put it away!' Throughout the tour it had been a regular request from the frontman.

The date at Detroit's Ogden Theatre on 6 May was streamed live for all those who couldn't attend. Then the gigs came to an end on 14 May with a hi-jinks night at the Warfield Theater in San Francisco. Pierce the Veil decided to play a game of beer pong during All Time Low's rendition of 'If these Sheets were States'. For the uninitiated, beer pong is a drinking game in which a set of plastic cups, filled with a refreshing alcoholic beverage, is placed in front of each player. The aim is to get a ping-pong ball in your opponent's cup and if you are successful they have to immediately down that cup's contents (minus the ball, natch). It's an exceedingly silly game, which can be played by two teams of two players each facing the other, and inevitably ends in a downright mess of booze.

Pierce the Veil had a good time – history has not recorded which band members won – but they were also to get their own comeuppance in their following set. The All Time Low lads started a game of catch – or, rather, a game of throw in which they were aiming for specific targets on and off stage. You reap what you sow …

A wrap video was released following the tour which showed scenes from the gigs, the usual lines of kids waiting to get in, people messing with silly string, and interviews with the guys. Rian revealed he had a new rock star crush on Pierce the Veil drummer Mike Fuentes, who he said was a softly spoken, lovely bloke. Jack said that the pre-show ritual involved the band dancing around, listening to Hip Hop like Lil Wayne or Jay Z. Alex said he fistbumped everyone before the end of the intro to the first song as a ritual. Zack's fitness regime was shown again – busying himself with press-ups throughout. Vic Fuentes commented that the tour really felt like the biggest and best thing that his band had ever done. Jack explained the importance of touring to bands in an interview with The Merch Dude. He said that the only real way to make money from being in a band was to tour constantly. 'All of our income comes purely from show guarantees and merchandise sales,' he explained. The guitarist added that a tour was a pretty expensive thing to do, particularly when your crew varied between ten and fifteen people. These would include tour managers, lighting and sound engineers, technicians, merchandise guys and all the people that made the magic happen. Because All Time Low always wanted to give the fans a new experience tour by tour, this meant investing heavily in the running costs.

'A good amount of what bands make on tour (more than you think) goes into the crazy lights we have behind us,' he said. 'And the amount of speakers we bring out. I like to think we do an awesome job giving the fans a different show every tour.' Jack added that the crew had been consistent for years, which was important, particularly travelling between different countries, different venues and different situations. Knowing that the shows would run smoothly was really important as was getting on well with the people that you are surrounded by day in, day out. 'Our drum tech [Alex] Grieco went to high school with us,' he said as an example. 'When we graduated we kidnapped him, taught him how to drum tech, and he's been with us for seven years.'

CHAPTER 28

KINGS OF
THE AIRWAVES

The latest video from the boys, *Backstreet Serenade*, was posted online on 9 May. Jeremy Rall was the director and he definitely delivered in terms of entertainment. The song begins with Alex eating some colourful breakfast cereal, dressed in a fluffy animal suit without the head on. Each of the lads gets his own creature and is seen dressed up cycling, skateboarding, using the toilet, waiting for buses and doing all sorts of everyday stuff. The juxtaposition of the utterly daft suits and the banality of their context is what makes it all the more effective as a piece of art. The live element sees the band playing in a casino, all flashing lights and JJ Abrams-esque lens flare. We see the furry people clocking in to their jobs, running to make it on time, before it's revealed that in fact our boys are the moles of the whack-a-mole game and are only there for a gang of girls to smack upside the head with a hammer as soon as they put their heads above the parapet. Finally, the lads don their fluffy suits to briefly play their instruments before we see Alex undressing from his suit and wearily getting into bed with his gal at the end of a long day of furry cosplay.

The video was filmed in part in Funtopia, Queens, New York and Fuse interviewed the lads about it. Alex revealed that some of the furry actors were actually hired from Craigslist. Rian said that it got quite surreal. 'In the catering room there's like a lobster, a dinosaur and they're all just sitting there on their phones, taking a cigarette break or whatever,' he laughed. Alex added that the budget had not been high enough to hire the whole of Funtopia for the filming, so there were instead just some roped-off areas. The song had become a live favourite, said the singer, since it had been unveiled at the UK gigs earlier in the year.

Alex and Jack ventured onto the airwaves in another new project with the 3 June debut of their brand-new radio show, entitled, provocatively, *Full Frontal*. The show would feature the lads chatting about pop culture every Monday through Idobi Radio and the advertisement had possibly the least sexy photo of Alex and Jack naked that there had ever been. The words 'Full' and 'Frontal' covered their more private parts, but this certainly was one that would be dodgy to paste on your high-school locker. Jack joked that as it was an online show it would allow the boys to swear. Engineer for the shows was Evan Kirkendall and executive producer was Jeff Maker, also the band's lighting designer. Jack explained that the show was even more fun than he'd imagined; he and Alex were hardly professional radio hosts and they were messing about so there was no guarantee of how it would work but it turned out really well. 'It's another way for us to interact with the fans and talk about weird news and it's completely natural, it's not forced and it's just very relaxed. So yeah, just an hour of uncensored, weird date jokes,' he explained to Kill Your Stereo. Maybe he meant to say 'dick jokes'.

The show was only really possible while the lads were on tour because Rian, who took charge of the engineering and editing, was based in Los Angeles while off the road. Alex and Jack still lived in Baltimore, so it was when the lads were together on the tour bus that they'd get it done. Rian was getting better and better at using ProTools – the industry standard recording software used by many studios – so he was definitely the right man to have at the helm. A born engineer! Aside from everything else, the show helped to pass the long hours of driving between shows.

The lads were in Europe when that show debuted, headlining the Main Stage at the Slam Dunk festival, which took place in Leeds, Hatfield and Wolverhampton from 25 to 27 May. Attending the Hatfield gig was *Rock Sound*, which posted a lengthy review online. As for All Time Low, the band provided a perfect end to the day, boosted by that great lighting and sound set-up that Jack was talking about. It was an hour or more of singing, jumping around and hugging your mates to the glorious sounds, the reviewer reckoned. There was plenty of screaming, as ever, both to the songs and to the bras added to Jack's mic stand. Most telling was the fact that other bands flocked to watch the Baltimore headliners. 'As what seems like every band member on site [clamours] for a space at the side of stage, it leaves you with the feeling that this is one of the most fitting finales of all' was the payoff.

After a quick jaunt to Austria for the Vienna-based Krieau Rocks festival, the band returned to London for one of the greatest moments in their careers to date. The first day of June 2013 saw the lads supporting Green Day at the Emirates Stadium, home of Arsenal Football Club. Kaiser Chiefs, featuring soon-to-be TV star Ricky Wilson, were the other band on the bill. While at Slam Dunk, Jack spoke to an interviewer from Jägermeister and explained what the gigs with one of their heroes meant to the band. '[It's] terrifying,' he said. 'Some of the shows it's just us and Green Day and [we] have to warm up the crowd and get 70,000 German dudes into it [...] it will be a good time and I think we are professionals at warming up crowds.'

It would be the biggest tour they'd ever done, but Jack was excited to be able to talk to Green Day about their career – and favourite sexual positions. He said he'd probably get his band kicked off the tour as a result. '[Green Day] is one of the bands that decided our fate,' Alex told *Kerrang!* in a podcast. Jack joked that the band had been forced to do some terrible things to get on the tour, a baton that Alex picked up gleefully before getting serious again and saying that as an eleven- or twelve-year-old he'd listen to Green Day. 'Definitely, it was defining [...] I remember going and buying the records and getting really absorbed by the band. My god, this is awesome, they are singing about my life.' It was the first time, he said, he felt like a rebel for listening to a band that talked about smoking weed and pissing their pants.

Alex also revealed that as a boy his favourite side was West Ham United, while Jack's allegiances were entirely up for sale. One person who was likely to be very jealous of the lads playing at the Emirates was Josh from You Me at Six, a major Arsenal supporter.

But it was music that was on the fixture list rather than footie, and 60,000 people turned up to get their fill. Among many reviewers on the day was the journalist from *Kerrang!* who expressed wonder that it was actually a sunny day. The 'agreeable' surroundings, felt the writer, were a good fit for the similarly agreeable All Time Low. 'Clearly new to this stadium lark, the Maryland band bounce around the stage as if it's a trampoline, while playing songs tailor-made for summer days,' the reviewer reckoned. That said, the lads were clearly unfamiliar with the stadium set-up and the writer felt that they were not quite ready for it either. The mag also carried a short interview with Alex in which he called the experience 'fucking fantastic: it was phenomenal, man!' His mind had been blown by stepping out there in front of the 30,000 or so that had already got into the stadium when they played. The band knew that there were a lot of people there who'd not previously heard of All Time Low so they went all out to give them the full experience. 'Time-Bomb', he said, had come across the best.

As for Green Day, they were simply awesome and showed exactly why they were such a hugely successful band. Their skills weren't all musical, either: Alex noted that Green Day's ability to work with the crowd and create interaction was something that All Time Low had always drawn inspiration from and to see it first-hand was bound to push the Baltimore band to up their own game to another level.

The lads from *Rock Sound* were also at the Emirates and remarked that All Time Low had taken the stage around

5pm, which was rather early. In contrast to their Slam Dunk headliners, it was clear that they were nervous at opening such an enormous gig. There were some issues with the sound and the guys were not as well known in comparison to the headliners of course, but they 'garner[ed] a huge response for the likes of 'Damned If I Do Ya (Damned If I Don't)' and 'Backseat Serenade' that sees fists pumping stagewards from goal line to goal line'. Alex and Jack dived into the crowd, enjoying the moment.

There were more huge dates to play in Italy, Germany, Poland and Russia, with the lads going on to festivals in Scandinavia and the rest of Europe at the end of a breathless tour which undoubtedly taught them loads about the next step to which they should aspire. They were doing pretty well already; it was the *Kerrang!* Awards 2013 on 13 June and All Time Low put another gong on the shelf by winning Best International Band. Jack accepted the award by pointing to Mark Hoppus and thanking him for letting All Time Low rip his band off for ten years without suing them. Alex said it was important to remember that it was voted for by the fans and thanked them sincerely. After the ceremony, he and Jack spoke to the magazine, award in hand, and praised Green Day. 'They are so cool to their support acts,' the singer said. 'They just take care of [us]. It's a very endearing quality in a headliner.' Jack said he was going to show his mum the award to convince her that he was actually in a band, in real life.

With no new material as such for a while, there were rumours all over the place. One such rumour was spotted by eagle-eyed fans in early July, who noted that *Amazon.com* was listing a release on audio CD by All Time Low scheduled for

1 October 2013. The title at that time was *Panic* but there were no indications as to whether this would be an album, a single, or an instruction in general. Around a week later, Alex tweeted the cryptic message that he would be flying out to Los Angeles on 20 July in order to track some vocals at the last minute for some unnamed project. At the same time, Jack told Kill Your Stereo that the band was 'focusing on touring and we have so many albums out at this point that we want to kind of slow down on the recording [...] We just made an album and the others are so close together, we are just going to focus on touring and getting a DVD.'

Alex also told May the Rock be with You that the band had a few aces up their sleeves, which were for the time being secret. He also mentioned that the band were still determined to make a sequel to *Straight to DVD* but that it was about 'finding the right moment to really hone in and put all the collected footage together'. Again, though, there was no timeline associated with the planned project.

Jack, meantime, hooked up with the guys from No Budget Movies to amuse himself and duly re-enacted scenes from various movies including *Home Alone*, *Scarface*, *Back to the Future*, *Moonraker* – where he played James Bond – *Jerry Maguire* and loads of other really, really, extremely silly scenes. *The Shining* is a personal favourite but seek it out – each one's a winner. Jack's mother's reaction to her son's career is not on record about this one, sadly.

There was some downtime because the planned four dates in Mexico and Brazil from 24 to 28 July had been cancelled due to unexpected circumstances. The shows had been pulled by the organisers so late that the group's team had even bought tickets and shipped gear over to South America. The dates would be rescheduled for December and would also feature 3OH!3, the electronic duo from Colorado. Also during July a session was aired that the lads had recorded for Guitar Center, including versions of 'Somewhere in Neverland', 'Dear Maria...' and 'Backseat Serenade'. Gigs would restart in mid-August with a jaunt to the Far East before the second world tour of the year kicked off properly down in Australia.

CHAPTER 29

OH DON'T PANIC, HOW YOU'VE GROWN SINCE WE SAW YOU LAST

The boys played five dates in the Far East: Taiwan, Hong Kong, Beijing, Indonesia and the Philippines. The Hong Kong gig was on 19 August and attended by *Dinosaur Journal*, the number one source for rock in the Chinese territory. It was the first time that the band had played the city but the crowd had a familiar demographic base of teenage girls throwing their bras on the stage. Alex was at his encouraging best, thanking the fans for their support and supporting them in turn as they tried to make their own dreams come true. As ever, Jack got in among the crowd and the lads stayed to sign autographs after the show.

'Generally speaking,' reckoned the writer, 'the show was fun and pretty fulfilling. They were very energetic and despite the venue was small [sic] they still gave all they could to put out a memorable show.' Jack spoke to the Australian press about how everything was coming along, telling Themusic that he felt that *Don't Panic* had been 'quite possibly the strongest comeback we've ever had, and I'm not really saying it's a comeback because we didn't really go anywhere, but I just feel like it really kind of re-energised our fanbase, and re-energised us as a touring band. I think it was definitely the perfect record to make at the perfect time.'

The live experience went down as well as ever with the Aussie lot, including a three-day run at the Billboard venue in Melbourne. Originally it was planned as a two-day residency but with tickets flying out for the under-age and over-age shows respectively, a third was added. The band was on killer form and full of their usual charisma. A reporter from Reverbstreetpress summed it up niftily after watching the gig on 2 September. 'What is truly amazing about this band and the way they perform,' wrote the gig-head, 'is that even though they have millions of fans around the world, you don't feel like you're seeing a band play in front of faceless fans, but rather a band playing to a group of their very own, personal friends.' Succinctly and accurately put. After flying back from Australia, there was a ten-day window before the latest leg of the United States tour took place.

The band was not standing still, as you'd expect. Jack also had explained in his TheMusic interview that the band were already working on new songs. At this stage of their career, he said, the group had found its sound and that was a little more rocky than poppy, albeit there was always going to be a pop edge to some of the songs. He said that the songs being written were in the same vein as the previous album and he felt that it was 'going to be a *Don't Panic* 2.0. At this point we've honed in on our sound and I think we've got it.'

Meantime, Alex was being coy about new material in his own interview with CoolTry. Referring to the *Panic* announcement on Amazon, he was adamant that it was 'all hear-say! Amazon never really knows what's going on, and as far as us releasing something called *Panic*, they're dead wrong. I'm not really sure what they were doing/thinking when they posted that album, but it certainly isn't something we've got in the works. Guess everyone will just have to wait and see what's next.'

The teases were numerous, not least a video of the band and Vic Fuentes of Pierce the Veil hanging out in a movie theatre. Given the video was posted to the official ATL site, tongues were certainly wagging. Alex had also been writing with the Aussie phenomenon, 5 Seconds of Summer, which had always captured his imagination. His creativity and energy certainly were in demand at this point and would continue to be so.

It was time, though, to release a new All Time Low track, 'A Love Like War', featuring Vic Fuentes. Aha! The song's video, directed by Drew Russ, debuted on 2 September and featured – hang on now – the band and Vic in a movie theatre watching a black and white movie. Well, that explains that one, in any case. It has to be said if Jack did indeed take his electric guitar into a showing of a movie in normal circumstances he'd no doubt be kicked out by the ushers. He set a bad example, clearly, 'cause the rest of the band were soon at it too, playing right in front of the screen. Sssssh you noisy pop-rock-punks at the front! Some of us are trying to watch the movie, ya know. The addition of Vic gives an edge to the sound and visuals that is a welcome addition of heaviness. Vic's screamed 'Let's GO!' is a rare OTT shouty moment in the All Time Low oeuvre. The single peaked at Number 17 in the US Hot Rock Songs and 22 in the Bubbling Under Hot 100 Singles, both Billboard charts, and reached Number 56 in the official UK singles chart. It was the lead single from the newly issued *Don't Panic: It's Longer Now!*, which was the actual release the band had been planning for a while.

There were no less than four new songs – an EP's worth, really. The second new track, 'Me Without You (All I Ever Wanted)', begins with some earworm singalong parts and a galloping, almost Iron Maiden-esque drum rhythm. It settles down into one of the band's tuneful, slightly softer pop-punk ditties with some tinkly piano and well-controlled riffery. Alex is in great voice on this one, singing beautifully and tenderly with a hint of Feargal Sharkey vibrato in among the more plaintive, pleading parts. (Check out The Undertones – they're great.)

Another addition for the new release was 'Canals', a self-reflective piece in which Alex looks deep inside and finds contradictions, answers through wine and worries. The spikier, almost post-punk riffs of the verses on the track show the band's ability to hold back and play with dynamics before exploding into the chorus. It's definitely the more rocky side of the Baltimoreans coming through and, as with the Vic Fuentes track, is a welcome addition.

'Oh, Calamity!' is the fourth new track on the rebooted LP, one of Alex's torch songs set in a minor key and nodding towards the epic 1980s rock sound with which All Time Low were increasingly flirting.

As well as the new songs, there were four acoustic songs: versions of 'For Baltimore', 'Somewhere in Neverland', 'The Reckless and the Brave' and 'Backseat Serenade'. One bonus extra to entice people to buy the record was the possibility that you could win dinner with the band – if you found the Willy Wonka-like golden ticket, which in this case was a special Polaroid of the guys in your album case.

Reaction to the reissue, or extended album, was reasonable, with Bringthenoise saying that the whole thing worked because the new tracks fitted with the flow of the original while giving a surprise when the new songs popped up. 'Bonus acoustic renditions of singles 'For Baltimore' and "The Reckless and the Brave" really explore a more emotion fuelled side to the songs, especially with the inclusion of beautiful string arrangements that quite frankly, we would love to have heard a little more rather than in the odd moment,' reckoned the site's writer, who also pegged the record as sounding strangely both nostalgic but concurrently extremely fresh.

A reviewer for Spinorbin began by saying that reissues with extra material often only pointed to the fact that there was a reason said songs didn't make the original cut, plus that record companies often re-released albums for purely commercial reasons. But in the case of All Time Low, the new tracks were definitely worth the effort. Again, 'A Love Like War' was praised and 'Oh Calamity!' also well regarded, Alex's expressive delivery and the smooth-wailing electric guitar contributing to a feeling of solemnity. 'Canals', meanwhile, had an introduction reminiscent of Maroon 5. In general, the lads had released one of the most fun albums of the genre, 'and it's only a matter of time [before] they come up with a new album full of new material to ignite a riot and excite a crowd as fervently as *Don't Panic: It's Longer Now* does'.

While on tour, Alex and Jack caught up with *Alternative Press* about the co-headlining tour, explaining that their stage set-up was relatively straightforward but the light show was spectacular, courtesy of Jeff Maker, the talented lighting designer (and nascent radio show producer). Jeff had begun in the lighting world in 2000, with a local Connecticut band called Throne. At a show he jumped behind the desk and started to press buttons. Later, he moved to Boston to attend college and got a job at The Paradise Rock Club as a barman. The in-house lighting designer, as it happened, was looking for an intern and so Jeff stepped up to train with him, before moving on to his own lighting job at a venue called Axis. His first tour was with The Dresden Dolls in 2006 and word spread. His favourite lighting to date, he said in 2012, was 'Too Much' by All Time Low on the Glamour Kills tour. When asked by Kids in Doubt about his lighting ritual, he explained how it all worked. 'Before tour I put together my lighting designs and work with lighting companies to make sure my vision is brought to life the way I want it to [be],' he said. 'Before each show, like right before the set, I make my notes on the set list next to each song and tell the guys to have a great set. Then I test all my fixtures to make sure they are all responding correctly and then I loosen up my fingers, wrists, and hands.' An artist, and a performer – illustrating how much talent there truly is in the All Time Low family.

The lads were playing only around forty minutes a set, which was starting to be tricky because by now they had such a great back catalogue to choose from. This time 'Coffee

Shop Soundtrack' edged out 'Jasey Rae' as one of the must-play tracks. Jack reckoned that the title of the new album hadn't been intended as a double entendre, in the same way that it wasn't until *Straight to DVD* was actually out on the streets that the band realised that in fact it spelt STD. Oops! 'This operation writes itself,' Alex joked. He also said that it was great to be able to perform 'A Love Like War' while actually on tour with the band of the dude that co-sung the song because Vic's live vocals really did add a huge dimension. The singer referenced the relatively short period between *Dirty Work* and *Don't Panic*, citing the release of … *It's Longer Now!* as helping to draw out the cycle of that album a little bit longer in terms of its currency. 'I feel like it's probably one of the stronger records that we've ever done as a band,' he mused, 'And it feels like it makes sense to keep trying to push it.'

There were definitely plans to make something new, perhaps a new album, which might happen in 2014, he said. The interviewer, Scott Heisel, managing editor of *Alternative Press*, posited that the reissue, or deluxe edition, was a little like George Lucas remastering the *Star Wars* movies. 'But with no fucking Jar-Jar Binks,' Jack insisted, once more referencing the CGI dimbulb that so marred the long-awaited Episode I of the franchise. The band's increased cultural embedding continued with Jillian Jensen – from the US version of TV show *The X-Factor* – releasing a cover of 'Therapy'. She did a decent job of it, albeit with a vocal absolutely shrouded in cathedral-sized reverb somewhat at odds with the intimate, self-searching lyrics.

As for the live work, the ironically named House Party

tour, which actually took the bands to a number of arenas, was going down well with fans and journalists. The brilliantly named Black Squirrel Radio attended the gig at Columbus, Ohio, and called the tour one of the biggest – maybe *the* biggest – of the year. Opening act The Wonder Years – a band that since 2010 had been actively climbing the pop-punk tree – kicked it off nicely. All Time Low were onstage next and the crowd lost their minds as soon as they hit the stage: 'While it was great to hear old songs such as 'Coffee Shop Soundtrack', it was their new song, 'A Love Like War', that stole the show. Vic Fuentes of Pierce the Veil came out to do his guest vocals, and the band sounded tighter and better than they had in the previous thirty minutes. Closing their set with mega hit 'Dear Maria' set the crowd into huge singalong mode and dozens of crowd surfers made their way to the barrier.' Pierce the Veil similarly smashed it and A Day to Remember headlined with a blasting set of their own.

The tour came to an end in the last week of October, when it was time to say farewell and good luck to one of the most instrumental members of the All Time Low team. Matt Flyzik, who had been there more or less since the start as tour manager, friend, brother and general all-round fixit guy, was to leave the camp after seven years and seventy-four days.

The twenty-seven-year-old Mickey Mouse fanatic spoke at length to Alter the Press! about his decision to leave. He explained that even before hooking up with ATL he had toured with other bands as well as his own, meaning he'd spent the majority of the last nine years on the road. He'd started feeling it was tricky being away from home quite so much and therefore he'd been pondering taking his leave for some time.

Touring with such a successful band meant that he'd got to see a lot more than some people ever did, he acknowledged, but it was the home comforts that he was beginning to hanker for. Having mates, a local pub, sleeping in your own bed and putting down roots were beginning to prey on his mind, he said. 'And you see a lot of these crew guys who are in their 40s and 50s and don't have a life. They don't have a wife, kids but have this cool stuff like some people collect cars but they are not able to use them.'

Matt had told himself that by the time he was thirty years of age he'd step out of the melee, but had decided to pre-empt that, partly due to the fact that All Time Low would be taking some months off after the House Party tour to rest and re-energise. If ever there was a good time to go, it was now in order that his friends would be able to find a replacement in plenty of time for the next set of gigs. It had been a decision that he'd mulled over for the best part of a year; he said that he'd given himself every chance to think about it; pondering, for example, that those tours might be the last time he ever visited Japan or Europe as part of the ATL family. He found, he said, that he was OK with those prospects in general, albeit that he was sad to go and the band were sad to see him go likewise. In fact, there had been talks in the camp of any possible ways to keep him involved but ultimately the band understood his decision. That didn't stop it being difficult, however, with all feeling the imminent parting deeply.

'They were pretty sad and there were some tears shed,' he said, 'but I'll still talk to them quite a bit. I still talk to their manager every day.' He likened it to breaking up with a girlfriend – except having to do it twelve times, in terms of crew members, the band, the management and so on. He reminisced that he'd been roped into appearing in videos, singing harmonies and doing all sorts of stuff since he'd first toured with the lads as a merch guy and said that he almost certainly wouldn't manage another band – he felt so close to All Time Low that it would feel like a slap in the face to them if he went on the road with anyone else. 'The guys are so family orientated, when the show was over, we all wanted to hang out with each other and when you work for bigger artists, there is such a separation between band and crew. I don't think I would enjoy working with someone else who would want to get straight to their hotel room, go see their baby-sitter. They just want you to be just their [tour manager],' he told the interviewer.

Thankfully, the talented Matt stayed in music, working for Idobi Network as events manager as well as tour manager for Showtek and Nocturnal Touring. He also has his own business, J.M. Flyzik Management. As of 2015, Time Low's tour manager was Brian Southall, who had played virtually every instrument onstage with various bands from 1999 onwards and tour-managed Motion City Soundtrack since 2009.

CHAPTER 30

A NEW HOPE

*T*he rest of 2013 passed in relatively sedate mode, with one more release to round the year off. This time, the band had a seasonal track on *Punk Goes Christmas*, a Hopeless Records LP that also featured the likes of New Found Glory, Yellowcard, Real Friends and Crown the Empire, who win the misery-guts title of the year award for 'There Will Be No Christmas'. The Baltimore boys' song, 'Fool's Holiday', was a little more user-friendly than their previous, irascible seasonal ditty. Opening with the traditional, cheesy sound of bells, the song goes on to talk about broken promises and the faults of the protagonist, who is desperate to win back the heart of a love that he's wronged through his own mistakes. It's another departure from what one might call the All Time Low pop-punk sound and far from a throwaway effort knocked off in five minutes for a seasonal album; it's a really good piece of music featuring a great solo by Jack and a very wintry middle eight.

On 3 December, Alex posted a video that showed the lads were in the studio once more, creating and writing tracks. Jack was fully recovered from minor surgery he'd had in November, having taken the opportunity to put himself in for the equivalent of an MOT once the car was off the road. I mean, Jack's the car, and the MOT ... I mean ... anyway he was better, so that was good. He also managed to catch his beloved Ravens (American Football team Baltimore Ravens), feed his pet turtles, catch up with his brother Joe and visit NYC as a tourist during the downtime.

Such are the vagaries of publishing that an interview that Alex and Jack had given to *NKDMag* a month or two previously had just hit the streets. The lads looked back at the band's career and Alex explained what the future would hold. 'I think we're going to write the best record we ever have,' he began. 'We're going to get all the radio success we've ever wanted, take over the world, and then break up.' Of course, as ever this was tongue-in-cheek, with the vocalist quickly affirming, 'That last part's not serious, we have no plans to break up in the next five years. We're having too much fun.' He also said that there was a tour of the United States to come, where the band would hook up with groups they hadn't previously toured with, plus some work abroad before the band would concentrate on new material. Given that 2013 marked a decade as a group with a consistent line-up, it was also definitively the case, he said, that if anyone quit the band then the band would break up. The family spirit, once again.

As the year ended, the lads' tour with Pierce the Veil,

Mayday Parade and You Me at Six, aka Spring Fever, was voted by Alter the Press! as their favourite one of 2013. On 19 December Jack posted a video on his Keek account, which enables short clips to be uploaded. In it he showed that he had taken receipt of his first ever customised personal guitar, courtesy of ESP. It's from the Eclipse range. He said it made him miss touring and he could not wait to get back out there. The axe in question featured his signature on the headstock and pictures of sinister-looking pumpkins on the fretboard. As he said, 'Fucking awesome!' Jack has used a range of different gear over the years including Gibson SG, Paul Reed Smith SC245 and the good old Fender Stratocaster. Not all at the same time; he's not Doctor Octopus.

Hopeless Records turned twenty that month too, with a party being held to commemorate a label that had succeeded for its own blend of talent-spotting, hard work, family atmosphere and business savvy. The event was in aid of charity, raising awareness for Foundation Fighting Blindness, one of many charities that the label had supported over the years. Louis Posen, who founded the label, summed it up:

There is a proverb that says, "If you want to go quickly, go alone. If you want to go far, go together." We recognize these past 20 years have everything to do with the fortune and opportunity to work with amazing fans, co-workers, artists, managers, agents, distributors, retailers, media outlets, individuals and organizations. There aren't words to describe the level of gratitude and appreciation we feel for all those who have supported Hopeless Records and Sub City these first 20 years. We hope we have given to you as much as you have given to us.

Amen to that, brother.

Jack was at the party and told *Alternative Press* that he loved the family atmosphere at the label. 'Every band on their label gets a lot of attention, which is really rare,' he explained. 'That's why we went back to Hopeless, because we knew that on Hopeless we were going to get the attention that we wanted.' The guitarist was hanging out with Marky Capicotto, who said that Hopeless were Glamour Kills' favourite label to work with. It was all under the friend umbrella, or as Jack coined it, 'Frumbrella'. Which kinda sounds like a weird GM food mashup, or at least a cream for sensitive intimate issues. 'It's not about gimmicks, it's about good bands who care about their fans. That's it, really, and it works,' he added. He reminisced about the notorious underwear photo shoots All Time Low had done, where the label were less than keen. Still, it all seemed to work out. Marky said that his mum loved Jack and all confirmed that she was, indeed, a very sweet lady. Hooray!

All the lads were suitably refreshed by their lengthy break from the road, which also meant that they were more than ready to get back out there. New songs like 'Me Without You (All I Ever Wanted)' and 'Oh, Calamity!' were in the frame for being performed as the lads set out on the A Love Like War European tour, running through February and March 2014. The gigs were loud as ever, as Smash Press noted when they attended the boys' show at the world-famous Paradiso club in Amsterdam. The band opened with 'Do You Want

Me (Dead?)' and cooled things down mid-set with the duo of 'Remembering Sunday' and 'Therapy'.

During 'Time-Bomb', two girls were invited onstage. At one point another fan fainted and Alex stopped the song so she could get treatment. The vocalist also had a go at twerking and he and Jack also put balloons up their shirts – instant bosoms. Another fan rushed the stage before security dragged them off again. Alex called the fan a 'ninja assassin' – tongue-in-cheek as ever. According to my translation (by way of the always entertaining Google Translate), the review ended thus: 'All Time Low still knows how to make the audience a great evening must deliver. There will today have put several people gaping at school (including yours truly), but it was well worth it.'

Jack also explained that he had three tattoos: 'I enjoy them very much but they hurt like a bitch to get,' he told Dutch Scene. He showed the camera his Blink-182 bunny, Rian's version of which had been so instrumental in the two bands meeting up. He also has Jack Skellington from *The Nightmare Before Christmas*, playing one of Jack's guitars. In the future, he reckoned, he would get more tattoos, including one of the Baltimore Ravens crest. The guitarist said that people did judge those with tattoos but maybe a little less than in the past. He added that it would be cool to have a lawyer with ink, if he was great at his job. Finally, he revealed that when he was seventeen he'd wanted to get his lip pierced but his mum advised him to wait a year – by which time he didn't want the procedure any more. If he wasn't in a band, he'd still get tattoos though. A lot of his mates back home who weren't involved with music had them, so why not? It wasn't something to rush into, of course, he noted.

Three days later, the tour moved to Vienna and Cassadee Pope joined our chaps onstage for 'Remembering Sunday'. The band was interviewed by a Slovenian journalist at the gig. Alex revealed that the new album was at a very early stage of the process. 'I don't know when anyone's going to hear anything,' he began. 'I think we would like to have a record recorded by the end of the year but it's kind of up in the air. We don't have any commitments to [a timescale], we're just going to let it happen.'

Jack announced that it would in fact be the best album ever. The lads also talked about the difficulties of scheduling co-headlining tours because all the bands involved had different release dates and commitments. Alex said that when it came to choosing where to tour, the band definitely had a say; for example, on the current tour a lot of Slovenian fans had made it to Vienna, so the next time around, that country would hopefully be added to the list. Promoter interest was also key, Jack added. As for touring Europe, the boys said that the crowds were great. 'There are some places where you play,' Jack mused, 'and the crowd, you need to get them to do it, but in Europe as soon as you play a song the crowd goes crazy.' He said that he didn't read the 'Jalex' fan fiction, which generally had the guitarist and singer in a gay relationship. 'I do love Jack, but not his butt,' Alex said. He also said that he wanted to be the first pregnant male, so messing about was never too far away.

A new season of *Full Frontal* began on 24 February – keeping the lads happy and out of trouble while on the road and concurrently giving them an outlet for their more strange jokes. The season finale was on 28 April and featured Mark

Hoppus and Sean Mackin, violinist with Yellowcard. The Paris gig on 5 March was notable for the rare performance of 'Guts', one of Alex's favourite All Time Low tracks, plus 'Vegas', which delighted the crowd. The boys also pulled out 'All the Small Things' and even 'Killing in the Name', by Rage against the Machine. It was a triumphant return to the French capital and this time Alex was in rude health rather than stricken as he had been on the previous visit. The lads managed to play in Dublin on St Patrick's Day, 17 March, and the tour ended with several dates in the UK, traditionally one of the most productive territories for the band.

The O2 Academy in Birmingham had the group bringing fans on stage, as had become customary during 'Time-Bomb'. *Riot Magazine* summed it up: 'All Time Low are more than just a great band with followers. As well as demonstrating their fantastic musical abilities, the band also demonstrated an intimate level of kinship with their fan base.' The band, reckoned the writer, were the best at what they did, and no doubt about it.

At the London gig, Jenna McDougall of Tonight Alive joined the chaps onstage for 'A Love Like War'. It was a celebratory occasion for the lads, with Jack using a bra as a headband as they launched into their set, which for this tour was the longest they'd ever played in the UK. Zack and Jack had a game of chase during 'Lost in Stereo' while the backdrop showed first the band dressed as knights then zombies. This time, the cover the band chucked in was Journey's classic AOR track, 'Don't Stop Believin'. That gig at the Brixton Academy in London was filmed by *NME*. 'The UK tour has been incredible,' Alex remarked. He said the venue was one of the most historic and cool venues out there and that it was great to play on the stage that had hosted so many famous names of the past. 'The two hours that we're onstage really define us as a band. We had taken a long break of four months off before this tour … we walk offstage every day and go, "Yeah, that's why we do this." It's people screaming lyrics back at you and having an amazing time.'

The vocalist added that the rest of 2014 was looking open-ended. The band, he explained, was in a good position in that they had a lot of music out there, including *Don't Panic*, which was doing really well. All that considered there was no need to force themselves to grind a record out just to have new material. After the American dates, he said, they would have some downtime, and rather than just go in to a studio and quickly bash out twelve songs it was better to have a narrative for the record, which fans always reacted better to anyway. A more immediate bit of trivia to share was that Alex and Jack also praised the catering while on tour in the UK; breakfast, lunch and dinner all laid on by Sugar & Spice On Tour Catering. Usually, the singer said, he'd lose weight on tour but this time around he was stuffing in the good eats, including a great Banoffee Pie. As a result he was putting on weight.

The States were next up as March turned into April, the tour now named A Love Like tour. Support acts for this run were Man Overboard and Handguns, the latter band having worked with Alex on some music. He was credited with vocal production on their 2014 release, *Life Lessons*, which had been produced and engineered by old mate Paul Leavitt. Brandon Pagano, guitarist with Handguns, said that the experience had been great.

At first, we really loved the songs the way that they were, and we made it to the point where we thought, 'This is the record. This is the one we wanted to hear back.' Taylor [Eby, vocalist] and I worked with him for a week straight almost every single day. It was awesome because he's worked with a lot of really big name producers, co-written with Hoppus and he's at the point where he knows his way around it. When he starts producing records it's going to be a cool thing because he's already got it down.

Eby also said in the interview with Substream that Alex had a brilliant ear for music, melody and vocal parts. Handguns, at a relatively early stage in their career, were also learning from being on the tour with All Time Low in terms of stagecraft, onstage banter and tightness of playing.

Everyone needs to pay their dues at some stage and the Baltimore boys certainly did their own share back in the early days. On 1 April – April Fools' Day – the lads were in Jacksonville, Florida, and their prank on the fans was to open the set with 'Dear Maria, Count Me In', which of course would almost always be one of the final encores. By All Time Low's standards that was a pretty lame one but it definitely would have wrong-footed long-time supporters. A reviewer caught the gig at Rialto Theatre, Tuscon. By 4pm there had been a line of fans two blocks long in the 95-degree Arizona heat, to the extent that venue staff went around distributing water to all and sundry, although some had already got ill from the queuing.

The gig was great, though, said the subsequent review in

Concertlivewire. 'This was a 90-minute non-stop show of relentless energy by both the crowd and the band. There were multiple episodes of crowd surfing as well as dancing, arm swaying and singing along. There was nothing passive about this insane crowd and the band did as much as they could to interact and keep the party going.' The next night, the lads pulled out a surprising cover version, this time 'My Own Worst Enemy', the 1999 song by Lit that had spent eleven weeks at Number 1 in the US Modern Rock Chart.

As the tour featured many new or under-served cities, the boys were able to explore a lot of places, including Milwaukee, Wisconsin. During an interview at the 19 April gig, Alex revealed that Jeff Maker reckoned he'd seen a ghost that day. 'He was in the room alone starting to set up lights,' the singer noted to The Rave TV. 'And he saw someone running across the floor but the room was empty.' Spooky! The tour had nearly all sold out, even in the towns and cities that the band had not previously visited and even though there was no new material to push. 'I can't understand why people aren't sick of us,' Jack joked. 'We tour a lot.'

After the tour, Alex said, the band was going to disappear for a bit in order to work on some new music. 'We don't really have any deadlines, which is a nice place to be,' he said. The group wanted to take the opportunity to let things grow more organically for the new album. Alex also definitively addressed rumours that the band would break up or go on hiatus after the tour. That was simply not true, he reassured fans. It had been slightly exacerbated by one of his own tweets, which some had taken as being of more significance than it actually was. 'I'm squashing that one right now,' the musician said.

Jack and Zack said that instead they were going to start up their own company: JZ Guacamole. Alex preferred Guac and Roll for the proposed name. And so the silliness returned from a serious moment. Phew!

The tour wrapped up with a hometown gig on 3 May. The show, at the 1,600-capacity Ram's Head Live in Baltimore, had been sold out for at least a month. The set was a bumper twenty-one songs long and the boys also played snippets of tracks by Blink-182, Green Day and Wheatus. Sight of Sound was in attendance and reckoned that 'All Time Low have been on a roll for the past three years, gaining more success with each sold-out tour they play and *A Love Like Tour* was certainly no exception.' It would be the last live show for a while but Alex did announce that the band would be playing a very special benefit gig on 12 July.

A Concert for Casey would feature the full band playing acoustically at Baltimore Soundstage in the inner harbour of that city. The performance had been set up to benefit The Center for Child and Infant Loss, which works with communities and families in Maryland that have tragically lost their children. Tiny Casey Leavitt, son of producer Paul, had gone to sleep on 5 July, five days before his first birthday. Tragically, the tot never woke up. A more worthy cause you could not find and All Time Low's involvement in this and many other charities is heartfelt and admirable.

CHAPTER 31

FROM THE HEART

*T*he group kept the music flowing and on 14 May put out a video for 'The Irony of Choking on a Lifesaver', which pulled together loads of clips from their recent touring antics, showing the band off in their most loved environment while the crowds went nuts as usual. Rian rightly gets a good amount of time because this song features some of his most beefy, driving drum fills, pushing the song ever further into rock despite its relatively pop-punk framework. Those *na-na-nas* are as irresistible as ever they were, too. And that was about it for the first half of 2014; the chaps went their separate ways, enjoyed some holidays and started to get their heads around a planned new record.

A month after the lads played the final show of their tour, they were briefly back in action for a special appearance at the gig on 11 June 2014 for the VANS Road To Warped Tour, at

Anchorage in Alaska. Alex explained the reasons for All Time Low's appearance there. 'When we heard Warped was doing a show in Alaska we really reached out to get here. It sounded like a great opportunity to get here for the first time,' he told local paper *The Frontiersman*. The partnership director of Warped said that it was all about discovering new acts: 'The local scene is so important to that, and it's really an honor to be out in Alaska to see local acoustic and rock acts in addition to some of our veteran bands that have come out with us so many years like All Time Low and Yellowcard.'

While up in the territory, the Baltimoreans had a quick mooch around the spectacular Alaska Wildlife Reserve. Alex was clearly inspired: on his return, 13 June, he announced on Twitter that he was getting back to work on the new record. He joked that he'd finish it that day and get it out with no fanfare, much as Beyoncé had famously done with her 2013, self-titled record that came out on iTunes with videos for every song, but with no pre-publicity. What we did know about the record was that it was to be produced mostly by John Feldmann and some by Mike Green.

A Show for Casey took place on 12 July. There were three support bands: 3PM, Cinder Wall and Like You to Me. In the highly charged atmosphere it was rather intense for an acoustic concert and Paul Leavitt joined the band onstage to play 'Hear You Me', an extremely emotional moment among many that night. That track, by Jimmy Eat World, is about wanting to sing a song just one more time to a person who has been lost. The gig raised $18,000 for the Center for Infant and Child Loss.

The guys played a few shows for United States troops over-seas during this period but were next seen onstage by civilians at the *Alternative Press* awards, 2014. They performed a medley of tracks including 'Dear Maria, Count Me In', 'Lights and Sounds' by Yellowcard, and 'All Downhill from Here', the Ne Found Glory song. Ryan Key of Yellowcard, plus Jordan Pundik and Chad Gilbert of New Found Glory, joined in the fun. All Time Low walked away with the award for Song of the Year for their mighty Vic Fuentes-featuring 'A Love Like War', which they also performed on the night. Alex expressed his thanks for the award and added that every song on the shortlist was incredible. He thanked the fans who had voted as well as Vic, who'd made the song so special. They also won the Artist Philanthropic Award for their work alongside Skate4Cancer, which had long had information stalls at the band's various tours of the States. 'This is not only for us, this is entirely for Rob Dyer and for Skate4Cancer,' Alex told the crowd. 'He has been busting his ass spreading awareness across countries and doing amazing things to change the world ... Every band that's out there standing for something fucking wins tonight.'

The chaps spoke to *Artisan News* a week or so later when attending an event in the Cleveland, Ohio, Rock and Roll Hall of Fame. A bestubbled Alex confirmed that there were a lot of songs being written at that point and that there was plenty of time to focus on music. When asked when fans might hear some of the new stuff he said, 'Some time next year. We're not rushing it out.'

Another odd but great gig was an after-party the boys played at San Diego Comic-Con, 2014, for the *Her Universe* Fashion Show. That brought together over thirty designers to promote their geeky fashion designs. As big fans of comic culture the Hot Topic after-party was a perfect event for the lads to get involved with. At the party, they met actors from the phenomenon that is TV series *Game of Thrones*, a big thrill for all concerned.

A new-but-old release hit the streets in July, too, with the re-release of *So Wrong, It's Right* as a limited edition of 1,000 copies of orange splatter vinyl. It's a beautiful thing and those who were able to get hold of one own a piece of art that you just can't get from a download, so there! *Put Up or Shut Up* was given a similar treatment that December in an even more limited edition of just 500, this time on white, green and gold splatter vinyl. It's a beautiful thing and ... well, you know where this one's heading, no?

August 2014 brought news that finally something would be actually done about that pesky long-discussed *Straight to DVD II*. Wembley Arena, no less, would be the venue for a concert on 25 March 2015. This special headlining arena show in the 12,500-capacity venue would be filmed especially for a new live DVD project. At last! As if to celebrate, Alex headed back to his birth country to join You Me at Six live at the Reading Festival. The frontman joined the UK act for 'Fresh Start Fever', which was fairly apt given the new writing sessions going on that summer. It was doubly apt that the bands' closeness was illustrated, as they would be touring the UK's arenas as co-headliners in February 2015.

Jack was keeping rather busy at this time, videoing himself being covered with a bucket of icy water as part of the ongoing ALS Ice Bucket Challenge, which raised awareness of Lou Gehrig's disease, or amyotrophic lateral sclerosis. The craze spanned the world during late summer and early autumn 2014 and raised many, many pounds for research into the currently incurable disease.

Jack had plenty of ice on hand, as he'd just started a new venture – co-owning the Rockwell Bar in Baltimore's Fells Point. He'd been involved with the venue more and more as 2014 went on, and he'd always frequented it because it played good music. Bryan Burkert, who also owned the Baltimore record shop Sound Garden, had asked him to come in on the project, which would be a bar dedicated purely to rock 'n' roll. The guitarist explained his motivation to *Alternative Press*: 'I go out a lot; I have a good time, I like to party. There haven't been that many bars I go that have a rock 'n' roll vibe like there used to be, kind of a craziness to them. It's all about hip-hop and pop and mainstream music. I was like, "Let's fucking do a bar that plays old '80s rock and metal, new rock, old school, whatever it is—just plays good music. We don't leave that genre. We don't have a night where we do club night or whatever. We just want it to be purely a rock bar."' He said that when bands came to play in Baltimore there weren't that many rock pubs for them to go to. He added that he wanted to establish post-gig DJ sets by visiting bands, which would start on 30 August with Alex Gaskarth getting behind the decks. The plan was to have a Jack party once a month where he'd hand out shots.

Another thing he wanted to do was to get the fans to come down for their birthdays. As All Time Low had been around for a decade, he figured that a lot of the long-time supporters would be turning twenty-one (the legal age for drinking in many US states) so why not have the party at the Rockwell? Jack even promised to give out free champagne. The Fells Point location would be tricky, he reckoned, as there are thirty or so bars within around four blocks. Getting people to try out a new place would be key, and to that end things like Taking

Back Sunday, The Starting Line and old-school Blink-182 would be the music of choice. He said that in the UK, where the legal drinking age is eighteen, crowds were younger and so there were loads of non-mainstream bands being played. 'I just love that. You don't have to play these massive Top 40 hits, and everyone can still have a good time. And if the bar doesn't care that it's not a popular song, I appreciate that they would go out on a limb,' concluded the whisky-loving musician.

Sessions were ongoing in the search for new material, with Pierre Bouvier of Simple Plan working on some material, along with Alex and Mark Hoppus on 17 September. Hoppus declared that the results were going to be 'disastrous'. Come 29 September, however, and work on All Time Low's sixth studio album was officially under way. Zack gave an interview to Glenn Clark Radio later in the year where he talked about charity work, including an event on 3 December outside Chick-Fil-A, at which people would be encouraged to bring spare jackets for the Helping Up Mission. That charity was set up to assist homeless veterans and other homeless men in need of food, shelter or help to recover from addiction. The bassist explained further: 'The people at Helping Up [Mission] introduced us to the whole building and the process, and they have an overnight shelter for people who need overnight [accommodation]. And then, they stay there long enough, they're kind of put into the whole program where everyone gets their own job. No matter what it is, everyone is doing something within the facility. So when you're walking around, you think it's all employees, but actually they're people who are trying to get their lives back together. And they have a responsibility, which is a big thing because they have to be accountable for something—and that's part of the process.' He said that while at the facility often people went out to try and get jobs and cited the example of a man he'd met wearing a suit, who was employed for motivational speaking in schools. It turned out that the guy had received that suit the previous day from the charity.

Talk turned to the band. 'We have just finished recording our new record,' announced the bassist. 'It comes out in March and we are touring it [from February in the UK] ... Everyone over there is [really into the band], it's so cool. The UK is where punk music was born so it really makes sense. All the venues have [history] to them. We played Brixton, Nirvana played Brixton; the Stones ... you can't find that as much here. We played CBGBs but now that's gone.' America was a relatively new country in comparison to some places in Europe, with buildings dating from five hundred years ago, he added.

Something else was new, too: the title of the album. It would be called *Future Hearts*, and would come out on 17 April 2015. But by early January of that year, Alex was ready to speak about it to *Rock Sound*: 'It's been really crazy. We spent a lot of time last year and even into this year writing, recording and setting up this record, so it feels awesome to finally hit it and hit it hard, you know?' He continued to speak about a new video, which hit the streets on 12 January for the new track, 'Something's Gotta Give', directed by Chris Marrs. It's one of the band's morning-after-the-night-before ditties with the protagonist having woken up in a stranger's bed – Alex is dressed as a giant pack of fries and meets up with a girl, other band members, guests and loads of people with whom he is being über-friendly, but none of them, not least his girl from the night before, wants to know him. The song even stops midway through the video so that he can catch his breath after getting a stitch. It is then revealed that in fact he's a zombie, something that spreads to the rest of the band, who are playing live. There's also lots of product placement for Rockstar energy drinks. Alex's character then proceeds to feast on the sweet, sweet flesh of all he comes across, including the poor little kitty of his lover (not a euphemism). Something did indeed give – she shoots him squarely through the head. Hell of a video, with splatter credentials as well as being very, very funny and with lyrics that talk about sinking in a town that's dying and wanting to get out and live properly, about doubt and dreams, about critical mass building up.

One slightly daft rumour that went around at this point was that the new LP would be called *Slappy Joe's Burgers and Fries*, the burger joint in the video for whom Alex's character is dressed up. He even recorded a thirty-second 'commercial' for the imminent opening said to be at Manhattan Beach, California. Sadly, on 13 January 'a representative' for the burger joint tweeted that plans to open had been permanently cancelled. It's almost as if it was someone messing about with social media profiles to amuse themselves, isn't it? Shame, really, because unlike an egg, you sure can't beat a good goddamn burger 'n' chips. The whole process had been tough to keep quiet, though, Alex remarked; he wanted to share things as soon as they were ready but the album was still three months away from hitting the streets.

It would, however, mark a progression rather than a departure from the previous album, so while there was some material that was in the vein of *Don't Panic*, there would be stuff that represented a step forward too. He added that All Time Low were absolutely raring to get out there on the co-headliner with You Me at Six because there was something of a friendly competition between the bands to really rock it, which would drive both groups to put on a great show. 'Also, we haven't played in a while. We haven't played shows in general since we've been making this album. It's a little intimidating to think we'll be knocking the rust off with a show to 9,000 people in Cardiff. That's the one where it's like, "Alright, let's give it a try and see if this thing still works!" It's a little nerve-wracking, but it'll be fun. It's a really good way to start the year. We'll start big and get in that mindset.'

Following the February dates, there was the looming prospect of that massive Wembley Arena show for the planned new DVD. It had sold out in just over a week, which spoke for itself. The lads also did an interview with *Alternative Press*, which aired on that mighty site the same week, in which Alex said that social media's reach directly to fans meant that these days everything had huge hype attached to it. He expressed his admiration for Beyoncé just putting out that famous surprise record. 'It was almost like, "Fuck the hype train",' he mused. 'Why build it up and sell it? Just put it out and hope that people love it.' It wasn't the same as getting excited about a new release after having read about it in a magazine.

Jack took over the thread and said that in days gone by there would be press releases or studio updates but now fans were firmly part of the process in that they could see where the record was at through the videos and posts on social media by the band over the course of the process. Rian said that once upon a time it was a case of trying to catch a new single on a specific radio show, which would be the first material from a new record. These days, one way or another you could get to hear new music way in advance.

Josh Francheschi of YMA6 and Alex sat down with Sugarscape on the eve of the largely sold-out tour. 'We did a tour together in America,' Josh said of how the co-headlining dates had come about, 'and we saw the benefits of putting together a strong package for the fans who come to the shows [...] there was more than one band they came to see but the hysteria [...] the energy in the room, people would really be reacting [to all the bands.]' The two bands had always been keen to bring that idea to the UK.

Alex explained that the reaction to 'Something's Gotta Give' had been great and that as the band had not been outwardly active and gigging of late he was genuinely excited to have something new to release. The album had a lot of depth to it and that song was the perfect one to bridge the gap between *Don't Panic* and what would be *Future Hearts*. He denied that 5 Seconds of Summer were listed on the album as co-writers, a rumour that had gained traction due to someone vandalising the album's Wikipedia page. He said he would love to work with them in the future on their own tracks, maybe. Alex and Josh both said that online they had both been listed as dead at one time or another, so you really couldn't believe everything you read online.

Back to work, then, and the bands began that tour at the Motorpoint Arena, Cardiff, on 9 February. Walk the Moon took the stage first, then All Time Low ran onstage with some excitement. 'An instant wave of ecstatic atmosphere sweeps the arena,' wrote *Buzzmag*. 'A nod to the lighting director is deserved: the pyrotechnics and eye-watering strobe lighting are fantastic, and add to ATL's fun-loving colourful vibe.' The writer also noted that Josh had broken his ankle, nearly leading to the cancellation of the gig, but that YMA6 played a charismatic set. The contrast between the bands, said the writer, made for a great night.

The date at Birmingham's Genting Arena was also notable for the lighting and production, said the *Birmingham Mail*. 'The band's stage presence portrayed confidence that was fueled by the ever-loving fans, who were ready to create one big party atmosphere,' was the verdict. The esteemed *Guardian* was a little more sniffy about it, saying that the bands were rarely covered outside the pages of the likes of *Kerrang!* or *Smash Hits* but that the arena nonetheless was filled with 'screaming teenage girls'. The reviewer reckoned that All Time Low were generic pop-punk, joking about wanking and getting everyone to sing along. That said, 'their Blink-Weezer-McBusted-y songs get hands in the air, and there's a certain zip about the tunes. These likable dorks are easy enough to warm to.' Still, it was all in good spirits and plenty of mickey taking and good honest fun was the order of the day.

Alex had got himself into a bit of a spat on Twitter, after watching a telecast by the Grammies which introduced the It's On Us campaign, an organisation that helped to raise awareness of and wipe out sexual assault. He noted that Chris Brown was in attendance at the event. Brown had notoriously assaulted ex-girlfriend Rihanna in 2009. Maybe people like Brown ought not to be invited, he tweeted. Brown responded by saying, 'you sound really perfect brother ... How can I get those VIP tickets to the pearly gates bro ... Seems like you have it down.' He subsequently deleted the tweet. Alex replied with two tweets, widely reported in the press: 'I'm not worried about the pearly gates RN, man. Worried about here and now … And double standards. And the messages we send.' The second was, 'Shouldn't target individuals. Uncalled for, maybe? Or maybe it had to be said. Either way, sleep! "Be excellent to each other," – Bill & Ted.'

The tour wrapped up on 14 February, Valentine's Day. Alex and the boys flew home for a few days, during which the singer announced that he had asked his long-term girlfriend Lisa Ruocco to marry him. Inspired by Beyoncé, he'd put a ring on it, he tweeted on 18 February. Sweet! It also put paid to long-term rumours that he and Taylor Swift were, had been, wanted to be, or should be an item. Shake it off, Tay-Tay.

The next live dates were imminent, however, so there was little time to get all that cosy: Australia's Soundwave beckoned once more. The first gig was at Melbourne, where *Music Feeds* caught up with Jack and Zack. The guitarist noted that it was the band's seventh time in Australia, which was some going as it was only ten years since they'd formed. 'Seventy per cent of our [lives] have been over here,' he half joked. 'You could not be further away from our house [in Baltimore] right now, technically.' The band had loved Soundwave since they first appeared there at the age of around nineteen and had always made a point of trying to get back regularly. 'The shows are great,' Zack smiled, 'The weather is great, the women are really great, the men are great …' Jack said that the lads were well rested after doing the album and really up for getting back out on the road. 'For eight months we were hibernating, like bears,' Zack added. 'Now you wake up, you hunt, you fish, whatever,' he concluded, tying up the metaphor niftily.

Alex was busy too, speaking with *Team Rock* about the

last time they'd played Soundwave in 2013, when Blink-182 also played, upping the enjoyment. 'The line-ups are really diverse,' he said. 'This year we're doing it, there's Marilyn Manson, Slipknot, Fall Out Boy: [...] it gives us the chance to play for people that may not come to an All Time Low show normally. If we can win a few of those people over, then great.' He rated Australian crowds as some of the best; like the States the audiences listened to a lot of stuff but down under they'd never stopped loving pop-rock, which meant the band really felt at home. The gigs went off in suitably raucous style, aside from the Sydney show on 1 March.

The lads always said that playing in the rain helped people shed their inhibitions, but concurrently there are obvious limits. In the case of the Olympic Park show, the downpour was so heavy and harsh that it irreparably damaged the band's gear, forcing them offstage and unable to play. There could be no rescheduling so Alex grabbed a microphone and headed out onstage, leading the crowd in an a cappella singalong first of 'Weightless' and then of Queen's 'We Will Rock You'. It was some consolation for the disappointed fans and band; Jack later tweeted that there might well be a future visit to Australia from All Time Low later in 2015.

There was also a quick visit to New Zealand for a couple of gigs, somewhere that the lads had felt they needed to make a priority after fans' repeated social media requests for a visit to that country. Alex added that the Internet had been good in lots of ways for music and musicians. 'I remember being a kid and you picked one genre and stuck to it and if you didn't you were a poser. Now, because of the internet and how much people are exposed to, they listen to lots of different music,' he told the *NZ Herald*. 'It's a cool age where kids are listening to One Direction, All Time Low, Lady Gaga and a country artist.' He also revealed that he was a fan of New Zealand gothy popstrel Lorde, who was even being produced by alternative pop and punk dude Joel Little.

In the meantime, fans were treated to the second single from the new album, 'Kids in the Dark'. The music was put out via Twitter on 9 March with the video the next day, this time directed by Sitcom Soldiers, who had also worked with the likes of Sleeping with Sirens and Of Mice and Men. This time, there ain't zombies but there are a lot of youngsters looking for meaning – the titular children are having a secret rendezvous unbeknown to their parents. Turns out it's an All Time Low-led party, with absolutely tons of glowing paint being chucked around in a celebration of life, of the outsider, of ploughing your own furrow. Lyrically, Alex sings about the hill crumbling – and sending people back down again. Leaving kids in the dark, he sings, means either burning out or lighting sparks – either way the world can do as it pleases but the kids will never surrender. As the various band members had been alluding to, it's definitely recognisable as an All Time Low song, with all the hooks and pulsating drums you'd expect while adding some epic singalong choruses. Timeless stuff.

Back in the here and now, however, there was the small matter of a few more dates across Europe before returning to the UK for that 20 March One Night in London gig at Wembley Arena, and with it the full-on long-rumoured recording for the maybe-sometime release-possibly of another live DVD. Woot!

CHAPTER 32

CONQUERING LONDON AND RELEASING THE ALBUM

'London is a really cool place to play,' Jack told *Music Scene*. 'Because people will fly from all around the world to get there. We hope it's gonna be all the biggest All Time Low fans from around the world all in one room.'

And so it proved. The atmosphere was electric as support bands Real Friends and Neck Deep ramped the atmosphere up even further. The huge production values were evident from the start, with pyrotechnics going off as the lads launched into 'A Love Like War' and then 'Lost in Stereo'. Rian had thankfully recovered from a severe migraine that he'd suffered on the way to a Radio 1 interview the previous day – he'd had to head back to the hotel and rest instead. The set pulled out all the favourites, with the band absolutely on top form. Even 'Weightless' went down relatively early before Alex moved to a second stage for his customary quieter performances, with Cassadee Pope joining him for 'Remembering Sunday'. 'Kids in the Dark' led to a huge singalong, this despite the fact that it'd only recently been unleashed to the world, and Josh Franceschi came on to add his vocals to 'Outlines'. The encore simply blew the roof off with the triple assault of 'The Reckless and the Brave', 'Jasey Rae' and 'Dear Maria, Count Me In'. It was a flawless performance from the lads and the banter was in full effect – at one stage Jack decided he was going to invite the entire crowd back to his hotel room. The boys stayed in the UK for some acoustic in-store performances and signings and departed back home at the end of March.

Music was flying out by now, with another new track, 'Runaways', streamed on MTV on 23 March and their Mark Hoppus collaboration, 'Tidal Waves', briefly popping up on Fuse three days later before being officially released the next day. There was an accompanying *Making of...* type video a couple of days later which featured the Blink-182 lad laying down his vocals, the boys playing with a dog and the musicians generally having fun getting the track together. It was yet another almost unbearable throw forward to the album that was about to come. Before it was finally out, though, the band had to get as high as possible ... with an acoustic performance at the top of the Empire State Building in New York City on 6 April. How goddamn cool was that? *Artisan News* was there to record the experience as the boys sang their little hearts out to 'Something's Gotta Give'. Alex said that he'd been up the Empire State Building when he was nine years old, on a field trip, but for Jack it was his first time ever. Alex also explained the title of the new record: 'It's kind of an ode to all of our endeavours; we almost feel like we are on the right path, on to something big. It's a representation of what you are shooting for and what you want from the future is worth it.'

Future Hearts was released on 7 April 2015 in the United States. The first track is 'Satellite', which opens with walkie-talkie-like chatter before launching into a segment with a truly epic feel, reminiscent of Queen's 'We Will Rock You'. Alex's voice is more gravelly than ever before on record as the track builds up critical mass. It's one hell of a way to open an album. Sonically it is *massive*: synth pads, rumbling bass, enormous reverb on the drums and a crescendo that builds up to a double-time coda, where Alex eventually screams that they are just kids, singing. The song was a co-write with Simon Wilcox, who collaborated on several other tracks.

'Kicking & Screaming' comes in after a quick 1-2-3-4 and brings things back into pop-punk territory. It's a track all about chasing after rock 'n' roll but having a dark side of loneliness at the same time and hankering after memories and goodbyes. Alex introduces Jack's solo with a truly rock, 'GO!' The middle-eight breakdown is reminiscent of a church choir, before the energetic track hammers right back in with a brilliant fizz about it with some unison riffing that is as close to old-school punk as the lads had ever been.

The brilliant 'Something's Gotta Give' is next, gang vocals upping the texture and call-and-response vocal-piano parts showing the band and the producer's superior skill with arrangements. This one was co-written with Andrew Goldstein, a huge hitter whose credits also include Celine Dion, Ne-Yo and the easily spooked Demi Lovato. By this point in the album it's clear that All Time Low have put together something pretty special; it's got all the ballsiness of

Don't Panic and the ambition of *Dirty Work* even after just three songs.

'Kids in the Dark' is next up, both nostalgic and a shout at the skies of the future.

'Runaways' takes up the theme of getting out there and not turning back: don't quit, you might be miles from home but together anything is possible. The naysayers and those out to trip you up will just have to look for other people whose hearts they can break. Musically it opens with a very 'Lucy in the Sky with Diamonds'-esque descending organ figure before settling down into an obvious radio single with hooks to burn. That galloping middle eight is a piece of pure pop heaven, heading towards another Beatles-y moment and the final, triumphant expression of individuality of the last chorus. In some ways this is the quintessential All Time Low track and its fadeout expresses the never-ending sentiment that there's still so much to explore.

Nicholas 'Ras' Furlong worked on this one with Alex, as he told the author in an interview for this book. 'I'd been a fan since I was a teenager just getting out of high school,' he explained. 'My friend John Feldmann told me he was doing a record with them. We'd just finished working with 5 Seconds of Summer prior to them going into studio with John and their stuff had gone over phenomenally, a Number 1 record in multiple countries. He asked me to come and meet the guys so I did and we all hung out. After a couple of days it was just cool – I got thrown into the mix of a couple of sessions and we just started writing.' Ras said he had an idea for a chorus and some lyrics, pop-punk but with a big epic chorus. 'We played around with the idea,' he added. 'And people have come back to me and said it's their favourite song on the album.' Not all bands are as open to ideas as All Time Low, he explained. 'Alex is a songwriter at heart, has always been, and is very open-minded. It helps that all of them are really nice guys, down to earth and low key. There was a mutual trust and respect there; they know I would never bring them something that would not hold true to their brand, as a fan.'

'Missing You' has a co-writer credit to Chris Leonard of Son of Dork and is based around various stringed instruments. It's very nearly a hoedown sound and features the banjo, ukulele, mandolin and additional guitar work of Matt Pauling, who also contributed editing, programming, engineering and additional production. How did we get from pop-punk to this?

David Hodges (Evanescence) and Cameron Walker co-wrote the instantly catchy 'Cinderblock Garden', which leads into that long-awaited Mark Hoppus-featuring 'Tidal Waves', written by Feldmann and Wilcox. It's another 1980s-sounding slab of emo-like pop-rock about liars, hidden feelings, feeling stuck but being bashed around by the titular tidal waves.

'Don't You Go', also involving Ras, is one of the band's future singalong favourites, with a driving beat featuring hand-claps which takes a relatively simple song and breaks it down and up again with multiple rhythms and beats, mosh-ready sections and life-affirming backing vocals all over the place. It's sometimes said that the test of a great song is whether it could stand up to being stripped right down or covered in completely different genres, and this is definitely a piece of creative work that fits the bill.

Ras said that he was delighted that both songs he was

involved with ended up on the LP. 'That doesn't usually happen, you know? It was such an easy and effortless process – those guys are so creative and prolific in their craft. They do a great job. You feel like you are hanging out with your buddies. They do what they love, for a living.' He said that during the writing and recording process John Feldmann would play acoustic and Ras would sing the lyrics over the top to see if the band liked it or not. 'Fortunately Alex said there was something there, for sure, so for the rest of the day we worked on it.' Ras is a big fan of UK rock and pop so he wanted to give it a Beatles-y undertone, he noted. 'There's just something about those doo-woppy, happy pop songs that just puts a smile on your face,' he added, citing the Fab Four as an influence on the track.

'Bail Me Out' was written with Joel and Benji Madden of Good Charlotte, Joel's more clipped vocal delivery upping the pop quotient as Rian lays down a skipping beat underneath choppy guitars. It's got a real sense of classic rock about it; that main guitar line could easily be from a track by 1970s UK rock band Free in another dimension.

'Dancing with a Wolf' comes next as the record enters its final furlong, opening with a horror film-like bar or two of organ before Rian's relentless tom-heavy drum rhythm kicks this one into shape. This time, there's a hint of *Thriller*-era Michael Jackson about the song, filtered through decades of punk and pop music and with Alex roaring his defiance about those who have lied to him. Someone is really getting both barrels on this record: cross the singer at your peril, folks. Again, there's a spitting, rough-edged angle to the delivery that brings massive energy to the song. But take a bow,

Rian Dawson: this is your moment and you absolutely kill it throughout. Bravo, sir, bravo!

'The Edge of Tonight', a Feldmann epic, begins with layers of diminished piano chords, heightening the desert-sized atmosphere of the opening loneliness. The main character of the song is being kept safe, sane and alive by the thought of his love, despite all the mistakes and the tiredness and the ever-long roads. It shares the sentiment if not the musical style of the classic 'I Drove All Night' by Roy Orbison. Some sentiments are clearly universal.

The record comes to an end with 'Old Scars/Future Hearts', with All Time Low in rock mode, including some ace robotic vocoder effects on some of the vocals. The sentiment is again that of escape, of not hiding, not being left behind, not fading away. Live your own life, it's yours: get out there and do it. It's a refrain that Alex and the boys had repeatedly stated as a *raison d'être* within their careers and through their music. There are scars on the band's future hearts, they sing and shout, but they will never look back. There is absolutely no doubt about it. This band is not going anywhere anytime soon; these people have a vision and the energy and the chops to realise that vision.

The Deluxe Edition of the record has three extra tracks. 'Bottle and a Beat', a nifty ditty looking back at a love in which all that's needed is indeed a beat and a bottle and a night to play in, includes more of that church organ stuff in the middle of the hymn to fun, youth and happiness.

'Your Bed', as the title suggests, is a plaintive and pleading one as Alex misses his lover. Swathed in synths, this is a full-on torch song in a minor key and it's full of regret and longing.

This time it's Zack who takes the opportunity to provide an interesting bassline that is sparse when it needs to be but when he lets go with smooth glissando turns he brings an additional level of feel to the song.

The last bonus track on the Deluxe Edition is an acoustic version of 'Cinderblock Garden', if you allow the inclusion of a synth as acoustic of course. Still, it's really nice stuff.

There is a different edition of the album out there, which customers of Best Buy, HMV and Suburban Records were able to buy. The extra tracks on that edition are different. They include 'How the Story Ends', another co-write with the Madden gents, which is absolutely injected throughout with rock and pop-punk. It could happily sit on any of All Time Low's LPs, not to mention Good Charlotte's, and it's a cracker. It's also testament to the quality of the album proper that it couldn't quite make it into that narrative. This edition of the LP also features an acoustic version of 'Something's Gotta Give'.

Whichever format the fans bought, they would have clearly and quickly found out that this is All Time Low not just back to their best but pushing the boundaries. It's got stadium-sized songs, intimate songs, pop-punk of course, top-notch guests, co-writers and production from John Feldmann (Alex's main collaborator on most of the tracks). It takes the blueprint of four lads with the classic set-up of bass, drums, two guitars and backing vocals, and adds sophisticated technical and aesthetic layers. Everywhere, the song is at the heart of the production and the time taken to sit down and let it happen organically has paid off in absolute spades. The fact is that this is the album that Interscope should have made with the band;

it truly has everything about it to make it a colossal crossover hit while still pleasing long-term supporters. That said, maybe this couldn't have happened with *Dirty Work*. Maybe the band needed to experience the frustration and patchy sessions and delays associated with that period in order to reappraise what they really wanted to do.

Don't Panic is a great album, full of fire and pith, elements which are also on show here, but there's a subtlety about *Future Hearts* as well as an acknowledgement of rock's storied history, while concurrently pointing towards the possibilities yet to come. By anyone's standards that's a tricky thing to pull off and there was little doubt that All Time Low had created something very special.

CHAPTER 33

TOP OF THE TREE.
HEY, THAT RHYMES. COOL.

With 80,000 sales in its first week, *Future Hearts* debuted at Number 2 in the Billboard 200. It was kept off top spot by the soundtrack to *Furious 7*, which sold significantly fewer units as an album but by some strange metrics, single sales were added to the soundtrack's total. Needless to say though on the Rock Albums and Vinyl Albums charts *Future Hearts* took top spot. With nearly 20,000 sales in the United Kingdom, the record shot straight in at Number 1 – the lads' first ever top spot in a territory they so love (which is mutual, natch). Australians bought enough for it to debut at Number 4 in the albums chart down there. Ras Furlong rates it hugely. 'I will listen to *Future Hearts* from front to back,' he said. 'There is not a song I want to skip. It really works.'

Reviewers also rated the album when it hit the streets. Good old *Alternative Press* was all over it, despite initially expressing reservations that John Feldmann's previous work on 5 Seconds of Summer's breakout album would impinge on the All Time Low sound. Luckily, it was the opposite, with Alex's influence on the Aussies having brought them into ATL territory. The mag praised 'tighter songwriting, more complex and layered arrangements and some of the most fully realized songs in the ATL canon'. 'Tidal Waves' was poignant and very effective, indeed one of the most effective of Alex's songs in that style. 'Kids in the Dark' reminded the writer of new wave arena rock, 'Kicking & Screaming' was a gritty Green Day-esque one, 'Bail Me Out' was more like a grooving, late 1990s alt-rock track, while the thrashy coda of 'Old Scars/Future Hearts' was the heaviest that the band had ever been on record. All in all, the album was their best to date because it had taken the album's sound and developed it.

Kerrang!, meanwhile, was of the opinion that it was 'pop-punk in its most unadulterated, carefree form'.

As ever, Alter the Press! was on hand for an in-depth analysis of the band's output. The writer loved the opening track and gushed that "Future Hearts' will not only go down as the band's best release yet, but also as one of 2015's top pop-rock albums. (If not the best.)' The singles, 'Something's Gotta Give' and 'Kids in the Dark', were the most reminiscent of *Don't Panic*, while both collaborations were a perfect fit. The record felt like 'Every era of All Time Low', and was purely and simply for the fans. It was an inspiration to many and would get people through hard times, concluded the writer.

The chaps at Absolute Punk saluted the band for having made it through the tricky years on Interscope and said that at that time it seemed to many as if they may have broken up. '*Future Hearts* is All Time Low finally finding its sweet spot,' read the review. The site said that 'Something's Gotta Give', 'Tidal Waves' and 'Missing You' were the three strongest cuts in an LP that was triumphant. It was a piece of work that had real value as an LP and there was a chance, too, that they could get that elusive smash single to dominate radio. One thing was clear though – this was a band with no intentions of going anywhere.

The august folk at *Rolling Stone Australia* pointed out the enormous difference between the lads messing about onstage and the craft evident in the songwriting. 'Frontman Alex Gaskarth has written for McBusted [on their December 2014 album], among others, and a song like 'Runaways' sparkles with shiny pop hooks, a lightweight counterpoint to some of the lyrical sentiment. *Future Hearts* is always catchy, but at times it's a little too flimsy to be satisfying,' was the ambivalent conclusion.

Also down under, the AU Review liked it and offered an excellent summary of the record: 'Growth is an important part of music and without its constant progression it's a struggle to keep up with the rest. All Time Low are elite athletes in their own marathon and with it comes the birth of *Future Hearts*; a record that has proven once again that they never once left the spotlight.'

The band themselves were chuffed at the release and reaction to it. Jack gave an interview to *Cooltry* just after the record was out. 'It's so weird to have our biggest week for any record we've ever had, out of like, six albums,' he stated. 'I think it's just weird. It's so rare and unique and a testament to how awesome our fans are because, fuck, it's not easy [...] It's a nice thing for any indie band; I think it's a big deal just to show that you can do it. Not saying that we're this big almighty, but if you work hard and write music you love it can happen.' He also revealed that there were a lot of songs that hadn't made it onto the final CD, such had been the organic nature of the process.

Alex spoke to The UK Official Charts Company about their Number 1 record. 'I'm just glad people like the songs. I definitely felt like our fans were ready for another album, but I didn't know it was going to be like this,' he said. 'There's so much nervous anticipation our end that we haven't even planned a celebration yet.' The singer went on to say that building things slowly had been key to the current success and that the UK really did understand and support the band.

Future Hearts was definitely an album that had allowed them to explore, he continued. 'For example, on 'Missing You', most people haven't heard us play the mandolin before. It was fun to try something new,' he said. The group was however aware that there was a certain 'box' All Time Low inhabited, but it was rather a large box for all that. To him, putting this record out had felt similar to releasing *Nothing Personal*, with the attendant excitement, and the band wasn't likely to slow down or stop any time soon. Gigging and consistently getting music out for the fans is central to the All Time Low *raison d'être*, so all the time they were laying down foundations to enable longevity. It wasn't about one smash hit then fading away again, that was for sure.

The busy frontman also chatted with *Rolling Stone*

Australia about a whole bunch of subjects including those Taylor Swift rumours, getting star-struck around Dave Grohl and having meltdowns when he got overheated. An example of that was a record store signing in the middle of the summer a while back, where there was no air conditioning. The band had been there a couple of hours and he was getting antsy. 'I felt horrible, 'cause I wasn't mad at the kids, but I was just being mean 'cause I was so uncomfortable. Kids are taking pictures and I'm dripping with sweat and feeling really gross, and I kind of unloaded on the people who were organising it a bit. I really try to rarely have moments like that, but I felt like an animal at the zoo,' he recalled – a very, very rare example of any of the boys losing their cool at all. He also revealed that three years previously he'd got into a fight with a dude who'd thought Alex had muttered something at him (which he hadn't). 'I hate fighting, but this guy was coming in so strong I don't think it was going to be a talking situation,' he explained. He concluded that he wanted to do some kind of YouTube show about cooking on tour; he liked to cook while at home and reckoned it would be great to see if they could turn whatever they had on their rider into good eats. An idea just waiting for a commission.

Alex also chatted with *Entertainment Weekly*, to whom he explained the title of the new album. 'It happened to be a lyric on one of the songs and we thought it was a really good title,' he began, 'summing up the whole record as far as feeling like we've been chasing this dream for our whole lives and living with this idea that we have parts that are bound for the future.' The theme was instilling a sense of hope as well as saying that carving out your own path could bring great rewards. The band, he assured the interviewer, were aware that they were building a legacy by this point.

Alex told *NME* that the UK Number 1 would be testament to the fact that bands could reach that height without needing a huge amount of created exposure or hype. The grassroots approach, he said, would pay dividends and also shows other bands that it would be possible to plough their own furrow. *Don't Panic* was a rock album but *Future Hearts* was the chance to do something more varied and with more dynamics. He also revealed that inspiration came from some sources that were outside of the pop-punk arena. 'I don't think people expect us to be talking about The Clash, The Doors, The Cars and lots of dub bands – Third Eye Blind ... there is nineties influence but in a song like 'Bail Me Out' we were trying to work out what The Cars would do now, what The Clash would do now. Maybe that's kinda sacrilegious to say that, but I don't know.' There was also a lot of hidden synthesiser in the album, lap steel and other instruments that All Time Low hadn't used before, he added. The analog synth, he revealed, was inspired by some of the sounds on the Sia record that he loved.

Rian was in demand, too, speaking to the AU Review about all things ATL. 'We've always been aware that we're not a band that reinvents the wheel with every record,' he said. 'We're not a band that no one's ever heard before. We play punk/rock music and alternative pop music and we know that another band could come along and do what we do any second [...] We have to take that extra step to be like, "How can we do this better and how can we make this a more unforgettable experience for these fans that come out to the show?"' The drummer also said that there might be an opportunity for the band to begin thinking about new material after July.

As for Zack, speaking later that year, he told *Guitar World* that John Feldmann had pushed the band, in a good way, to work hard without it being overly serious. He revealed that his first instrument had been the alto saxophone before zipping over to bass. As for the live dates later that year (and after their *Future Hearts* dates) to push the album, he said that in terms of a set-list, 'We do a bunch of new songs off *Future Hearts*. It's split. We have so many records out and we only have, like, an hour and a half. Being that it's the *Back to the Future Hearts* tour, we wanted to play some songs we haven't played in a while. I'll play a little acoustic guitar, even. People are going to enjoy it. We will be playing all the songs people want to hear and a few people won't expect.'

Early April saw the lads continue with in-store performances plus the news that 'Dear Maria, Count Me In' had gone platinum. Cover versions at this point included Sia's 'Elastic Heart' at the BBC Live Lounge and Alex duetting with Lynn Gunn on 'Say Something', the Christina Aguilera song. The Future Hearts tour began on 15 April in the United States with support from Issues, Tonight Alive and State Champs. On the tour, the boys made use of the vocal talents of Jenna McDougall of Tonight Alive for the Vic part in 'A Love Like War' and also made the day of fans by inviting some lucky people onstage during 'Time-Bomb'. At this point there were three live tracks taken from the new album: 'Satellite', 'Runaways' and 'Missing You'.

Her Campus attended the Lowell gig, where the lads opened with the same track that opened the record, explained the writer: 'Once the black curtain dropped and lead singer Alex Gaskarth sang the opening lines, the crowd went wild. An elaborate light sequence in which spotlights shone into the crowd, making the band members only visible in silhouette, was a perfectly dramatic way to start the show.' The whole caboodle ended with oodles of confetti raining down on an ecstatic crowd. The boys were back in town.

All Time Low's longevity was pointed out by a McCall writer at the Bethlehem gig a day later: 'The group has actually been around long enough to be nostalgic: The song's lyrics of "we were just singing" had to hit their older fans, who now are in their 30s.' The reviewer also likened 'Runaways' to a lighter U2, and 'Missing You' to Mumford & Sons. More unlikely reference points for a band that began as a straight-up Blink-182 covers messaround.

At the House of Blues gig in Orlando Alex spoke of the power of togetherness, saying, 'You have friends in the room right now. If you feel alienated, your friends are here.' The lads also were rotating covers in the encore. This time it was 'My Own Worst Enemy' once more. Great news came for the band on 19 April when *Future Hearts* was the biggest-selling record in the United States that week. As had been often the case with the hard-touring group, the only thing that could possibly trip them up was Mother Nature – on this occasion, heavy rain and the very strong possibility of thunderstorms forced the Atlanta gig to move from the outdoor Masquerade Music Park into the Civic Center. That didn't put the band off their stride, and the gig went off with no problems.

Sadly, the Milwaukee show on 16 May did have to be rescheduled due to the band having been invited to the KROQ

Weenie Roast Y Fiesta in California. Alex explained that it was something they had always wanted to do and the show would now take place on 29 May, with Knucklepuck and Real Friends in support. There would also be an acoustic performance plus signings for the first 1,000 people, and a special item of merchandise to make up for the rescheduling.

Alex spoke to KROQ about the event. 'It's gonna be a blast,' he said. 'We've always had an amazing amount of supporters out that way so it should be a great time.' And so it proved, the Saturday fiesta being a huge party featuring Mexican feasts, mariachi bands, loads of dressing up and the economical but impractical throwing of half a bra at All Time Low by one particular fan. Brilliantly, Mark Hoppus climbed onstage to perform 'Tidal Waves' with the gents before wandering off again and smacking a cymbal with his mic as he did so. Vic Fuentes was also in da house for 'A Love Like War'. The line-up for the festival was one of the strongest of the year with Muse, Florence + the Machine, Of Monsters and Men, James Bay, Death Cab for Cutie and loads more alternative types performing.

Back to the tour proper and Jack noticed something at the Philly gig: food trucks. 'Hey, when we've got fucking food trucks, we've made it!' the guitarist observed. This time, the guests on stage included a giant hot dog, a Tellytubby and Superman. Encores included American Idiot and All the Small Things plus an impromptu singalong of the theme to *The Fresh Prince of Bel-Air*. The tour ended at Baltimore on 24 May (aside from the Milwaukee gig), where Justin Tucker of the Baltimore Ravens joined the group onstage.

Sticking on a sport kick, Alex found himself invited to do

something very special two days later at the Baltimore Orioles vs. Houston Astros gig when he led the crowd in singing 'The Star-Spangled Banner'. Seek it out on a video-sharing site of your choice. It's a genuinely spine-tingling moment from a boy who was born in the UK but found the States embraced him and his talent. He is also one of those rare characters who knows that a bag of chips in the UK is not the same as chips in the United States.

The very same day as that anthem experience, an interview with Alex, Jack and Rian aired on MTV in which they reverted to silly mode. 'Jack spent a couple days out on the road with the 5 Seconds [of Summer] guys last year when they were touring and they're convinced that Jack might have gone poo poo on their bus,' Alex said. 'That's a big no-no on tour buses, by the way,' added Rian. 'You can pee pee, there's no poo poo.' In the same interview Jack said he'd never seen a band get so naked so quickly. All Time Low were a pretty naked band, he reckoned, but after ten minutes everyone was dancing around with no clothes on. Rian said that the success of 5 Seconds of Summer hadn't gone to their heads though – they were still the same guys that they were when they first started out.

As for the now-veterans, All Time Low, it was a festival summer with a series of dates in mainland Europe to occupy them through most of June 2015 as the word continued to spread about the band's latest hit album. They signed off from the States with a typically awesome, and daft, statement. Fans at the Karaoke Cave in New York City were astonished to find the band onstage to perform 'Dear Maria, Count Me In'. Alex commented that it was in a higher register than the group now played it, so it was tricky. 'I don't know why I'm looking at the screen [for the lyrics],' he joked about a song he had sung literally thousands of times. In an interview with *New York Magazine* he later revealed that his karaoke go-to was usually boy band stuff rather than rocking out to a pop-punk classic, which made the occasion even more special for those who were present. If you watch this one without smiling, there is something seriously wrong with you.

While the chaps were away from the States, the movie *Fan Girl* debuted at the LA Film Festival. The independent teen comedy starred Meg Ryan and Kiernan Shipka, the latter playing a character setting out to make a film about All Time Low in order to enter it in her school's movie contest. It premiered on TV in October 2015. Alex later told *Alternative Press* that the script came out of the blue from the writers: 'It was basically pitched to us because the movie was written around our band—and I guess the band would have been interchangeable, had we turned it down. But we just thought it was something different and cool. It was rad to be a part of,' he told that fabulous magazine. While the performances by the band were familiar ground, the acting was a lot of fun and it was great to try something different. Playing themselves helped the process, of course.

The awards kept coming; *Kerrang!* yielded both Best International Band and Best Event for the co-headliner earlier that year with You Me at Six. Alex looked set to win awards with his latest hair colour – a lovely, shiny, bright aquamarine. Jack had also been busy, co-creating with Represent a range of merchandise including T-shirts, sweatshirts, tank tops and even phone covers under the banner Free the Nipple. A percentage of the money raised went to the Bahamas Breast Cancer Initiative Foundation.

Following Europe, Alex and Jack were given the opportunity to host the 2015 *Alternative Press* Awards, at the Arena in Cleveland, Ohio. The lads scooped up three awards themselves: Rian was named Best Drummer, Zack best bassist and the ever-loyal Hustlers rightly named the most dedicated fans. The All Time Low set was something of a romp through some absolute classics: 'Bad Reputation' by Joan Jett, 'Blitzkrieg Bop' by the Ramones, 'Should I Stay or Should I Go' (The Clash), Nirvana's 'Smells Like Teen Spirit', 'Basket Case' by Green Day, 'The Middle' (Jimmy Eat World), 'What's My Age Again?' (Blink-182, of course), 'Sugar We're Going Down' by Fall Out Boy and their own 'Something's Gotta Give'. Phew!

In his acceptance speech, the sometimes-shy Zack said, 'I know I don't talk much, but thank you to you guys for letting me speak through what I do.' Also at the ceremony, a shirtless Trace Cyrus called Alex out for something he had said about one of Cyrus's songs. It was something and nothing because the song Alex hadn't rated ('Shake It' by Metro Station) had in fact gone multi-platinum. So, y'know … Sorta silly.

It was to the Far East once more as August dawned, with a quick stop-off in Honolulu on 9 August before the Philippines, then dates at Summer Sonic festival in Tokyo and Osaka, Japan. The Philippines gig was attended by *PopInquirer*, which reported: 'Pop punk band All Time Low got the scenesters headbanging and fist pumping as they played their show.' The Summer Sonic line-up was headlined by Pharrell Williams, The Chemical Brothers and Imagine Dragons, and All Time Low were joined on the supporting stages by huge names including Manic Street Preachers (from Alex's mother's birth country of Wales) and the oddly popular Babymetal. In total, nearly 250,000 people were in attendance over the two festival dates. Such huge crowds were becoming increasingly common for the Baltimore champions.

The festivals carried on through August, including a return to the Reading and Leeds Festivals over the August Bank Holiday weekend. This time the lads were right up the bill as third support to headliners Mumford & Sons on the main stage. At Reading, *Kerrang!* asked Alex how it felt in a video interview. 'The preparation is about the same,' the singer explained. 'Just a few more butterflies in me. Everybody usually gives a good fist bump before we go out there, but that's about it.' The short video then followed the lads onstage, where literally tens of thousands of fans screamed for them. A tiny taste of how it feels; a small indication of why this pop-punk band thing is so irresistible both to All Time Low and of course to the fans. And as if to illustrate the point further, the group invited various colourfully dressed fans up to join the 'Time-Bomb' party. Jack, as had become his trademark, passed his guitar to one youngster, who strummed away while he played the chords from behind her.

Rock Sound live-blogged from Reading and began with the thought that once upon a time All Time Low were in between superstardom and being just one pop-punk band among many, but that was now all in the past. 'The band onstage today not only sound amazing but draw the best reaction the main stage has seen all day,' wrote the reviewer. 'This is a set that proves that Alex Gaskarth and Co. can easily hold their own amongst the likes of Fall Out Boy and Blink-182. Not only one of the best pop-punk bands, but one of the best bands in the world.'

CHAPTER 34

FORWARD TO THE FUTURE

The world premiere of the latest video from All Time Low, *Runaways*, was hosted by none other than Team Coco – the site of superstar Conan O'Brien. The film is based around the lads playing the song live at various festivals and gigs and shows the gents signing autographs, meeting fans and messing about, in and on the water. When Alex sings that coda about running away and the sun going down, the pictures of the kids going wild tell their own story. The band's confidence in their craft is palpable and their connection with the fans is stunning. The lads also announced their new tour, Back to the Future Hearts, which would bring them again to the UK during February 2016. And the tour mates this time? None other than Good Charlotte. Another awesome line-up awaited UK fans.

Before that, though, there was the small matter of keeping

the American fans in the loop. South America, that is: the lads hit Mexico, Argentina, Chile and Brazil at last in a whirlwind week below the equator. The boys then headed to Canada for the first time in two years. The band was at full-throttle, something that a journalist from *Confront Magazine* was in awe of at the Montreal gig, where Cody Carson of Set It Off joined the chaps for 'Jasey Rae'. The writer explained that 'it has been a long time since I've seen a crowd singing from the first minute until the last. All Time Low have proved once again that they are here to stay and will still have just as much energy as they always have. I still haven't seen another band with that much energy and presence on stage.' You said a mouthful there, comrade!

The Back to the Future Hearts tour of the States began in Orlando on 9 October. It was a set with much more new material to it. 'It's nice to be able to plan a tour like the Back To The Future tour, where we're focusing on new material and have the response be really positive,' Alex told The Aquarian. 'So it's really cool for us to be able to grow as a band and have others support that. But we can't really play all of our songs, which is a bummer, because it'd be a three-hour show.' We don't think many people would complain, to be honest.

Alex also mentioned that it was tricky to write on the road because there was so much other stuff going on, be it interviewing, enjoying a stroll in the city or simply the distractions of the tour bus. He said that he would be trying to find some peaceful spots to get the creative juices flowing again. With the latest album still feeling fresh, there wouldn't be a lot of forays into new music for a while but there definitely would be some to look forward to as time went on. Alex also revealed one big change in his life to take place in 2016 – his marriage to Lisa Ruocco.

One significant date on the tour was 25 October 2015. This was the date that Marty McFly travelled to the future in *Back to the Future II*, a world of flying cars, hoverboards, 3D ads for *Jaws* and all sorts of cool stuff. On that date the lads were at the Monster Energy Aftershock Festival, which was headlined by Faith No More, Jane's Addiction and Deftones – three bands that were firmly from a past era, returning to the present day. It was another foray into a more metal-tinged context for the group, keen as ever to play to potential new fans. Jack, of course, ended up in the crowd, this time with the help of a photographer in the pit. The energy was undiminished: look out for plenty of sequels in the future.

The band's connection with their fans was confirmed by Alex in an interview with Fuse, during which he evaluated how far they had come and also how they had become a force for good with many of their young fans. Often these kids would look up to them for inspiration not just musically but in their personal lives, he said. 'The fact that our music has been able to connect with people on that level is insane and awesome. We've always written from a very personal place, so the things that we're singing about have affected us, too. It proves that we're all interconnected and it's the process of living that makes us all the same. [...] We're here doing our thing and we absolutely want to help people. It's so rewarding to know that anything we've put out there into the world has been able to pull someone out of a dark place.' He also alluded to the fact that *So Wrong, It's Right* would turn ten years old in 2017 and the *Three Words to Remember...* EP would do so in 2016. He added, maybe, that something might happen to commemorate those anniversaries.

And there's no doubt that as time rolls on its inexorable path there will be many more anniversaries to celebrate: this is a band that began in high school and has taken on a true life of its own. A band with four people so close they often refer to each other as brothers. A band from Baltimore, via the Lebanon, the United States and the United Kingdom. A band with a back catalogue so extensive that they are now finding it difficult to put together a set-list without leaving out some of their most loved tracks. If only they had a more positive name, things would be perfect!

Old friends and new alike see something special in the group. 'Honestly, right from the start, I knew ATL was going to be something,' Hometown Anthem's Stephen Dufresne told the author. 'I had no idea how big they would get, but after listening to "Noel", "Hometown Heroes" and "The Party Scene" I had no doubt. They constantly impress me with their songs. It's cliché to say, but there's been a maturation with each of their releases. "Paint You Wings" still gives me goosebumps to this day.' As people, they hadn't changed either. 'They were always humble,' recalls the musician. 'I saw them after a show at Nokia Theater in LA [years later] and it was hugs all round, almost like there had not been years between the last time we saw each other.'

David Kahne, producer extraordinaire, worked with the lads a little further down the line. 'I saw them play at Irving Plaza, and their fans are die-hard,' he recalled. 'And the band delivers to them. There's a great personal vibe that the band gives out, and the fans appreciate it immediately. Seems like the fans go there knowing they're gonna get a great show. And they did!'

Scott Stallone is a real All Time Low fan and he explained why: 'They're the absolute state of the art in the genre. They've got great songs and they're so good live. Also, they always look like they're having so much fucking fun doing it! How can you *not* love All Time Low?'

Ras summed it up. 'The guys are so personable that they are hard not to like. Their reputation not just in the industry but also with their fans [is great]. These guys are normal dudes and they don't try to be anything that they're not. They don't try to be above anybody or anything like that. They are just happy to be there, making music, playing shows. They are appreciative of everybody, super-gracious and all of that comes through in their personality as rock stars. What you see is what you get and that is why people gravitate toward them.'

As for the future? 'You will hear some more really great music coming from them. They continue to write as they always do. *Future Hearts* was a big step up for them and challenged them to get even better. They are inspired by the success of that record and that will only help them to continue to grow and develop as a band. As I look at the charts there are more bands with guitars and real music, less synthesised music and that is just showing that rock is making its way back into the limelight. All Time Low will definitely be a big part of it.'

We may not have hoverboards quite yet. The aliens might not yet have made contact with us (although some people do make us wonder) but when they do, it won't be because politicians have instigated it. It won't be the military machine.

It won't be the haters and the doomsters and those who trudge the weary path towards the mainstream.

It will be because of the hustlers, the lovers, the musicians and the funsters. It will be because of the reckless, the brave, the champagne poppers and most of all because of the bands who bring such joy, hope, love and magic into people's lives. Remember those three words? Here's a reminder:

All.

Time.

Low.

SELECTED WEBSITES

The ALS Association: http://www.alsa.org/
Campaign Against Living Miserably: https://www.thecalmzone.net/
Cancer Research (UK): http://www.cancerresearchuk.org/
Center for Infant and Child Loss: http://www.infantandchildloss.org/
Childline: https://www.childline.org.uk/Pages/Home.aspx
Helping Up Mission: https://helpingupmission.org/
It's On Us: http://itsonus.org/
PETA: http://www.peta.org.uk/
RSPCA (UK): http://www.rspca.org.uk/home
Skate 4 Cancer: http://dreamlovecure.org/

ACKNOWLEDGEMENTS

*T*hanks and love to James Hodgkinson and all at Music Press Books/John Blake Publishing; Martin Roach; all those who were interviewed for this book and those who helped but stayed anonymous; Suzy; Shoomans and Faulkners everywhere; Zoë and Bangor University; all those who plough their own furrow.

Respect and love to the punks, the skunks and the noise-loving monks. All the bands I've played with, recorded, watched, got drunk with and listened to over the years. Not least: Rabo de Toro, Vaffan Coulo and Zombie Dub. The outriders and the lovers. Brothers and sisters lost in the music. All those who were lost along the way. You mattered. I raise my glass in gratitude and admiration to the reckless, the brave and the different. The future is yours: use it well. You matter, too. The power of music to bring people together in an atmosphere of sheer joy and shared hope proves (most) politicians are opportunists and thieves. Always punch upwards. Love thy neighbour. *Hasta la victoria siempre.*

'The arts are not a way to make a living. They are a very human way of making life more bearable. Practicing an art, no matter how well or badly, is a way to make your soul grow, for heaven's sake. Sing in the shower. Dance to the radio. Tell stories. Write a poem to a friend, even a lousy poem. Do it as well as you possibly can. You will get an enormous reward. You will have created something.'

KURT VONNEGUT

OUTRODUCTION

You turn your ship around. The numbers show you have returned to the present day. What a ride it's been!

Your balibberskibber banks are now chock-full with this strangely compelling earth music. You take one look back at the blue-green orb you've been studying. Several of your shoulders shrug. What a place!

You set the controls to your home coordinates. The multiverse folds into itself as you zoom into hyperspace. Chuckling, you realise that you can never tell the real story.

The folks back home would never believe how doggone weird that planet in the slightly unfashionable western spiral arm of the galaxy is. You'll have to make something else up that's more feasible, like a population of mirrored anti-matter eaters all called CLANG, who reproduce through magnetism. (Of course, if the universe is truly infinite then this is actually true, somewhere. Also true, somewhere, is that Trace Cyrus owns some shirts.)

But by the beard of Aragararar the Pan Galactic Gargle Blaster Mixer, the guys back home are sure gonna be knocked out when they tune their dimensional earagrams into what you're bringin' back.

One of your multimouths begins to sing a melody. Some of the others join in, harmonising beautifully:

Merry Christmas, Kiss My ...